Contents

Part I. The Antiwar Strategy of the SWP and the YSA 5

1. From 'The Next Phase of American Politics' 7

2. The Antiwar Movement (Excerpts from a Discussion in the SWP Political Committee, June 25, 1965) 10

3. Revolutionary Policies in the Antiwar Movement, by James P. Cannon 20

4. A Reply to a Criticism of Our Antiwar Policy, by Lew Jones 28

5. From 'Some Comments on Party Policy and Tactics in the Antiwar Movement,' by Tom Kerry 35

6. The Fight Against the Vietnam War 39

Part II. Revolutionary Antiwar Policy and Practice 55

1. Socialists and the Antiwar Movement: A History, 1965–69, by Gus Horowitz 57

2. May 1970—A Student Upsurge Without Precedent 66
   - *a. The Impact on Capitalists, Unions, and Students, by Jack Barnes* 66
   - *b. From 'After the May Upsurge: Young Socialists and the Student Movement'* 70

3. Disputed Issues in the Antiwar Movement 74
   - *a. Mass Action vs. Calculated Confrontation, by Doug Jenness* 74
   - *b. Mass Action vs. 'Multi-issue' Reformism, by Larry Seigle* 78
   - *c. The Communist Party and the April 24, 1971 Demonstration, by Larry Seigle* 81
   - *d. The Communist Party's Peace Policy, by Dave Frankel* 84
   - *e. Why Moscow and Peking Favor the 'Sign Now' Demand, by Barry Sheppard* 87

Appendix 91

Introductory Note 92

I. Revolutionary Strategy in World War I: Three Articles by Lenin 94
   - *1. The Conference of the Russian Social Democratic Labor Party Abroad* 94
   - *2. The Question of Peace* 98
   - *3. The Military Programme of the Proletariat* 101

II. Proletarian Military Policy, by James P. Cannon 107
1. Resolution on Proletarian Military Policy 107
2. Military Policy of the Proletariat 111
3. Summary Speech on Military Policy 121
4. Militarism and Workers' Right 128

III. 1945: When U.S. Troops Said 'No!' 133
A Hidden Chapter in the Fight Against War, by Mary-Alice Waters

Introductory Note

This Education for Socialists bulletin brings together materials outlining the strategy followed by the Socialist Workers Party and the Young Socialist Alliance in the anti-Vietnam-war movement that emerged in the U.S. during the eight years from the bombings of North Vietnam in February 1965 to the signing of the Paris accords in January 1973. The first part presents key political documents in which this strategy was developed. The second part deals with the application and defense of that line at key conjunctures.

In its essentials, Trotskyist policy in the antiwar movement was adopted in 1965, and maintained consistently ever since. The three essential elements of this policy were: (1) placing the main political stress on the demand for immediate, unconditional withdrawal of U.S. forces; (2) mass action in the streets independent of the capitalist parties; and (3) the building of broad coalitions on a nonexclusionary basis to organize the mass actions. The most complete statement of this strategy can be found in the resolution adopted by the 1969 SWP convention, "The Fight Against the Vietnam War," which is included in this bulletin.

The war in Vietnam and the struggle against it have profoundly altered American politics, energizing a mass radicalization that continues to develop today. All political tendencies and organizations were tested in this struggle—from the Social Democrats to the pro-Moscow and pro-Peking Stalinists. In this test, the SWP and the YSA far outdistanced rival groups.

The SWP and the YSA participated far more energetically than any other political organization in the antiwar movement, and quickly became leading components of it. They were recognized in wide circles for their determined efforts to keep the movement on a mass-action course. As a result, the SWP and the YSA experienced rapid growth. The ranks of revolutionary Marxists in the U.S. today are several times larger than they were when the movement began and the SWP and YSA developed into leading groups in the American left. Further, the experience gained by SWP and YSA members in building a mass movement, in developing a correct policy towards this movement, and in combating all the varieties of reformism and ultraleftism within this movement will continue to stand them in good stead as the radicalization deepens.

Although the mass anti-Vietnam-war movement in the United States was unprecedented, the fundamental principles that underlay the approach of the SWP and the YSA were not new. They were a specific application of the revolutionary-Marxist strategy worked out by Lenin during World War I and further developed by the SWP during World War II.

The appendix to this Education for Socialists bulletin includes selections from Lenin's writings on World War I and documents on the SWP's proletarian military policy in World War II.

PART I

The Antiwar Strategy of the SWP and the YSA

1. FROM 'THE NEXT PHASE OF AMERICAN POLITICS'

The following is an excerpt from "The Next Phase of American Politics," the political resolution adopted by the 1965 convention of the Socialist Workers Party. The resolution assessed the political situation in the U.S. after Lyndon Johnson's landslide victory in the 1964 presidential elections. Johnson had the overwhelming support of labor, the Black community, and the radical movement largely because of his promises of "peace" and popular fears that his conservative Republican opponent, Goldwater, would escalate the Vietnam conflict into a major war. An exception to the stampede to support Johnson as a lesser evil was the presidential campaign of SWP candidates Clifton DeBerry and Edward Shaw. The SWP campaign denounced the war, warned of further escalation under Johnson, and demanded immediate, unconditional withdrawal of all U.S. forces.

Published in May 1965, the resolution predicted that "the key to the next phase of American politics lies in the fate of the unstable coalition of diverse and basically incompatible social forces gathered around the Johnson administration." The bombings of North Vietnam had already produced the first cracks in this coalition, expressed in student demonstrations and teach-ins and the first large anti-Vietnam-war protest in Washington, D. C. on April 17, 1965. (The complete text of this resolution can be found in *SWP Discussion Bulletin*, Volume 25, No. 2.)

Experience makes it ever-plainer for all to see that Johnson's real war is not against poverty but against the poverty stricken colonial masses. Each step he takes in foreign policy shows that at all hazards he is out to stem the tide of revolt against capitalist exploitation and imperialist domination. Johnson's real policy was actually exposed right in the middle of last year's election campaign. Using the Tonkin Gulf incident of August 1964 as a pretext for naked imperialist aggression, he savagely ordered the bombing of North Vietnam. At the same time a bipartisan resolution was rushed through Congress backing Johnson and giving him a free hand for further acts of aggression. Johnson and the Democrats, no less than Goldwater and the Republicans, were proven ready to risk war to serve imperialist ends. Even before the 1964 elections, Johnson's conduct had refuted practitioners of lesser-evil politics who persisted in touting him as a man of peace and the Democrats as a party of peace.

Once elected Johnson lost no time in applying the Goldwater foreign policy line which the voters had rejected at the polls. Within three weeks he intervened militarily in support of the hated imperialist puppet, Tshombe, in the Congo. U.S. planes airlifted Belgian paratroops for an assault on Stanleyville. There the Belgians, aided by U.S.-armed white mercenaries in Tshombe's employ, launched a murderous assault on the Congolese freedom fighters. Subsequent disclosures revealed that the whole thing had been done with a prearranged plan which had obviously been worked out while Johnson was campaigning for election as a man of peace.

Last February Johnson launched what has proven to be a continuing series of bombing assaults on North Vietnam. Use of American air power against South Vietnamese freedom fighters has simultaneously been stepped up. In both cases death and destruction is being rained upon the civilian population and their possessions. A big new buildup of U.S. ground troops has begun in South Vietnam. All these acts of aggression bring closer the danger of another Korean-type war in Southeast Asia, the possibility of a direct military confrontation with China which now possesses nuclear potential, and the peril of a general nuclear war.

With the whole world already apprehensive over the war danger in Vietnam, Johnson proceeded to order a massive U.S. military intervention in the Dominican Republic. The first excuse of protecting American and foreign lives quickly wore thin. Washington policy makers then shifted toward explanations adding up to the assertion that the United States will not allow another Cuba in Latin America. Taking no chances on another Castro evolving out of a bourgeois-democratic revolution, Johnson has intervened in support of the military dictatorship and against the Dominican *constitucionalistas* who appear to have widespread popular support. The basic aim is to see that no new government takes power in the Dominican Republic, or anywhere else without U.S. consent. The intent will be to bend the *constitucionalistas* to this policy through whatever combination of political maneuvers and military pressures the situation may require. Johnson can afford to be flexible about the exact composition of the Dominican government provided its members pass a CIA-FBI security check. His main aim will be to disarm the insurgent masses and restore firm police rule over them.

The Dominican intervention marks a new stage in the imperialist drive to crush all revolutionary upheavals. Johnson's cynical bypassing of the OAS in his unilateral military action exposes the imperialist hypocrisy concerning inter-American "cooperation." Little pretense remains of supporting an "Alliance for Progress" to bring about needed social reforms. The Dominican intervention shows that any social reform movement undertaken without Washington's authorization faces the threat of direct U.S. attack. It also raises grave new dangers of a counterrevolutionary assault on socialist Cuba with direct U.S. participation. Through the Johnson doctrine, U.S. imperialism is taking a further long stride toward setting itself up as world policeman over the limits to which any social reform will be allowed. In keeping with that perspective the Pentagon is presently reevaluating the draft policy that will be needed to provide a bigger conscript army for the purpose.

Parallel with Johnson's new long stride toward the nuclear brink, Washington propagandists have been resorting more and more to McCarthy-type charges of an "international communist conspiracy." That tune is being played in all keys in the Dominican Republic, as it has been in Vietnam, the Congo, and as it will be wherever freedom fighters revolt against the puppet regimes of imperialism in their countries. Use of the hateful McCarthyite technique in matters of foreign policy implies parallel attempts to employ it within this country in an effort to gag critics of the bipartisan imperialist foreign policy. Similarly, it is not accidental that the Supreme Court's decision upholding the ban on travel to Cuba coincided with Washington's military intervention in the Dominican Republic. The Johnson administration's present gestures toward public discussion of its Vietnam policy with critics at home does not mark any departure from the long-established policy of witch-hunting critics of foreign policy. It simply reflects differences within the ruling class over Johnson's tactics in opposing the colonial revolution. It also reflects empirical resort to a temporary expedient which they hope will blunt swelling criticism. The ruling powers have no intention of setting foreign policy through public discussion.

Growth of internal opposition to the bipartisan foreign policy reflects the mounting impact of the colonial revolution upon the people of the United States. From its inception, the Cuban revolution has aroused considerable sympathy within this country, especially among students. A number of young people were thereby drawn into general opposition to Washington's policies, some moving all the way to acceptance of socialist ideas. Today an even-larger new wave of opposition to the antidemocratic foreign and domestic policies of imperialism is coming into being around the Vietnam issue, its forces composed of a broad layer of activists in the student movement itself. Centering on the campuses, the protest movement over Vietnam is attracting greater numbers of students than in the case of Cuba in the early Sixties, and there is a marked rise in faculty support as well. The brutal application of the Johnson doctrine now unfolding in the Caribbean is bound to broaden and intensify the movement even further. It lends cogency to the central issue brought to the fore by the teach-in movement, namely, the right of the American people to decide questions of war and peace. No thinking person would take seriously the old argument that "there wouldn't be time" for a vote about military intervention in Vietnam and U.S. occupation of Santo Domingo.

Development of the teach-ins over the Vietnam issue offers a vehicle which, despite its amorphous nature, can be used to help build a genuine opposition to imperialist war. Originating out of sentiments against imperialist policy in Vietnam, the teach-ins are essentially an integral part of the antiwar movement. They are not to be viewed as substitutes for, but rather as catalysts leading toward, various actions of an avowedly anti-imperialist nature. Assemblies like the teach-ins serve primarily as a forum where a meaningful anti-imperialist policy can be argued out, provided that all viewpoints have the right to be heard. Our task in such forums is to refute fake peace advocates who call upon the imperialists to be more "democratic," who exonerate the imperialist aggressors by blaming "both sides," who seek to keep the peace movement mired down in the swamp of capitalist politics.

As against such peace fakers our task is to explain that U.S. imperialist policy, and that policy alone, obstructs peace. There can be no peace until all U.S. troops are withdrawn from abroad and the peoples of other lands are allowed to settle their own affairs without U.S. intervention. Such a peaceful policy cannot be attained through either a Democratic or Republican administration. Both parties are capitalist parties and are therefore irrevocably tied to the imperialist policies inherent in the capitalist system. Peace can be won only by breaking definitively with capitalist politics and taking the road of independent, anticapitalist political action.

We fully support demonstrations which are explicitly against imperialist foreign policy, no matter how limited the specific demands may be. As in the case of the student March On Washington, a flat demand that Johnson end the war in Vietnam affords a principled basis for united action toward specific anti-imperialist ends. The March also set a further good example through its nonexclusionist policy toward all who supported its central demand and through recognition of the right of all participating groups to distribute their own literature. Such insistence on a nonexclusionist policy is tending to become the norm in the committees and organizations which make up the movement, and it is precipitating a healthy differentiation between serious antiwar militants, on one hand, and social democrats and right wing peaceniks, on the other. Our aim must be to take advantage of such opportunities to broaden the protest actions against imperialist policy and in the process to deepen the political consciousness of antiwar militants.

As in the case of student youth, the colonial revolution is making an impact upon the Freedom Now movement. An example is support from SNCC to the student March on Washington demanding an end to the war in Vietnam. Awareness of issues in the colonial revolution and acts of solidarity with the colonial freedom fighters will bring the Negro vanguard to a higher level of political consciousness. Through observation and experience they will perceive more clearly the interrelation between imperialist resistance to liberation movements abroad and the parallel resistance in this country to Negro demands for Freedom Now. Our task is to help develop that perception all the way to the indicated anti-capitalist and prosocialist conclusions. Those efforts will lend impetus to the present incipient revolt against Negro misleaders who acquiesce in the capitalist government's criminal acts abroad and who preach reliance on that same government in the civil rights struggle here at home.

2. THE ANTIWAR MOVEMENT

Excerpts from a Discussion in the SWP Political Committee, June 25, 1965

The following remarks by Farrell Dobbs, Jack Barnes, George Novack, and Carl Feingold, are reprinted from *SWP Discussion Bulletin*, Volume 25, No. 5.

Dobbs: In discussing the strategy and tactics of the present antiwar campaign it seems useful to review the proletarian military policy adopted at the party's September 1940 plenum-conference held in Chicago. Those of us who participated in the decision need to refresh our recollections about it, and comrades who have since come into the party should find it helpful to have the decision reviewed in its main lines. If we also recall the historic setting in which the policy was adopted it should aid us in determining what parts of the 1940 tactical considerations remain applicable today and what parts require reevaluation in the light of present objective conditions.

The 1940 resolution on military policy was adopted after leading party comrades had discussed the subject with Trotsky during a visit with him in Mexico and after the draft resolution setting forth the policy had been discussed for two months within the party in advance of the plenum-conference. The resolution made clear that it maintained uninterrupted continuity with long-established Marxist principles in the fight against capitalist militarism and imperialist war. At all times we maintain irreconcilable opposition to imperialist war. Our war is one of the workers against capitalism, ours the concept of an uninterrupted struggle to win leadership of the working class, carry through a fight for power, and establish a socialist society. Toward that end we stress at all times the importance of building a Leninist-type party, and our military policy was viewed as one which applied those principles under conditions of World War II.

The resolution, as Comrade Cannon pointed out to the party at the time, represented a continuation, but not a mere repetition, of Lenin's policies during World War I. It signified further development, deepening and sharpening of Leninist strategy and tactics. Taking the totality of the existing world situation for its point of departure, as Trotsky had taught us, the plenum-conference undertook to chart a strategic and tactical course in military policy commensurate with the needs of the day.

In September 1940 World War II had already been raging for a year, peacetime conscription had been introduced in the U.S., and this country was only a little over a year away from entry into the war. It was a time of great change in the world, a time in which we saw capitalism entering into a state of permanent crisis which heralded an epoch of uninterrupted militarism and war. No peaceful solution could be seen to any social problem. All great questions would have to be decided by military means. Capitalist militarism had to be taken as an established reality which we were not strong enough to abolish. We had no choice but to adapt our strategy and tactics to the existing reality and to shape a course which took its start from the facts of capitalist rule over the working class. Our object was to counterpose a working class program to the imperialist program at every point.

In its origins, unfolding and outcome World War II was basically an interimperialist war. The Nazi-Soviet conflict and Japan's invasion of colonial China were extremely important but subordinate to the overall character of the global struggle. The characteristics of World War II were in the main akin to those of World War I and much different from those of imperialism's present assaults on the colonial revolution and its antagonistic military postures toward the workers states. Even though the Stalin-Hitler pact was still operative in September 1940, we already saw signs of the coming Soviet-German rift and the Soviet shift to the anti-Hitler side, which did occur in June 1941. Our policy decisions therefore assumed that U.S. armies would not be fighting the Soviet Union, at least until after Hitler had been defeated. We expected that the U.S. conscript army would be fighting in an essentially interimperialist war and would not in the immediately foreseeable period become involved in a military attack on the Soviet Union. Under those conditions we applied strategic and tactical concepts which brought up to date the policies of Lenin during the interimperialist war of 1914–1918.

As revolutionary optimists we challenged any notion that U.S. imperialism would succeed in its ambition to dominate the world. We visualized social revolutions erupting directly out of the interimperialist war and our policies were oriented toward such an outcome. Only with the masses would it be possible to conquer power and, in those times, it appeared that the masses in the military organizations were destined to play the decisive revolutionary role. To meet the anticipated course of history, we developed the proletarian military policy.

A massive force of young workers was to be drafted into the U.S. army. We knew they would enter it with anti-Hitler patriotic sentiments, but we also took into account the struggle potential they brought with them in terms of their own class interests, especially from their background of militant labor battles during the thirties. Our military policy was conceived as a bridge toward these worker-soldiers, designed to protect and develop their class independence in the capitalist military machine. It was viewed as a military transitional program supplementing the political transitional program adopted in 1938.

Starting from the fact that the workers were for compulsory military service, we counterposed to the capitalist draft policy the concept of conscription by the workers organizations to form well-armed and well-trained labor detachments. We called for compulsory military training under trade union control with the capitalist government paying the bill. Stressing the class need, we called for election of worker-officers by the worker-soldiers. The aim was to build in the army a class-conscious workers movement capable of defending working class interests under conditions of capitalist militarism and war.

We thought that revolutionists should be prepared to go with the masses, become soldiers with them, and go to war with them. In doing so we felt it important that revolutionists strive to become the most skilled among the worker-soldiers. Military skill was looked upon as a necessity since all great questions were up for decision by military means. As skilled hands at the military trade, revolutionists would be so much the better able to win the confidence of worker-soldiers and influence them with socialist ideas. Such influence would help to lead them in a revolutionary direction and to advance the leadership role of revolutionary socialists.

It was deemed necessary to work toward these objectives in stages as the anticipated social crisis began to unfold. It was considered important to begin in a careful, cautious way, making no premature moves that might separate the socialist militants from the masses. At all stages, however, the aim was to participate in the military machine for socialist ends, seeking to win a majority over to the idea of transforming the imperialist war into a struggle for socialism.

Today, no one needs to be reminded that the unfolding world revolution took a different course than we had expected. World War II did not lead directly to social revolution in the advanced capitalist countries. Instead an expanding wave of colonial revolutions developed and a combination of historic factors postponed the coming workers revolutions in the imperialist strongholds. Capitalism has consequently been able to mount a sustained cold war offensive against the workers states and it is carrying out brutal military interventions against colonial uprisings. With these changed circumstances in the permanent crisis of capitalism, we still face the problems of capitalist militarism and imperialist war.

Starting from the totality of the world situation that results from these basic objective conditions, it is necessary to think through the policies required at the present conjuncture. As in the 1940 decisions, the aim must be to maintain the uninterrupted continuity of Marxist-Leninist-Trotskyist principles in the fight against war; to counterpose a working class program to the imperialist program at every point; and to shape current strategy and tactics with a view toward a struggle for workers power and the creation of a socialist society.

The political criteria for current military policy are qualitatively different from the considerations that were applicable in 1940. Today the U.S. armed forces represent a counterrevolutionary dagger aimed directly at the colonial revolution and the workers states. The present conscript army is growing, but it is not yet one of the massive proportions attained during World War II, and it does not have the decisive mass weight considered so important under the conditions of 1940. The ranks of the present army do not tend so much to consider themselves a crusading force, as did the conscripts who thought the country went to war in 1941 to rid the world of fascism. There are numerous signs of the present conscript army becoming a disgruntled army, as revealed by reports in the daily press, an army that can be expected to share in increasing measure the sentiments of the growing antiwar movement here at home.

In view of the changing conditions which led to the general situation prevailing today, we dropped the slogan of military training under trade union control back in the early fifties, and there is no basis at the present conjuncture to contemplate its revival. In recent years the approach to the question of the military draft has been one of stressing opposition to capitalist conscription, with no mention of conscription into workers military formations. The plank on military policy in our election platforms has set forth such slogans as full democratic rights for the military ranks, election of officers, trade union wages for servicemen, etc.

Policy on the draft remains unchanged in the sense that revolutionists do not as individuals refuse conscription, as do conscientious objectors, and thereby isolate themselves from the stream of life while serving a term in prison. Revolutionists exercise their constitutional right, however, to refuse compliance with the loyalty oath procedures attached to the present conscription process. If conscripted, it is also one's constitutional right to express one's views in the armed forces. It is simply a matter of using good judgment in the exercise of that political right. For instance, citizen-soldiers are under no obligation to accept uncritically the biased imperialist propaganda presented by brass hats in the guise of "political orientation."

In exercising the constitutional right to political expression inside and outside the armed forces, opposition to capitalist militarism is only a point of departure toward larger questions. Serious thought must proceed from there to an analysis of militarism's parent, the imperialist foreign policy. That in turn leads to questions about the basic characteristics of capitalism, about the need to abolish capitalist rule and reorganize society on a socialist basis. The application of revolutionary strategy and tactics in a transitional approach to these basic questions, especially as required in the main arena of struggle against war which exists today outside the armed forces, will be taken up in a separate presentation by Jack.

BARNES: First it might be a good idea to review the character of the movement we are dealing with. In a certain sense it is a pacifist movement, a general revulsion against war. On the other hand, (1) it is not led by professional pacifists, (2) it is political, and (3) it is more antiwar than it is pacifist in the general sense. It is focused on a specific war, the war against the Vietnamese revolution waged by the regime in Saigon and the Johnson administration.

It is a movement which thus far has utilized direct action. Its tactics were learned in the civil rights movement and in various student actions of the last half decade. For example, there is now a lot of talk about direct action in the future with large elements of civil disobedience. You have to watch carefully the language that participants in this movement use. The terms "civil disobedience" and "nonviolence" are often used in a different way than we have been used to using them. Some people in the movement considered the March on Washington an act of civil disobedience in which certain small rules were broken. When someone suggests any kind of action, they will often speak of it as a "nonviolent action." Because the civil rights movement is the only mass movement the students in the antiwar movement have known, they copy its language and tactics.

I think what Farrell said in his report is striking: The young people involved in this have never seen in their lifetime any example of the working class as a class in motion. Unless they are historians or members of the radical movement, the modes of struggle and types of organization which are characteristic of the working class are unknown to them. The lessons and backlog of understanding of those who were conscripted into the army in the early forties are totally absent in this generation.

The traditional peace organizations, and the Communist and Socialist parties are not in the leadership of this movement. New student forces and new student activists are in the leadership and dominate it at this stage. These activists are in no way oriented toward the Democratic Party nor do any of the movement's leaders propose taking it in that direction. Quite the contrary, one of the searches on now among the left wing leaders is for an alternative of some sort to political subordination to the activities of the Democratic Party.

The *ad hoc* committees which have been the main organizing centers for the movement have been nonexclusive. The protest has taken on a quasi-united-front character from the beginning. The main layers that are involved are four. The first is the students. They are the largest and they are in the leadership. Second, a surprisingly large number of young professors, instructors, and teaching assistants are involved. Third, a lot of those who have been in the peace movement are taking part even though their leaders are dragging their feet and often even opposing the more militant actions. Fourth, of course, are the radicals: members of the socialist organizations.

The antiwar movement began, has its roots on, and still has its major strength on the campus. It is very new. The first teach-in was March 24, the first major demonstration, the March on Washington, took place April 17th. Right now it actively involves more people than the fight against the Algerian war ever involved in France. That gives you something to compare it to in our own decade. It is bigger and larger and deeper at this stage than any other American antiwar movement in the past.

Along with the movement have come some surprising developments. You have such things as the court martial of the lieutenant for refusing to be reassigned to a more dangerous area in Vietnam. You have the spectacle of the governor of New Jersey saying that an open Marxist [Eugene Genovese] has a right to teach, has a right to take part in the teach-ins, has a right to say that the Vietcong ought to win, and still be a professor. Far from bowing to pressure from the administration, so far, the young professors as well as the students have stuck to their guns, refused to capitulate and to see their colleagues victimized.

What are the circumstances under which this movement has arisen? There is the dual character to the war threat which we face today. First, there is the threat of nuclear annihilation. That is, the fact that at any time a conflict in the world can lead to a nuclear showdown. While this has not been the major propellent of this movement, it has been in the background continually, and is often referred to. The fear of nuclear war has helped give a sense of urgency to the movement.

Second, is the type of war that is actually going on, the anti-guerrilla, counterrevolutionary war. In Vietnam there is the fear of escalation of the war to the scale of Korea. The generation that is protesting this was not politically conscious during the Korean War. They were 5, 6, 7, 8 and 9 years of age at the time of Korea. They can hardly even remember it. This is their first conscious war and it is their first confrontation with their own government as world policeman.

The war is taking place after five years of a slowly maturing and growing radicalization of the American students. It takes place when there is a thin layer of organized socialist youth. It takes place after a half decade of growing sensitivity and opposition to antidemocratic moves by the federal government in the South and North. The various protest actions and characteristics of the student movement which have developed in piecemeal fashion; the protest against restrictions on campus, activity in the civil rights movement, and sympathy to the colonial revolutions have merged in this fight against the Vietnam war.

It takes place under the protective umbrella of a split to one degree or another in the ruling class over the Vietnam war. The newspapers, the columnists, the cartoonists, and commentators on radio and television are by no means unanimous in their support to the Johnson administration and the war. While they don't take the radical positions that the students do, they still raise a lot of questions, and it is obvious that they are deeply divided over the questions of whether Vietnam should become a Korea-type conflict and whether Vietnam is worth the chance of a nuclear war.

The question of democracy, the question of how the decisions on war are made, the question of why people aren't told the truth, these questions are almost as important to the movement as opposition to the war in Vietnam itself. Protest against the falsehoods and the lack of democratic decision-making are important themes of the teach-ins and the protest literature.

Much of the antiwar activity is being organized by the Committees to End the War in Vietnam which have proliferated since the March on Washington. These are non-exclusive committees in which the organized radicals and the unaffiliated antiwar students can come together. The committees have generally been campus-based but they haven't been restricted to the campus. There are at least two places, Los Angeles and New York, where there has been significant adult involvement almost from the beginning. In L. A., a high percentage of the committee which organized support actions around the March on Washington, the cavalcade to Berkeley, and the city-wide teach-out was made up of nonstudent forces.

The committees against the war usually stress education and action. There has been no tendency thus far to carry on blind activity, or picket lines as ends in themselves. There has been a heavy emphasis on what we would call propaganda. There has been the idea that the movement should try to involve more students, through educational campaigns using teach-ins, street meetings, discussion groups, rallies, and literature. In the New York committee, the Minneapolis committee, and probably many others, much of the summer activity revolves around arming the antiwar people with more literature, information, and education.

The fact that the radicals have not been excluded and are an accepted part of the movement represents a complete about-face in the relation of forces and the attitudes that dominated the "peace movements." Always before we found ourselves having to prove that we belonged in such groups as Student Peace Union. These anti-Vietnam war committees have been just the opposite. The burden of the proof has usually been on the Americans for Democratic Action, the Committee for a Sane Nuclear Policy (SANE) types, the right-wing Socialist and Communist party members to prove why anyone should be excluded. The third camp and exclusionist stands of the right wing liberal and SP elements have tended to force them to exclude themselves from the protest. They have nowhere been successful in excluding the radical forces. In Los Angeles, the Women Strike for Peace was split on the question of whether or not SWP member Theodore Edwards should have equal time at the teach-out to speak. He ended up getting time to speak and those others who wanted to exclude themselves did so.

Most of the youth locals were deeply involved with the March on Washington Committees, and remained active in the committees which came out of the March activity. We've been the firmest supporters of the non-exclusive basis of the committees. The youth have had a campaign around the antiwar movement since late January and have tended to tie in their other activities around their participation in the antiwar campaign. In the future they will be trying to relate their election campaign activities to the antiwar movement.

On the war question itself, we should continue to emphasize three major points: First, is the demand for withdrawal of American troops as the central slogan as opposed to any other formulation, especially negotiation. A surprising number of the students involved in this movement will support the basic concept of immediate and unconditional withdrawal of the American troops. It's not ordained beforehand that a majority will go along with the idea of negotiations as a basic plank. It's really important for us to be very clear on the question of negotiations. We do not put down any absolute rules for a liberation movement, for a revolutionary army, that they cannot negotiate. In point of fact they do have to negotiate. But it is the responsibility of those in this country to oppose the American intervention and demand the withdrawal of U.S. troops, and to do nothing to suggest any legitimacy for unilateral imperialist actions.

Second, is the absolute character of the right of self-determination for Vietnam and for all nations. People of all nations have the right to determine their own destiny regardless of their size or military strength.

The third point is basically educational. It is the fact that not only are we for the withdrawal of American troops, we're for the victory of the peasant guerrilla forces in the Vietnamese civil war. We applaud those professors like Genovese who come out openly not only for the withdrawal of U.S. troops, not only for the ending of moral injustices, but for the victory of the forces of the peasants and the workers of Vietnam who are fighting against decades of oppression. While this is not something that is being raised or can be raised as a central point in the committees, it is something that in conversations or in our press we can discuss openly, frankly, clearly. In a war against a colonial revolution, there is a thin line between being opposed to the war itself and being favorably disposed to the guerrilla forces fighting against the American army as a reactionary army.

We are in favor of deepening the teach-ins, not as a substitute for protests, demonstrations, and rallies against the war, but as a justifiable mobilizing educator in and of themselves.

We should continue to take advantage of the strong attitude against the antidemocratic character of the Johnson administration's running of the war, by raising the concept of the right of the people to decide on war. When I joined the movement the slogan "no secret diplomacy" seemed to me to be a way-out slogan. I didn't really understand what it meant. It has a more concrete meaning now when the administration spokesmen put forth ideas like "well, we can't tell you all the details of this, because we've been negotiating secretly, we've been talking to the French and they're talking with the Swiss and they're talking with North Vietnam and your knowing what is being said would jeopardize the negotiations." When Arthur Schlesinger tried this approach at the national teach-in, he was attacked.

Many students are saying, "It is not secret negotiations which are needed, but an open decision by the American government in the full view of the people to get out or to negotiate with the National Liberation Front. Everything should not depend on a small coterie, representing a small layer of American society, making secret undemocratic decisions affecting the lives and deaths of everyone." We educate about the need to get rid of the warmakers as the ruling class and simultaneously while propagandizing for this, we do everything possible to support every popular initiative towards making it more difficult for the ruling class to make war behind the backs of the people. We should do everything possible to tie the hands of the ruling class until they are replaced.

The question of community work has come up. By that I mean simply the desire by layers of students involved in the protest not only to educate and agitate against the war on the campus, but to involve broader layers of the American people. We should support this as long as it doesn't involve them in adventures (as it did a couple of years ago when students passed out a leaflet demanding that workers not go into a war plant for some moral issue) and so long as it does not become a substitute for continuing work on the campuses.

One of the things that's different about the "new left" and the "old new left" is that the attitude and mood of the students involved in this movement is the opposite of the elitism which Comrade Novack pointed out lurked behind C. Wright Mills' concept of the professorial new left. Their desires to organize the broader community are healthy although they may be intertwined with social-work attitudes and with attitudes having to do with saving their own souls as opposed to organizing a change in society. It would be a big error for us to put ourselves in opposition to the desire to turn to the community. We should look for realistic ways to help the antiwar movement do so. The naivete of many of those involved can easily make any turning to the community either adventuristic or demoralizing.

On the question of civil disobedience: It's important to remember that we've no principle whatsoever against civil disobedience. We have been very cautious and careful, consciously so in the past period, not to let our small forces get involved in actions which would involve heavy fines and heavy court battles for which there is no preparation. We avoid actions which merely involve the victimization of a handful. What we may see in the future though, unless the antiwar mood declines, is large scale, almost mass acts of civil disobedience of one kind or another. Such large scale actions have little in common with the actions of a handful of pacifists who sit down in the streets and get arrested and heavily fined and accomplish nothing. We should avoid the acts of civil disobedience which will be proposed by professional pacifists which substitute individual or small acts of civil disobedience for acts of education, propaganda or meaningful action. At the same time we must take each act of civil disobedience, just as we take each rally or picket line or teach-in, as a thing in itself, recognizing that tactical decisions have to be made.

The same type of thing faces us on the whole question of the draft. Right now there is no large scale movement in the antiwar movement to burn draft cards or to refuse to serve, but it's not out of the question that there might be in the next school year a significant opposition to the draft and to ROTC on the campus. It could take the form not of individual pacifist acts but of large scale organized acts against the war.

Since the March on Washington the proposal for a national mobilization that has generated the largest acceptance in the antiwar movement has been the idea of a Continental Congress. It provides a focus for the next large-scale mobilization in the nation's capital of thousands against the war. It raises at least indirectly, the question of power, not in the sense of dual power as we know it, but in the sense that it is based on the concept that one way or another must be found to get around or to replace the "decision-making apparatus" of the American rulers. The call for the Continental Congress also makes an explicit attempt to mobilize layers of the American population outside the students against the war in Vietnam who also are not "represented" in any real way in Washington.

There seems to be no reason whatsoever not to give the idea of a Continental Congress support. Quite the contrary, it has the potential for being the best forum thus far projected to exchange ideas. It comes from within the movement and has been proposed by those who are in the radical wing of the movement, from those who are the firmest and strongest supporters of a nonexclusive approach to demonstrations and rallies against the war. The call for a Continental Congress and the discussion engendered by the antiwar movement raises a question that we didn't expect to be dealing with a year ago: That is the turn by a section of this movement, outside of ourselves, away from the Democratic Party and its rejection of Democratic Party politics. This turn has not taken the form of a proposal to form an alternative political party. To the contrary, it has taken the form of an attempt to (using their language) find and organize "an alternative apparatus," that is, alternative organizations which will eventually make the decisions and run the country.

The most important statement since the SDS March on Washington call, (which helped to set the tone for the first stage of the antiwar movement) is an article by Staughton Lynd, the young Yale professor who was the head of the Freedom Schools in Mississippi in 1964 and who is one of the leading young spokesmen for this movement. It is an article in the June–July 1965 *Liberation* entitled, "Coalition Politics or Nonviolent Revolution" which all comrades should read. It opens up a polemic against Bayard Rustin, and against those who would side with Rustin, on four major counts: (1) It attacks the idea of working in the Democratic Party. It points out that the Democratic Party not only is *not* the way to progress in the future, but that the history of the past has shown that it never has been. (2) It attacks openly and explicitly third campism and social-patriotic pacifism in the antiwar movement. (3) Lynd attacks those who seek to castrate new movements, such as the civil liberties movements, Negro movements, and the antiwar movement by tying them to the Democratic Party. He compares this to the way the labor movement was politically castrated in the thirties. (4) Lynd attacks coalition politics. He writes, "Coalitionism is also elitism. Its assumption is that major political decisions are made by deals between the representatives of the interests included in the coalition. Negro protest, according to the Rustin formula, should now take on the role of such an interest. And men like Rustin will become the national spokesmen who sell the line agreed-on behind doors to the faithful followers waiting in the street."

The article represents more than the opinions of Lynd. In the article he refers to Bob Moses [Robert Parris] of the Student Nonviolent Coordinating Committee and to Tom Hayden, leader of the Newark SDS community project, as two of those who helped formulate these ideas. The mood and attitude of the article reflects in many ways the current mood of the antiwar activists.

In describing a view of "nonviolent revolution" Lynd writes, "Robert Parris has sketched out such a scenario as a possibility in Mississippi. What, he has asked, if Mississippi Freedom Democratic Party voters elected not only legislators but public officials as well? What if the Negroes of Neshoba County, Mississippi began to obey the instructions of the Freedom Sheriff rather than Sheriff Rainey? What if the Freedom Sheriff impaneled a Freedom Grand Jury which indicted Sheriff Rainey for murder?"

The worst possible approach we could take to those people with this attitude would be to begin by berating them for not seeing that they should be for a labor party or for not proposing an alternative socialist party. We begin by wholeheartedly supporting their rejection of the Democratic Party and support them against the Bayard Rustins and Norman Thomases. We should see any rejection of the Democratic Party as a very significant thing, something we have had a monopoly on for decades. We should stress first those things we have in common with the radical youth in the antiwar movement; the common rejection of secret diplomacy and the elitism of the ruling class, the common rejection of the idea that Congress is representative of the great mass of people in this country, and the common rejection of any attempt to tie the Negro movement and the antiwar movement to the Democratic Party. And we should help push these common ideas in the movement itself and win new people to them.

It is within this framework that we should put forth our view that it is only through the organization of a new party with a socialist program that any real alternative can be given to the political apparatus of the ruling class.

An understanding of the class character of society will be one of our contributions. For example, we will be pointing out to the movement that those people that they call the poor, the disenfranchised, and the disinherited, and the Negroes are part of the working class. We can point out to them why it is that "the system" which they speak of which is carrying out counterrevolution around the world is capitalism.

There are all kinds of contradictions in the positions of these radicals. Lynd thinks that Bayard Rustin just came to his conservative ideas in the last two years. He points out that to really understand Rustin's position now you have to look at what Bayard Rustin has done in the last year: his selling out the Mississippi Freedom Democratic Party, his recent statements in favor of coalition politics, and his attacks on the March on Washington. Lynd and the others in the movement have not begun to grapple with the political roots and antecedents to the policies of the social patriots, social democrats, Stalinists, and coalition politicians. That is our job.

We can and should support unconditionally the building of a Continental Congress. Such a congress could be a forum for our ideas and we should consider what kinds of proposals we would want to put before such a gathering. First, we would want to put forth our ideas on the war itself: the withdrawal of troops, the rights of referendum, the right of self-determination for nations, and our opposition to militarism. Second, because of the character of the antiwar movement and the attitude of those involved, we can raise sections of our transitional program that tie together the interests of the Negroes, the poor, the working people with the antiwar protests. The desire to tie together the interests of *all* the "unrepresented peoples" is a dominant one and should be taken advantage of.

We should pay close attention to the cleavages which are taking place within the left and within the antiwar movement. They'll be over the question of exclusion versus non-exclusion and the question of unconditional opposition to the war. They'll take place over the question of subordinating the demands of the antiwar movement to the demands of "progressive" politicians.

The role of our press is of crucial importance. The paper is the organizer and educator for our own ranks as well as our vehicle for bringing our ideas to those outside our movement. The press should raise the questions I've raised today. It can help to educate our comrades on how to best present our ideas to the antiwar movement and thus take part in the programmatic debates that are taking place. It is important for our press to take on at every opportunity the social democrats, the Stalinists, the coalition politicians, and the professional patriotic pacifists. We must hammer away at our opponents at every opportunity, hammer away at their false conceptions and misleading programs within the antiwar movement.

At the same time we should approach in a different way the militants and leaders of this movement, like the Lynds, embracing and developing the ideas which they put forth that are correct and discussing their contradictions and our proposals for solving them. When we discuss our views in the press or in conversation within this movement it's always much better to find a concrete illustration, a statement by a professor at a teach-in, an attack by Norman Thomas on the movement, an article by Staughton Lynd, or a statement by George Meany to use that as a polemical peg or an educational peg around which to develop our ideas.

Activity in the antiwar movement must not be confined to the youth. The youth cannot have one campaign orientation and the party "adults" another. How large the movement can become remains to be seen. We have no way of predicting. But we must (1) participate in the movement fully, (2) join the debate in the movement by supporting the rejection by the movement of those things we've been opposed to and within this framework present our program, and (3) present our general ideas on socialism and talk over which of the points of the transitional program we want to present and translate them into the language of the movement—just as we have done with our participation in the Negro struggle.

NOVACK: We're confronted here with something new in American history of the twentieth century. That's the emergence of defeatism at the beginning of an ongoing military action. Wood correctly said this antiwar movement is not predominantly pacifist; i.e., I believe it is an embryonic defeatism in its implications and ultimate direction. When a professor like Genovese, who represents its extreme left wing, says he's for the victory of the Vietcong, that's about as defeatist a political stand as you can take. This is something quite different from World War I or World War II. I recall reading about the history of Russia in 1905 and 1917 and wondering what it was like to live in a country with powerful defeatist sentiments in the midst of war. In the two wars our generations went through, we never saw any defeatist sentiment on a large scale. Opposition to the war was confined to a handful of revolutionaries. Now we're experiencing the beginning of a political phenomenon formerly reserved for other peoples.

This is a new and higher stage in the reaction to imperialist warmaking in the postwar period. What came forth toward the end of the Korean war now makes its appearance in the first steps of the Vietnamese conflict. Although this is not yet called defeatism even by the war hawks that's what it is, although of course it's still in a budding stage. This is a development of considerable portent. The bulk of the participants in the antiwar forces certainly don't grasp its significance and consequences. They're fresh, unsophisticated, unpoliticized, like all new generations and new layers of the masses that enter the arena to challenge the ruling powers. In a way it is good they don't really grasp what they're engaged in or it might deter their initial audacity. But the more advanced will come to understand the implications more and more as the war costs and casualties mount. Proceeding from this definition of its potential character, what we're trying to do is to extrapolate the lines of development and comprehend the entire prospective course from its very first steps. Defeatism starts as a mood and an attitude and then passes over into other and higher forms of action. We must foresee more antigovernment acts as the logical consequence and manifestation of this budding movement.

This is a political issue of the utmost gravity in which every word and action has to be carefully weighed and plumbed to its foundations. This position we're working out here ought to be seen in its connection with the resolution on organization. If any comrade takes a frivolous attitude toward the question of organization, I think that consideration of the new phase of antiwar sentiment apparently ahead of us is an additional argument for the type of organizational resolution we are presenting to the convention.

FEINGOLD: I think we have all the conditions developing for the first time in many years for the rise of a mass movement in this country around the opposition to war. Now it takes the form of radicalizing students, but it can go on to the Negroes who have less to gain from a war than anybody else, and eventually the mass of the population, the working people of the country. The conditions that exist, which show the possibility of a mass movement against war developing for the first time in so long, are a lot different, as a number of the comrades have pointed out. This is not the Second World War. There's no patriotism in this country for the war. It's not the same situation as that of the Korean war which was a very unpopular war. Comrades who were in the army during the Korean war are aware that there wasn't a great feeling of opposition to the war in a political sense. It just was an unpopular war that people felt was a dirty war. Much of the opposition to the war came from those that returned from Korea. If you could talk to any of those, they were very much against the war. But there was a big political obstacle. There was McCarthyism, which swept right into the army. You don't have that today and it loosens up the whole situation both outside among the intellectual community and in the army.

Also different today from several years ago are the conditions affecting pacifist organizations which have been mainly in the leadership of these antiwar movements. People who have mainly a fear of the bomb tend to develop pacifist attitudes toward the bomb scare. But today you have a revulsion toward the war, toward American foreign policy, that should have profoundly revolutionary implications. There's less of a tendency to move in a pacifist direction in that kind of revulsion against the policy of your own country, and you have the possibilities of developing a revolutionary approach toward the war. These conditions are different from the past wars, and from the peace movements of several years ago which were under pacifist influence, even though the majority of the people involved in those movements were not pacifists. There were young people involved, but the leadership was controlled by these pacifists.

That no longer holds today. It puts us in a position of making a central turn of the party at this coming convention, a turn toward a central campaign, an antiwar campaign, wherever possible. The party and youth can provide leadership. I'm not talking about leadership in the sense of mass demonstrations, but leadership in the sense of a propaganda and educational campaign, using the press and, of course, actually participating in and where possible leading, actions in opposition to the war. Now we're for putting an end to the imperialist foreign policy, and that's the mood and the idea that we have to get across wherever our comrades participate in the developing movement. Another thing we have to popularize is recognition that the main enemy is at home, that its political representatives are also in the Democratic Party. Nat Weinstein made an important point that in the election campaign we can challenge the whole imperialist political structure. There are many forms the effort could take.

We have to begin approaching two audiences. Those not yet in the army, that is the young people mainly, and those who are in the army. Among the students it can develop into a propaganda campaign aimed at millions of people. We've never had in this country such a large student community as has developed in the past several years. Out of these millions, hundreds of thousands of them will be going into the army. The elections in this country give us a way of pushing for independence from the capitalist politics. On the campuses themselves, elections take place. The youth can promote antiwar slates running in the campus elections. Elections of this type, and proposals and referendums on the campus can then be aimed at the National Student Association, which has national conferences where big discussions can take place on the war issue. For the first time in many years, teachers are involved in this movement. Traditionally teachers have been a brake on the student movement in this country. Now the teachers have a great deal of influence all over the country. Such moves can be considered as demands for a referendum vote, say like the case of the Ludlow amendment that came up in Congress before the second world war.

One other variant. The election campaign also gives a vehicle to approach people in the army. One of the things people don't lose in the army is their right to vote in elections. If they don't lose their right to vote, then political parties have a right to talk to them about election policy. One other point to raise is that the 18-year-olds, who are old enough to be soldiers, do not have the right to vote.

What comes clear to me is that we're in a situation where the party has to begin a major turn, so that we can begin playing a leadership role, especially in a propaganda and educational sense, in the antiwar movement.

3. REVOLUTIONARY POLICIES IN THE ANTIWAR MOVEMENT

By James P. Cannon

In the summer following the first sizable antiwar march in April 1965, an informal "Congress of Unrepresented People" met in Washington and announced the formation of a National Coordinating Committee to End the War in Vietnam (NCC) which was to hold a conference in late November. This first national conference of the antiwar movement coincided with a national antiwar march sponsored on November 27 by SANE, which the conferees built and participated in.

The NCC conference called for local actions in March, 1966. These demonstrations proved to be highly successful, dramatizing the further growth of the antiwar movement.

The NCC conference also proved to be the arena for an intense political struggle over perspectives for the antiwar movement. At that early stage the majority of the NCC leadership favored concentrating their efforts on pressuring liberals in Congress to take a stance in support of negotiations with the NLF. The Communist Party provided the central leadership for this tendency.

The left wing at the November conference was represented by the members of the action-oriented local independent antiwar committees that had sprung up during the preparations for the SDS march on Washington in April. They favored concentrating efforts on demonstrations in the streets. The demand they favored was "Bring the Troops Home Now!" These activists realized that they did not yet have majority support in the movement as a whole for their position, but they hoped to win further support for their slogan within the NCC and to form a national organization to coordinate their activities around this slogan, an organization which would also participate, like other national organizations opposed to the war, in the NCC.

The conservative conference majority bitterly opposed the immediate withdrawal demand. Moreover, they refused to permit the independent local committees to even meet together to discuss forming an organization despite the fact that most of the other organizations represented at the conference already had their own national structure which the independent committees did not.

The Trotskyists of the SWP and YSA participated in the conference as allies of the local committees, urging support for the "Bring the Troops Home Now!" demand and fighting for the right of the local activists to meet together in a workshop to discuss the formation of a national organization. When the presiding committee denied this right, the representatives of the local committees decided to hold a workshop anyway. The conference leaders made a great uproar about this, denouncing the local activists and the Trotskyists as "splitters." A slander campaign along these lines was carried on in various left periodicals for weeks afterward. In the midst of this controversy, James P. Cannon participated in a discussion in the Los Angeles branch of the SWP in December 1965 on the outcome of the NCC convention and the future of the antiwar movement. The following is a transcript of his remarks.

The correctness of Cannon's evaluation may be judged by the actual course of events. The caucus of local committees formed at the NCC conference launched the *Bring the Troops Home Now Newsletter*, which helped to rally the forces that later formed the Student Mobilization Committee to End the War in Vietnam in December 1966. The SMC became the most dynamic section of the mass antiwar movement. The demand for immediate withdrawal was eventually accepted by the majority of antiwar activists and became widely popular. The NCC collapsed in less than a year.

Cannon's remarks are reprinted from the October 1974 issue of the *International Socialist Review.*

I presume the assumption is that I was only 3,000 miles away from Washington so I would know all about it, and that I can give you all the dope. The fact is, when the meeting occurred last week I knew very little about the events in Washington, but just enough from the general reports to make me curious as to what had happened and decide to get a picture of the whole situation and the forces at work before coming to a conclusion about it. That's the best way to proceed on all questions.

What happened in Washington two or three weeks ago had to be regarded as an incident in the long, drawn-out struggle in which we are going to participate from now on. A struggle under conditions of constant urgency the like of which have never before been known by our movement or any other movement. Above all what's new and different and what almost everybody understands is that the bomb hangs over the world and the war we're talking about is the nuclear war we are trying to head off. It's an atomic war which would not be just another war like the last two world wars in which America got fat and prosperous, but a war that could very well mark nothing less than the end of the adventure of the human race on this planet.

I recall that when the formula for the production of the H-bomb was perfected and had been tested, Einstein wrote a memorandum to the president in which he said that it is now theoretically possible to destroy all life on the planet Earth. That seemed like a far-fetched assumption at the time, but it has since been repeated by practically all disinterested scientists. The movement against this war—what is sometimes rather incorrectly called the peace movement—which has grown up out of this new situation must be recognized also as a new phenomenon; a new movement which is taking forms and intensities that we have not known in previous wars. I am talking now about the war in Vietnam.

It's the first time in the knowledge of the present generation that there has been an open, active protest movement against a war in wartime. Prior to World War I there was a tremendous opposition against the entry of the United States into the war, but when the shooting started the movement evaporated. There was nothing left of it except the Socialists, the IWW, and the Anarchists, who were ferociously persecuted and suppressed from the very beginning. In the Second World War there was no vocal opposition at all except for some conscientious objectors and our party. In the Korean War, the press of our party was the only press that attacked America's action.

Now we have a very widespread and diverse protest movement against the war while it is going on. That, I say, should be recognized as a new phenomenon.

Another new thing is that the dynamic militant action, and even the leadership for the opposition to the present war, comes from the campus—primarily from the students. And that, as far as I know, is something quite new in this country. The academic world never led anything of any social consequence in this country before. We have not had, as the other advanced Western countries have had, a radical and socialistic student movement such as we now see developing in this country.

There is also a new type of pacifism. The classic pacifism we know, which Lenin denounced as worse than useless, was a pacifism that denounced war until it started and then rallied around the flag. I don't know whether many of you present here have seen that characteristic of the old pacifism, as I recall it, especially from the First World War. At that time there was a tremendous movement of opposition to America's entry into the war. So strong was the popular sentiment that Woodrow Wilson was reelected to the presidency primarily on the slogan "He kept us out of war."

Many public speakers, politicians, and, of course, preachers, spoke against entry into the war. I can't forget the effect it had upon us militants. We thought we had the population with us in our opposition—until the declaration of war. Then everything went out of the movement and the loudest pacifists became the loudest patriots, right away. They said you don't fight the government when it is at war. So the pacifists had simply led the people up to the expectation of opposition and then led them down immediately.

We have a sort of pacifism today that is still operative after the shooting has started. We have an active war in Vietnam, rapidly escalating since last February when they began bombing right and left, but there is still a considerable segment of the pacifist movement that does not cease to protest. That's new.

Now this peace movement, as I have undertaken to examine it, has many components and it behooves us as Marxist revolutionists to analyze the different segments of this movement and see which are useful, which can be considered as possible allies of ours, and which are not and not to confuse the one with the other. At first glance it is a very heterogeneous assortment of all kinds of people. You even have a few people who are part of the political establishment, such as Senator Morse. They are against the war in Vietnam not by any means as opponents but as advisers, on the ground that it is not a profitable war for the U.S. There is even, in my opinion, a considerable segment of the ruling powers that has grave doubts about the wisdom of the policy of the administration on the same grounds; that it's the wrong war in the wrong place. They are not against the government or against American imperialism, but on the grounds of tactics, maneuver, time and circumstance, they think this is not the way to begin a showdown.

Then there is a big assortment of others like the SANEites[1]—is that the right word for them? Those who make up this respectable body of middle-class people held the march in Washington a few weeks ago. They want to make it clear that they are not against the government and they are not in favor, by any means, of the revolutionary people of Vietnam, but would like the government to get out of the situation through negotiations. This implies that Americans have a right to be there in the first place, and it's just a question of bargaining back and forth as to how long they stay, how much they keep of that country, and how much of it they destroy.

Now I don't consider these people allies of the revolutionary workers. On the contrary, a year or so ago they conducted an enormous witch-hunt in their organization to drive out everybody suspected of being reds. The Communist Party people had been sneaking into their local assemblages and calling themselves SANEites, and all that was needed was for one Jim Crow senator to get up on the floor of Congress and denounce one of the people in an organizing committee in New York to just scare the daylights out of them and they started a wholesale purge of their organization. And the march they held in Washington a few weeks ago was a very polite affair. They had some trouble with the people who wanted to carry genuine antiwar slogans like the central slogan: Bring the Troops Home Now, and even some who wanted to carry the flag of the National Liberation Front. They were in a quandary as to whether they should call the cops or counterbalance this "scandalous" performance some other way. So they worked out a system of surrounding the flags of the National Liberation Front with little American flags. This was to make it clear to the president that they were with him and not with them.

The Social Democrats and the Stalinists are also negotiators, not real opponents of the war. There are some independents and these are some of the most important people in the movement, especially young people who have never been a part of any of the sectors of the traditional radical movement and who are sincerely opposed to the war and want to do something about it but have not yet found any definite political ideology. And then, of course, you have the revolutionary socialists represented by our party.

I think the party is proceeding correctly in its attempt to cooperate in action with anybody who will help to make a demonstration against the war, while at the same time making it clear we stand for certain definite slogans which really mean opposition to the war. Especially a slogan which means that America has no right whatever in South Vietnam—and that is the slogan: Bring the Troops Home Now. In my opinion, that is the correct slogan. I don't see how any revolutionist could oppose it. It is a revolutionary slogan. And it is the one the party and the youth think is the proper one around which to rally the really militant and earnest opposition to the continuing war.

This slogan appealed to me right away, partly out of nostalgia because this is not the first time it was raised by the socialist movement in this country. When Wilson sent American troops across the Mexican border in the period just before our entry into the First World War, the Socialist Party called an emergency meeting of its National Committee and adopted a manifesto which bore the title: "Withdraw the Troops." That was the essence of the demand upon the government: Get out of Mexico and stay out of Mexico. That was all the situation called for, and it created both the basis for organizing the broadest opposition of people who

1. Members of the liberal Committee for a SANE Nuclear Policy.

were really against this monstrous attack upon the Mexican people, and at the same time made no concession whatever in principle because the withdrawal of the troops signified the victory of the Mexicans.

When we entered the Korean war, as far as I know the only paper in the country that came out with a forthright denunciation of the war and a demand which incorporated all that was necessary from a revolutionary point of view, was our paper, *The Militant*. I was appointed by the Political Committee to write an Open Letter to the president and the members of Congress. And this letter contained the demand: "Bring the American soldiers out of Korea and let the Korean people alone to settle their own affairs." It never entered anybody's head, so far as I know or heard, to suggest that this was not fully adequate as an expression of our support to the Korean people and our opposition to our own government.

So I think that slogan which our comrades have settled on as the central, motivating agent for the building of a genuine antiwar movement, stands up both historically and for the needs of the present day. I don't think that's the purpose of the political elements in the so-called peace movement beside ourselves and some of the pacifists and independents. As far as I can make out both by past experience and present operations, the Stalinists and the Social Democrats are primarily concerned with gearing the so-called peace movement toward the next election campaign for "peace" candidates, and peace candidates can be any kind of political faker who will say he is in favor of negotiations while the troops are still there and still bombing the people. It's an important question whether they will be able to take this inchoate and unclearly defined peace movement down the blind alley of coalition politics or whether a big section of the movement will respond to a different slogan and a different line of action.

I was greatly impressed by the reports that we got from the Washington conference. I am not speaking now of the march organized by SANE but of the conference called by the National Coordinating Committee, with delegates from various elements of the peace movement. I was impressed by the feeling that this was a new political experience for the younger generation of revolutionists. This is the first time they have had a serious confrontation with political opponents on a national scale. This marks the emergence of our small party from previous isolation toward the center of what radicalism there is in the country. It is the first opportunity they have had to learn at first hand what it means to deal with political opponents who are presumably all united in the same wonderful camp—unity, gosh, it's wonderful—but in actuality have entirely different objectives. They learned how to handle themselves when they meet these opponents at close range. That I consider a great victory for our young comrades. They were an active part in the preparations of this gathering and they participated in it as revolutionists. And they learned something that could not be learned fully out of books. Some things have to be learned in experience, although the books help to prepare for them.

I recall talking with Trotsky—on a delegation that went to see him in 1938 in preparation for the Founding Conference of the Fourth International—about the experience we had just finished in the Socialist Party.[2] We were drawing the balance sheet on what had been achieved or not achieved, and he wanted a very full and detailed report. I recall his remarking that he was well pleased with the practical results; with the recruits, the fact that we had kept our own forces intact and had gained some new forces. And he said, the principal gain is the experience. Those who have been through this experience of a direct confrontation with centrists and right-wing socialists have acquired something that cannot be lost. That is necessary for the full development of a revolutionary political leadership.

I think that is the big gain out of the Washington conference. And even mistakes that could have been made or defeats suffered can be turned to good account if it's all understood and assimilated as part of the experience.

As to what really happened in Washington, we

---

2. The American Trotskyists joined the Socialist Party in 1936 in response to a left turn by the SP and its recruitment of a number of radicalized workers and youth. They remained in the SP until the end of 1937 when they were expelled by the conservative leadership. The Socialist Workers Party was founded on New Year's Day 1938 by the expelled branches of the SP.

had conflicting reports. At first I was surprised to hear our delegate come back and say we had done very well there. Then I heard other reports, some comrades thought a terrible mistake had been made and a catastrophe had overtaken us because we had run head-on into a battle with the majority of the steering committee and others there. So I thought the best thing I could do was to try to find out what had happened.

I read in my attempt to inform myself about all aspects of the event. I studied the *National Guardian*. I studied *The Militant*, the *People's World*, and the *New Republic*. I heard the reports of Comrade Derrel and I read the account of the conference in this *Newsletter* of the national caucus for the organization of independent committees united on the slogan of withdraw the troops now. And I also read—you don't know how thorough I am when I am looking for information as to who really hid the body—I even read the circular letter distributed by a united combination of two people here, the *Spartacist*, and the Wohlforthites, and the Phillips tract. I even read a couple of copies of the *"Bulletin of the Fourth International"* printed by a couple of other people in New York. And everything I read except *The Militant* seemed to point directly at the Trotskyites in Washington as the people who had committed the crime. And I was just about to say it looks like a perfect case—because it was so unanimous—until I remembered that I am a Perry Mason fan and that I have often noticed the one who is accused of the crime turns out to be innocent, and the dirty dog who did the job fixed things so that he could clear himself and throw the suspicion on an innocent man.

The minute I read the *Guardian*—being a politician and knowing what the *Guardian* is and how it has been evolving—I said, that's a poisonously slanted article. It's aimed with deadly malice to compromise what they call—quoting others—the "Trotskyite splitters." That put me on guard. Then I later got hold of the *People's World*, published up in San Francisco, and I read their account; how everybody was for unity except some disgruntled and disruptive minority that they didn't even dignify by naming. The *Guardian* did; they said we had been denounced as "Trotskyite splitters."

The *People's World* informed me that Dave Dellinger and Professor Staughton Lynd of *Liberation* magazine worked with Communist Party delegate Arnold Johnson and Irving Beinin of the Lower East Side Mobilization for Peace Action, and many others to find a common ground for agreement. Now the minute I saw just that paragraph informing me that Arnold Johnson was working down there, and that he was backed up by Beinin, I knew there was something crooked going on. Because I know who Johnson is; he's the organization secretary of the Stalinist party. I know who Beinin is. He's the ex-Cochranite who has been making a profession of baiting Trotskyism ever since he got kicked out of the party twelve years ago.[3] I know that he's identified not merely with the *Guardian* but with the right-wing group which has recently conducted the swing of the *Guardian* to the right.

Another report I got was of a meeting down in Houston, Texas, which one of our comrades by accident attended. He told me they had received before the conference a letter from the SDS office in New York tipping them off about the Trotskyists and preparing them for a fight.

So out of all this a clearer picture emerged. And if I would criticize our comrades who were in charge of the fight in Washington, it would perhaps be for a fault that is hard to avoid in the absence of experience of this sort. That is, the underestimation of political opponents; an assumption that everything is going to be on the level, which is a very bad assumption when you have Stalinists and Social Democrats to deal with. They may possibly have been caught by surprise.

I didn't doubt for one minute about the ambush being prepared after I heard that several weeks before the conference was held the *Daily Worker* and the *People's World* suddenly began to promote the conference in high gear. I know what that means. I don't have the slightest doubt that they stacked the convention with every kind of delegate from every kind of paper organization they could mobilize. I don't doubt that they stacked the steering commit-

3. During the Korean War and the McCarthyite witch-hunt a group of young party leaders headed by Bert Cochran and George Clarke began to seek shelter from the political climate through adaptation to the trade-union bureaucracy and Stalinism. They were expelled from the SWP for acts of indiscipline in November 1953.

tee, that they rigged the agenda, in such a way that the delegates of many independent committees and our own people ran into a prepared fight in which there was room for everything except the one thing they were most interested in. That was promoting the real slogan of the antiwar movement, "Bring the Troops Home Now." And of the right and necessity of the independent committees organized under that slogan to unite themselves nationally.

Our operations and those of the caucus were called a "splitting move." If you examine the evidence of that convention, it's the most fantastic accusation imaginable. Splitting what? Every tendency represented in that convention had its national organization. There were the DuBois Clubs, SDS, Women Strike for Peace, the Committee for Non-Violent Action, the Communist Party, and many others. But the independent committees who have adopted the central slogan which tests whether you are really serious about opposing American imperialism, the war, or not—that is, the withdrawal of the troops—were denied the right to organize themselves. There was no provision on the agenda or any of the workshops to even discuss that question and take it to a vote.

I'll admit my ignorance—I asked, what is this National Coordinating Committee anyhow? From the reports we got about splits, splits, splits, I thought maybe there was a national organization that we were breaking up. It's not a national organization at all. It's just what its name says: it's a national coordinating committee. And where did it come from? Where was it elected? It wasn't elected anywhere. It's a self-appointed committee constituted in Washington a few months ago at the Congress of Unrepresented People. It has headquarters in Wisconsin, and it has as its president or chairman a man named Emspak.

Now that rang a bell for me. I have heard that name before. It isn't the same Emspak, I am told. He's the son, and from all accounts, a chip off the old block. Emspak was a Stalinist hack; he was the secretary of the United Electrical Workers Union. Emspak was the central figure in 1941, when we came to open warfare in Minneapolis in the split with Tobin, who blocked the issuance of a CIO charter to the Minneapolis Local of the Teamsters who wanted to join the CIO.[4] But the charter was issued to us—not by the CIO; there it was blocked by Emspak. It was issued by District 50 of the United Mine Workers Union. So in order to get into the CIO in the heyday of the Stalinists, the Teamsters had to join the Miners.

All this aroused the natural suspicion that proved to be a reality: that the NCC is in fact stacked and rigged and controlled by Stalinists, and it's not an organization. It's a committee, an unelected committee. It's not like a union or a political party or a cooperative or fraternal order; it's just what its name says—a coordinating committee to coordinate the activities of other organizations in the peace movement. And all tendencies have the right to have their own national organization. But the independent committees to end the war in Vietnam, who adopted the fighting slogan, Bring the Troops Home Now, when they asked to have a gathering to discuss the proposal that they should organize themselves nationally, they were denounced as "splitters."

Well, I think that is crooked. I think the slogan of Bring the Troops Home Now is an absolutely correct slogan, the one upon which you can organize an antiwar movement that really means business. Anybody who will not adopt that slogan isn't really fighting the war. Because if you agree to leave the American troops there, with all their equipment, there is never going to be any peace or independence for the Vietnamese people.

I think our comrades were correct to adopt that slogan and their militancy at the conference and their refusal to be bluffed or bulldozed is quite admirable. All the more so that they were perhaps taken by surprise and hadn't had previous experience with what the perfidy of Stalinism and the Social Democracy is really like. I will guarantee you that they will never be taken by surprise again.

These are permanent assets which speak well

4. In the 1930s the Teamsters International Union was affiliated to the AFL. The head of the Teamsters, Daniel Tobin, was seeking to regiment the union in preparation for Roosevelt's entry into World War II and as part of this process he launched a violent attack on the Trotskyists in Minneapolis. The Minneapolis Teamsters in response sought affiliation with the CIO, which was blocked by the Stalinists in the CIO national council but finally achieved through the intercession of John L. Lewis of the United Mine Workers.

for the future. Whether some error or misstep of a tactical character was made in the heat of the fight I would not be competent to judge at this distance. But even so, tactical mistakes or setbacks or defeats can be corrected as long as the principal line is correct and as long as we don't get stubborn, when we do make a mistake, trying to rectify it by doing the same thing over again.

Nothing definite as far as I know was settled at this conference. No policy was adopted; no slogan was approved or rejected. They just met; they talked—and attacked the Trotskyites—and the only motion of any consequence that was passed that I could discern from what I studied, was to call some new demonstrations in March and to support the demonstrations in the South in February. I presume we will participate in that.

No formal organization was constituted. So how can you split the NCC? It's only a coordinating committee. And not only was it not elected when first constituted, it was not even elected at this conference. It's rigged and stacked with representatives of god-knows-what kind of organizations. With a Stalinist at the head of it. And anybody that will put any confidence in the fairness and justice or revolutionary militancy of such a committee has my sympathy. He badly needs attention—and not the kind I can give, because I am not what they call a head-shrinker.

No definite program. Anybody that's for peace is entitled to be represented on the committee. No formal organization; all the local organizations have their own autonomy. No elected national officers. Just a National Coordinating Committee. I wouldn't worry about accusations on trying to split that outfit—because our people didn't split. The accusation is false. They stayed in the convention to the end, and they openly announced they were organizing a caucus of people who stood for the idea and the slogan: Bring the Troops Home Now. And the right of these independent committees operating under this slogan to form a national organization of their own and to affiliate to the NCC like the other national organizations, such as the Women Strike for Peace and others.

Now, I read the first *Newsletter* and thought it was well written, very intelligent and an honest report of the convention. Their proposals seemed sound to me from a revolutionary point of view. It remains to be seen whether they will be successful in their endeavor to create a national organization of independent committees on this slogan, or whether they will receive a setback. Experience will tell us. But if there is a setback or defeat, I think our comrades will know how to recuperate from it and plan other tactics. Tactics can be changed. If you've got the right line and know how to be a little flexible in your tactics, you're not easily destroyed.

The whole antiwar movement is, as I see it, at a very critical stage, because the war is escalating. The more the war escalates the more pressure will be brought upon the movement to conform. The weaklings and the negotiators and all the others will talk in softer and softer voices until you can't even hear them whisper any more. And the militants will get hardened and they'll get new recruits because every time the word gets out of another soldier killed, there are his family and friends who hear about it. And the public opposition to the senseless slaughter will grow up and there will be new recruits. And the end of the movement, as far as I can see it, can only be toward more militancy and more assertion of the type shown by our caucus and our associates in Washington. And they will then have to seriously look from the campus where things started to the sources of power of the social struggle—among the less privileged workers in the first place and eventually toward the organized workers.

And out of that I think we can see the beginnings of a new radical movement which raises great perspectives of world-historical significance for America, the most backward of countries in all things that concern culture, political intelligence, and social awareness. That America finally is producing a revolutionary and radical grouping on the campuses of this country. From the beginning of the socialist movement we have understood, and our fathers before us, that the power that can change society is the working class. But we understood also that from other classes could come what the *Communist Manifesto* calls elements of enlightenment and progress.

We should not forget that Marx and Engels began as students. We shouldn't forget that Marx and Engels and Lenin and Trotsky—and practically all the leaders of the Russian Revolution—began as students in the colleges. And it really almost takes your breath away—the prospect that we may be on the verge of a period when a new elite is taking shape among the student bodies across this vast country. They will find their way to collaboration with the working class in this country and bring with them the benefits of their talents and education. They will contribute new thinkers, new writers, new orators, and new agitators who know how to identify themselves with the working-class movement. I think we will not neglect that field and I think that we have made a good start already with the organization and development of our Young Socialist Alliance.

I think that the experience in Washington—regardless of what mistakes in tactics here and there might have been made—has to be regarded as a great achievement for our movement.

4. A REPLY TO A CRITICISM OF OUR ANTIWAR POLICY

By Lew Jones

The following article was written in reply to a criticism of the policies followed by the Young Socialist Alliance in the antiwar movement. The criticism, which was submitted to the YSA preconvention discussion in 1967, was written by Steve Chase, Eloise Linger, John Barzman, and Linda Sheppard. Subsequently Chase, Linger, and Sheppard changed their views and decided that the antiwar strategy adopted by the SWP and YSA was correct. Barzman went on to develop much deeper differences with the YSA and SWP, and eventually left the SWP in 1974.

The criticism, entitled "Minority Antiwar Resolution," can be found in *YSA Discussion Bulletin*, Volume 10, No. 7, published in March 1967. The reply by Lew Jones is reprinted from *YSA Discussion Bulletin*, Volume 10, No. 8. This document has been abridged for publication in this collection, omitting a detailed treatment of events in the antiwar movement in 1966.

The Vietnam war's central importance to world and national politics and our leading role in the antiwar movement make the antiwar discussion and decisions at the coming convention crucial for our work in the next period.

The submission of the minority resolution underscores the importance of the discussion. The YSA is now presented with what the authors contend is an opposing general line for our central arena of activity.

We will first reiterate briefly the general line which has guided our activity in the antiwar movement since its inception and which is embodied in the NEC [National Executive Committee] draft resolution. Second, we will deal with the minority version of the history of the antiwar movement. Third, we will examine the alternative course for our antiwar work implied by the minority resolution.

I. OUR LINE

From the beginning our attitude toward the antiwar movement has been based on the characteristic which makes it unique compared to past pacifist movements. Classical pacifism opposed war in time of peace, but when war broke out, used its authority to mobilize patriotic support for "this particular war." That is, classical pacifism always voiced its opposition to *war in general* but always found an "exceptional reason" for supporting its "own" government after the outbreak of armed conflict. The crime of the pacifist leaders was that they used their authority as advocates of peace, to turn the wholly progressive pacifism of the masses, who are opposed to war, into its chauvinist opposite when war broke out.

The present antiwar movement is distinguished from classical pacifism above all by the fact that it has developed and grown in explicit opposition to the shooting war being waged *now* against the Vietnamese. This is the first time in American history that such a movement has developed during a war. This fact dictated from the beginning the necessity not only of our participation but a willingness to shoulder leadership responsibility in this movement. It precluded intervening by simply condemning the movement as pacifist and "making the record" as to where we stand.

Proceeding from this premise, and from the knowledge that the movement was made up of conflicting tendencies, we have from the beginning fought for a policy of nonexclusion. Nonexclusion is the basis of our participation in the broad united-front-type coalition that makes up the antiwar movement.

As we interpret the concept of nonexclusion it embodies, not only the principle that no tendency shall be excluded because of nonconformist ideas, views, and opinions, but that we reserve the right, for ourselves—and others—to advance such slogans and demands within the movement that we feel can best advance the struggle in opposition to the war. We do *not* issue ultimatums to others to accept our views as a condition for joint action in the struggle against the war. Nor do we tolerate such ultimatums from others. We are confident that given a democratic milieu our views will prevail among substantial numbers of young militants and antiwar activists. This basic framework of nonexclusion and a serious attitude toward working out specific agreement for joint action dictates the necessity of arriving, within strictly defined limits, and wherever possible, at decision by consensus. United action would otherwise become impossible. It is within this general concept that we have, from the beginning, advanced and vigorously promoted our central slogan, Bring the Troops Home Now!

Our insistence on a "single issue" antiwar movement has been grossly misunderstood in some quarters. The "single issue" around which the coalition has been built was never intended to be the *single slogan* of withdrawal of U.S. troops but joint struggle *in action* to end the war. It is around this issue that the widest possible unity in action has been mobilized against the imperialist war in Vietnam and against the capitalist class that is waging that war.

We never considered, and we do not now view the antiwar movement as a united front of propaganda with a general program. It is a united front of *action*. Opposition to imperialist war is tested not in words, which come easy, but in deeds, in marches and in periodic mass demonstrations. It was around this axis that we concentrated our efforts to keep the movement from being channeled into class-collaborationist politics, community organizing projects, individual antidraft gimmicks, research projects, etc.

It is this that has characterized our "single issue" approach to the antiwar movement.

Within the broad united-front-type coalition organized around struggle against the war, we have been able to build and maintain to this point a working bloc with the radical pacifists. The bloc has rested upon agreement on the following points: 1) The most important question of the day is opposition to the war, and it is around this issue that the broadest coalition of diverse tendencies can be formed. The movement must be nonexclusive. 2) The movement should engage in mass actions, and not subordinate such actions to the so-called "multi-issue" projects of particular tendencies. 3) The movement's propaganda should reach out to the labor movement, the civil rights movement, and the G.I.'s. 4) Within the broader coalition, we seek to convince as many as possible to demand immediate withdrawal of U.S. troops. This demand is a concretization of the right of the Vietnamese to self-determination and links up the immediate interests of the G.I.'s in Vietnam with the antiwar sentiment at home.

This is *our political line,* embodied in resolutions of past conventions and national committee plenums, conferences, articles, and editorials in our press, in pamphlets, brochures, speaking tours, etc. From this general line flows our tasks, as outlined in the NEC draft resolution.

The minority comrades contend that they represent a tendency with a contrary line which they present in the form of a minority resolution for convention decision as a substitute for the line of the majority. Unfortunately, nowhere in their document is their alleged "line" clearly set forth.

Except for some casual, unsubstantiated "criticisms" in their first few paragraphs, they do not critically examine the line of the NEC draft resolution. Instead, we are presented with an "indictment" of the leadership for being derelict in carrying out the line adopted by previous conventions. Yet, although not explicitly stated, the logic of the views expressed does lead to a contrary political conclusion from which flows their charge of tactical "adaptation," unwarranted concessions, deviations, etc., etc. . . .

II. A REVIEW OF THE LAST YEAR

Section II is omitted from this document, except for the following:

The Current Conjuncture

Where does the antiwar movement stand today? Our perspective for it has in good measure been proved correct. The process of reaching out to other sections of society has moved forward, drawing in representatives of both wings of the civil rights movement, a few unions, and the conservative peace groups. The addition of James Bevel [of the Southern Christian Leadership Conference] as executive director [of the Spring Mobilization Committee] symbolizes and further aids the process of organizing antiwar sentiment in the ghetto. The addition of Cleveland Robinson, secretary-treasurer of District 65, as a vice-chairman and the formation of labor subcommittees within the Spring Mobilization Committee, and local union support on the West Coast indicates the growing labor support and the expanding opportunities in this area.

It took time and constant campaigning by our forces to set the Spring Mobilization in motion. The call, delayed by long political debates, has finally been released containing the demand for withdrawal of U.S. troops and no demand suggesting that the U.S. has the right to negotiate the future of Vietnam. *This call is the most militant of any of the previous days of protest.*

Around the mobilization a campaign spirit is developing, promising to make April 15 the largest demonstration in the antiwar movement's history.

The Effects of New Forces

There is a contradiction involved in the entry of labor and civil rights groups into the movement, of course. As organizations from the labor movement and the Negro struggle begin to become involved in the protest movement, they move through their own organizations and leaderships, and at their present level of political consciousness. These leaders are for the most part class-collaborationists.

The leaders move toward the movement because 1) they feel antiwar pressure from their own ranks and 2) they see a growing radical movement that threatens to go over their heads.

Their entry is welcomed by us, because it signals the beginning of antiwar activity by working class forces. Of course the entry of bureaucrats adds to the specific weight of reformism in the movement and will lead to increased attacks on withdrawal, nonexclusion, and radical influence generally. If such forces do come into the movement in sufficient numbers, it is likely we will have to refight some of the prior battles of the antiwar movement.

In such circumstances our conjunctural role will begin to change. It will tend to shift from one of direct leadership in a relatively small mass movement to one of fighting to build a class-struggle left wing among larger organized masses.

But we do not approach this conjuncture nervously and fearful that we will lose our integrity, talking about "girding" ourselves and "we must fight even if it means merely 'making the record'" as the minority does. No, we welcome, urge, and actively solicit the entrance of new forces into the antiwar movement, confident that we will not merely "make the record" but will reach out to even more people with our ideas and build a class-struggle left wing.

There is no contradiction between the leading role we are now playing and what *may* be our role 3–6 months from now. On the contrary, by building the Spring Mobilization we maximize the possibilities and opportunities for our ideas and influence in the future.

There are other factors which will or could influence the development of this contradiction: the 1968 elections, the possibility of negotiations, the escalation of the war, a new revolutionary upsurge in the world, etc. Our job will be to watch the objective developments closely and gauge our tactics realistically to the movement as it develops in order to reach our strategic aims.

The central tenets of the analysis of the antiwar movement in the minority resolution are completely wrong. The movement has not declined. It has continued to grow, reflecting the deepening sentiment against the war in the population, particularly in the labor and civil rights movements. The last year has seen the growth of united fronts of action based on nonexclusion on national, local, and even campus levels. The liberals and pacifists have not taken over, and the movement has not lost its "independent thrust" since March 25–26. Just the opposite is the case. The independence and anti-imperialism of the movement has deepened and will reach its highest point so far on April 15. At this time new forces are beginning to enter the movement which will give increased opportunities to disseminate our ideas to greater numbers of people. Our past activity has prepared the YSA to play such a role, contrary to the position of the minority. Had their approach been followed during the last year we would now be isolated from the present openings.

III. THE GENERAL LINE OF THE MINORITY RESOLUTION

Underneath the tendentious and false charges made against the YSA leadership, the counter-resolution contains an *implicit* general line which runs counter to the line the YSA has been following for the past two years and which the NEC resolution projects for the next period. This line is nowhere made clear and explicit, but can be deduced from their document.

They state, "Bring the Troops Home Now . . . is the only principled basis of opposition to U.S. imperialist war." On the same page, they say, "Therefore it is our main task to build an organizational form in the antiwar movement which can adopt this slogan (withdrawal of troops) as its central demand." And they say, speaking of the Student Mobilization Committee, "In reality this formation is not based on the demand for withdrawal. Again, as in the Spring Mobilization Committee, withdrawal is just one of three demands which are subordinated to the central task of building the mobilization."

(This last statement contains the absurdity that the Student Mobilization Committee is "not based on the demand for withdrawal," because "end the draft" and "end university complicity" are also slogans the committee supports. This almost defies comment. Are they suggesting that we should not support these two demands? Are these demands in contradiction to the withdrawal demand? The committee, in fact, *is* based on withdrawal and the other two slogans are good ones which help to build the committee.)

These three quotations, as well as the thrust of their criticisms in general, indicate that they do not understand the essential character of the antiwar movement.

The antiwar movement, by which we mean the whole coalition which has been built up around the single issue of struggle and action against the war, is deeply, profoundly anti-imperialist in character. It is not true that the withdrawal wing is the anti-imperialist wing within the larger movement—the *whole movement* is anti-imperialist. The test of anti-imperialism in a period of war is *action* against the imperialist war in Vietnam; this is the *concrete test* of anti-imperialism in the present period.

This fundamental appraisal of the thrust of the movement against the war has been the basis of our whole approach since the 1965 SDS March on Washington. This is why we are for the broadest possible coalition around action against the war, and why we *do not* make acceptance of the withdrawal slogan a condition for our participation in and leadership of united actions. From this view of the antiwar movement's deeply anti-imperialist character, our *primary task* is not now to "build an organizational form in the antiwar movement which can adopt" the withdrawal slogan. Our primary task is to continue to build mass actions against the war to achieve the greatest *unity* in action of a continually expanding antiwar movement. Yes—the "central task" of the Student Mobilization Committee is to build the April 15 Mobilization!

They say, "By this time [the November, 1966 Cleveland antiwar conference] almost every major opponent had given lip service to the slogan of withdrawal. This position had been clearly adopted by the previous Cleveland conference on its own initiative. Yet our fraction did not even attempt to have this statement *reaffirmed officially* (emphasis added) by this conference." That's right—we decided that rather than register a purely formal victory for verbal radicalism at Cleveland, it was *more important* to get agreement to launch the next antiwar *action* and to lay the groundwork to bring the largest possible numbers of people out into the streets against the war.

We had enough support to carry the vote at the conference, but did not have that majority among the antiwar forces we wanted to bring into the April 15 action. We should also note that far from contradicting our line of Bring the Troops Home Now, our tactics beginning in Cleveland have not only helped consolidate the largest action against the imperialist war in Vietnam to date, within which we have complete freedom of action, but for the first time in any national day of protest, the formal call "makes the record," if you please, for withdrawal of U.S. forces from Vietnam.

Throughout their document, they denigrate the concept of the antiwar coalition, belittling our efforts to build the widest possible unity against the war. The Parade Committee is referred to derogatorily as the "catch-all Parade Committee." We are *for* "catch-all" committees like the Parade Committee, to organize the widest possible unity in action against the war. We want to build the "catch-all" antiwar movement. We hope it eventually "catches all" of the labor movement and Negro movement.

Following through on their belittling of the united actions against the war, they say: "Furthermore, to confine ourselves to finding activities which divert their attention away from political conflicts, conflicts which would threaten the alliances between us and petty-bourgeois organizations, is to throw away the lessons of the revolutionary working class tendency in the united front." And, "we must fight even if it means merely 'making the record' or isolating ourselves from the petty bourgeois organizations we oppose."

Implicit in this approach and behind this advocacy of verbal radicalism and "making the record" (what record?) lies the concept of *reversing the priorities* in our antiwar work.

Instead of the primary task being to build the widest possible unity in action against this imperialist war, and fighting for our slogans, demands, ideas, etc., within this framework, they would have us open a *fight* to make withdrawal the central demand and not "subordinate it to" building mass actions!

This approach could have only one result and effect, whatever the authors subjectively intend. That effect would be to *split the movement* against the imperialist war in Vietnam.

Implicit in their position is that we begin laying down conditions, making ultimatums—*fighting* "even if it means merely 'making the record' or isolating ourselves." From this we can only conclude that they want us to demand that the antiwar movement adopt our line and to thereby *exclude* those who refuse to go along. But this would be the wrong turn at the wrong time. The next "moderate forces" who will come into the antiwar movement are sections of the labor movement and Negro movement! This is just what we want. What we want then is only the right to express our views as a minority within a mass movement, not be standing on the sidelines, safely wrapped up in our purity, smugly content for having "made the record."

The whole thrust of their line, intended or not, is to jettison a basic plank in our approach—nonexclusion. A fundamental tenet of nonexclusion is that we do not force others to accept withdrawal as a condition of joining the movement, just as we demand to be included in the broader movement against the imperialist war with the right to educate about and advocate the slogan for withdrawal of U.S. troops.

The counter-resolution lists a series of truisms everyone agrees with on the united front. "The united front," they say, "is not a partnership with the reformists but a form of struggle against them. We must not rely on them but mistrust them." That is true—but the logic of their position leads in the direction of abandoning the point of departure for the application of Leninist concepts within the united front; that point of departure is the united front itself.

Our Bloc with Muste and the Radical Pacifists

On the question of the militant pacifists, they say: "The 'radical' pacifists who are sympathetic to the liberation struggles play the role of fence sitters and mediators, but at *every* critical turn line up with their fellow reformists on the crucial dispute over withdrawal as a central demand, as Muste has done time after time." (Emphasis added). Again, they see the question of whether the withdrawal slogan is the *central demand* as the central issue. Not only Muste, but *we*, the YSA, have not forced the withdrawal slogan to be the central demand of the massive national actions against the imperialist war in Vietnam because we understood that not everyone agreed with it who could be mobilized in *action* against the imperialist war, and it is this action against the war which is our central objective. This is the correct, anti-imperialist approach.

They repeat their criticism of the radical pacifists: "It appears that the pacifist leadership in the Spring Mobilization Committee are sympathetic to the Vietnamese revolution and they agree with us on this level. But it must be remembered that they continually waver on the key questions of withdrawal and self-determination, and generally fail to aid us at *any* critical conjuncture." (Emphasis in original).

In the first place, this is factually incorrect. If it

were true that Muste and Dellinger and the other left wing pacifists fail to side with us at any critical juncture, the movement would not have been able to establish unity on the militant basis that it has. The radical pacifists support the withdrawal demand. Time after time they have sided with us on nonexclusion, withdrawal, broadening the coalition, and the single issue basis of periodic actions against the war.

The latest time was in the Spring Mobilization Committee, when the CP and other class-collaborationist forces on the West Coast succeeded in passing a resolution recommending that the Spring Mobilization drop its withdrawal position in favor of advocacy of U.S. negotiations to end the war. The radical pacifists among others blocked with us to kill this move.

Muste and the SWP "Peace Candidate"

Another factual error: they state, "The *Newsletter* contained an article in May raising the question of peace candidates, but since then contained not a word publicizing or exposing peace candidates—not even on the minimal basis of their antiwar platforms being for or against immediate withdrawal. Why not? Because now we were to use the *Newsletter* to form an alliance with Muste who supported peace candidates."

Muste supported no capitalist party peace candidates. He did support Judy White and Herbert Aptheker—two working class candidates—or does the minority consider White and Aptheker in the same category as capitalist peace candidates? Within the antiwar movement, Muste was the main single force outside of ourselves fighting to prevent the movement from being diverted into support to capitalist peace candidates instead of building mass actions.

The whole question of peace candidates was handled by the *Newsletter* through its fighting for the alternative policy of actions against imperialist war. The *Newsletter,* as an organ of the antiwar movement, could not present the full Trotskyist analysis of the question. This was done in the *Young Socialist* and *The Militant* in articles directly on the question, articles explaining the Judy White campaign, articles explaining our critical support of Aptheker, and articles on our opposition to the petty-bourgeois "peace" candidates. The SWP election campaigns, which we supported, provided us with an important avenue to fight on this question. It was by bringing these campaigns to our coworkers in the antiwar movement that we made some of our biggest gains.

Again, what is the implicit line contained in this position on the radical pacifists? Although they don't come out and say so, the logic of the minority position is that we should not be in a bloc with the radical pacifists, and we should now break that bloc. This, too, just like their implicit position that we give up non-exclusion is another piece of sectarianism bordering on abstentionism. Without our bloc with the radical pacifists neither the antiwar movement nor our movement would be where it is today. *Of course* this bloc has its frictions. *Of course* new events may upset it and maybe sooner than we would prefer. But we are going to hold onto it as long as we can, and won't lightly break it up in order to "make the record."

"Making the record" appears to be the essence of revolutionary politics to the minority. What we fear is hidden behind this verbal radicalism is a position that objectively approaches that of PL, Wohlforth, Spartacist, and the other ultralefts. They "make the record"—from A to Z—and have used that as a springboard to launch themselves completely out of the movement. That is the logical extension of the implied "line" in the minority resolution, and the road which we unqualifiedly reject.

The antiwar movement has been the first large movement the YSA has had an opportunity to work deeply in as builders and leaders for a sustained period of time. It is important we approach this movement correctly, by understanding its inherent anti-imperialist character, by understanding and applying the concept of nonexclusion to build the broadest unity in action against the imperialist war, by learning how to present our ideas and build the YSA without losing sight of the tasks of building the antiwar movement itself in struggle against the class enemy. In this movement we are learning valuable, if incomplete, lessons on how to intervene in the working class movements and great class battles to come.

No, our task is not to "make a clean break from the policies of the leadership in the past year" as the minority says. Rather it is to reaffirm the general line we have carried out in the past, affirm our tasks for the future, and deepen our understanding of the class-struggle approach of this line. We must reject the line implicit in the minority resolution—the line of isolating and splitting ourselves off from this movement.

One final point. The general line of the counter-resolution is unclear, and is not spelled out. The authors insist that they have a counter political line to that of the NEC draft resolution, however, since they place their resolution in opposition to that of the NEC. We have discussed the logic of their position, and have demonstrated where it is leading them. Supporters of the counter-resolution should seriously consider whether they actually agree with the political implications of their resolution or whether they are in actual agreement with the political line and tasks of the NEC resolution, with perhaps reservations and criticisms on how that line was carried out. If that is the case, the principled course for such comrades should be to vote for the *line* of the NEC resolution, making their criticisms and suggestions concerning implementation.

MARCH 12, 1967

5. FROM 'SOME COMMENTS ON PARTY POLICY AND TACTICS IN THE ANTIWAR MOVEMENT'

By Tom Kerry

The following is an excerpt from Tom Kerry's answer to an article by David Fender entitled "Remarks on the Antiwar Movement," which appeared in *SWP Discussion Bulletin*, Volume 26, Number 9, October 1967. Kerry's reply appears in *SWP Discussion Bulletin*, Volume 26, Number 12, October 1967. Fender left the SWP in 1971 as part of a tiny sectarian grouping styling itself the "Communist Tendency."

Just what is the character of the formation that has arisen in the course of development of the antiwar movement and what is our relation to it? It can be said at the outset that even if we grant there is nothing unique about some aspects of the antiwar movement, the formation itself is decidedly unique: i.e., nothing like it has been seen before in this country. When comrades cast about to find some analogous experience in the history of the party they find none to serve as a secure mooring upon which to anchor our tactical approach.

Obviously, the so-called "classical" form under which the united front tactic was applied in the past does not appear relevant to the existent formation. If not a united front then what is it? A coalition, a bloc, an alliance, a confederation, or some combination of these, just what is it? Unfortunately, like with some other things, language does not keep pace with the historical development. There just is no *new* word, that I know of, to adequately define this new phenomenon. It would certainly simplify matters if there were, terminologywise (in Madison Avenue jargon) if not otherwise.

For the simon-pure sectarian this poses no problem. Looking back in history, he "discovers" that the united front tactic as projected by the Bolsheviks was intended to apply to agreements between mass organizations. Finding no replica of the past in present day reality he washes his hands of the whole mess and takes refuge in the limbo of infantile leftism there to await the day when history finally catches up with doctrinaire prescription. A prime example of this type of sectarian approach is Gerry Healy, general secretary of the British Socialist Labour League (SLL).

Writing a series of two lengthy articles in *The Newsletter*, Jan. 7 and Feb. 11, 1967, under the general title: "The Real Meaning of the United Front," Healy explains why the SLL will have no part of any "united front" antiwar movement in Great Britain. "The united front tactic," he affirms, "was developed in order to deal with a situation where you had a mass communist party and a mass reformist organization." Here we have stated the alleged "classical" formula for the united front tactic. (I say "alleged" because it is an extremely oversimplified definition, but let it pass for the moment.)

Healy then proceeds to elaborate on this theme. The united front, he avers, "was essentially conceived of as a tactic governing relations between mass organizations and not groups or small parties who did not represent the mass of the working class." As the Labor Party, which includes the trade unions, is the only mass working class organization in Great Britain, you can readily see how this effectively rules out any "united front" antiwar action. A rather dreary outlook. But hold, there is yet hope! In a second article in *The Newsletter*, under the title: "How NOT to Defend the Vietnamese Revolution," (a very appropriate title, I thought) Healy offers a straw to cling to:

"If," he blandly assures his constituents, "the Socialist Labour League was a mass organization it would endeavour to involve the Labour Party in a joint campaign against the war in Vietnam, but this is not the case." And in the meantime?

"The Socialist Labour League," he concludes, "is, therefore, forced to confine itself to a propaganda political preparation for the struggle in defence of the Vietnamese people." If everyone will just be patient enough to mark time until Healy's SLL develops into a mass communist party so that he could then enter into a united front pact with the mass reformist Labor Party the whole problem will be neatly solved. What tripe! We expect the Vietnam war to go on for a long time—but not THAT long!

Meanwhile, the British working class is not reconciled to waiting for Healy's "mass communist party" to materialize. Their impatience was expressed at the recent Labor Party conference, voting a resolution, 2,752,000 to 2,633,000, calling upon the Labor Government to "dissociate itself completely," from U.S. policy in Vietnam. The *N.Y. Times,* Oct. 7, reports that: "The audience cheered a number of highly critical speeches on Vietnam. Alan Campbell McLean, a Scottish delegate, compared the United States action in Vietnam to the German bombing of Stalingrad in World War II. He said that American troops had no legal or political or moral right to be in Vietnam."

The vote is indicative, but not truly representative of the feelings of the British working class who, in their overwhelming number support the sentiment expressed by the majority resolution voted by their representatives at the Labor Party conference. This is good so far as it goes. True, it is no substitute for effective action. But it does present the antiwar forces in Great Britain with an opening to press for implementing actions by the trade unions and Labor Party constituency groups. And it is at least one thousand times more effective "propaganda" than all of Healy's ultraleftist gibberish.

Healy's defense of the "classical" form of the united front against "revisionist" corruption is a prime expression of the tendency of infantile leftism to use the cover of "Marxist nomenclature" to cloak a policy of abstention from the real struggle. Or, as Lenin put it: "The surest way of discrediting and damaging a new political (and not only political) idea is to reduce it to absurdity on the plea of defending it." This is precisely what Healy does to the idea of the united front.

Let us examine the idea of the united front from the viewpoint of "terminology" or "nomenclature" if you will. It may come as a surprise to many comrades to learn that the "nomenclature" came some time after the idea had been long in practice. In a speech to the Executive Committee of the Communist International held in November 1922, Zinoviev pointed out that: "The slogan of the United Front [was] first formulated by our Executive in December, 1921," when a united front campaign was launched on an international scale.

The theses on the united front were formally adopted by the Fourth Congress of the Comintern. (Comrades will find the text of the theses, which were drafted by Trotsky for consideration by the Feb. 1922 plenum of the ECCI, on page 127 [2011 printing] in volume 2 of *The First Five Years of the Communist International.*) But, as pointed out above, the idea of the united front had been part of the tactical arsenal of Bolshevism for some time before.

Lenin's important treatise on communist (Bolshevik) tactics, *Left Wing Communism, an Infantile Disorder,* published in 1920, never once employs the term, united front. Yet, in this classical polemic against the disease of ultraleftism, is contained a rich exposition of the united front idea as applied throughout the whole history of Bolshevism dating back to its very inception at the turn of the century. Consistent with his whole method, Lenin pinpoints those social, class, and political divisions which capitalism engenders, which make necessary the application of the united front tactic, although he does not call it that:

"Capitalism would not be capitalism if the 'pure' proletariat were not surrounded by a large number of exceedingly motley types intermediate between the proletarian and the semiproletarian (who earns his livelihood in part by the sale of his labor power), between the semiproletarian and the small peasant (and petty artisan, handicraft worker and small master in general), between the small peasant and the middle peasant, and so on, and if the proletariat itself were not divided into more developed and less developed strata, if it were not divided according to territorial origin, trade, sometimes according to religion, and so on. And from all this follows the necessity, the absolute necessity, for the vanguard of the proletariat, for its class-conscious section, for the Communist Party, to resort to manoeuvres, agreements and compromises with the various groups of proletarians, with the various parties of the workers and small masters.

"The whole point lies in *knowing how* to apply these tactics in order to *raise,* and not lower, the *general* level of proletarian class consciousness, revolutionary spirit, and ability to fight and win. Incidentally, it should be noted that the victory of the Bolsheviks over the Mensheviks demanded the tactics of manoeuvres, agreements and compromises not only before *but also after* the October Revolution of 1917, but such manoeuvres and compromises, of course, as would assist, accelerate, consolidate and strengthen the Bolsheviks at the expense of the Mensheviks. The petty-bourgeois democrats (including the Mensheviks) inevitably vacillate between the bourgeoisie and the proletariat, between bourgeois democracy and the Soviet system, between reformism and revolutionism, between love-for-the-workers and fear of the proletarian dictatorship, etc. The proper tactics for the Communists must be to *utilize* these vacillations, not to ignore them; and utilizing them calls for concessions to those elements which are turning toward the proletariat—whenever and to the extent that they turn towards the proletariat—in addition to fighting those who turn toward the bourgeoisie. The result of the application of correct tactics is that Menshevism has disintegrated, and is disintegrating more and more in our country, that the stubbornly opportunist leaders are being isolated and that the best elements among the petty-bourgeois democrats are being brought into our camp." (All emphasis by author.)

In another section, Lenin declares that "the whole history of Bolshevism, both before and after the October Revolution, is *full* of instances of manoeuvring, making agreements and compromises with other parties, bourgeois parties included.

"To carry on a war for the overthrow of the international bourgeoisie, a war which is a hundred times more difficult, protracted and complicated than the most stubborn of ordinary wars between states, and to refuse beforehand to manoeuvre, to utilize the conflict of interests (even though temporary) among one's enemies, to refuse to agree and compromise with possible (even though temporary, unstable, vacillating and conditional) allies—is not this ridiculous in the extreme?" (Emphasis by author.)

Lenin uses the terms bloc, alliance, agreements, etc., interchangeably throughout his work, in content synonymous with the tactic of the united front, though the latter term had not yet come into common usage. And nowhere does he suggest that the tactic was intended to apply only where there existed rival mass communist and mass reformist parties. In fact, prior to 1917, there were no such mass formations in Russia. Further, even in the early 1920s, after the first spontaneous revolutionary surge in Western Europe failed to conquer power and the Comintern, under the prodding of Lenin and Trotsky, was constrained to sound the call for a temporary retreat, such mass formations existed in only a few countries.

Yet, when the Comintern launched its campaign for application of the united front tactic, it was specifically designated as an "international campaign." For example, in the above mentioned speech by Zinoviev to the Nov. 22, 1922 meeting of the ECCI, he declared: "The United Front was really the first international campaign which the International attempted on a large scale." As such it was to be applied in consonance with the relationship of forces in each country, taking all subjective and objective factors into consideration.

Tactics are always concrete. Or, as Lenin observes in his work on "Left Wing" Communism: "Tactics must be based on a sober and strictly objective appraisal of *all* the class forces of the particular state (and of the states surrounding it, and of all states the world over) as well as of the experience of revolutionary movements." (Emphasis in original.)

So much for Healyite historiography. To return for a moment to our young critic from afar. He is upset no end about the interchangeable application of the terms "coalition, united front and bloc," and what is worse, of "even combining them—'broad united front type coalition'(!)." (The parenthetical bang is his, not mine.) He considers it highly improper to take such liberties with "traditional" Marxist nomenclature. The word "traditionally" applied exclusively to "coalition politics." Does this mean that we are no longer opposed to coalition politics? Or as he puts it with another of his loaded "questions": "Is it still proper for us to denounce coalition politics?" Off hand, I would say yes, it is.

For, if memory serves me, it seems that *The Militant* does just that in almost every issue and no one, to my knowledge, has yet registered an objection. Where is it written that the word "coalition" must be expunged from our political lexicon unless it applies exclusively to "coalition politics?" Why this ritual genuflection to linguistic dogma? According to my copy of Webster's Collegiate dictionary, the word coalition is defined as, "a temporary alliance for joint action." The same can be said of our "traditional concept," the united front. It seems to me that the word "coalition" as defined by Webster, an acknowledged authority on such matters, is quite appropriate.

I am afraid that our critic suffers from the affliction that Trotsky once diagnosed as "philological scholasticism." What a dismal method, this juggling of words, this twisting and distorting of words, phrases and sentences to laboriously set up spurious straw men to serve as a substitute target for the real thing; this use of the loaded question which is no real question but is designed to absolve the questioner of responsibility for an affirmative statement; etc., etc., etc. And all in the name of "clarity, precision and firmness."

Which of these terms shall we employ in defining our tactic within the antiwar movement? Any and all, either separately or in combination, interchangeably or together, so long as we are certain that our objective appraisal of the phenomenon is correct. The forms it assumes are complex because the movement is unique. There does not exist in this country a mass communist party and a mass reformist party so the so-called "classical" form of the united front tactic obviously does not apply. That is, it is not based on *formal* agreement between formally constituted organizations, mass or otherwise.

The antiwar formation is composed of diverse organizations, groups, and individuals, always shifting, rarely the same, knit together at moments of action in a temporary coalition for a limited objective. After each major action the centrifugal tendency inherent in so heterogeneous a formation threatens to make it fly apart. The cement that holds it together is common opposition to U.S. administration policy in the Vietnam war. How long it will endure in its present form is anyone's guess.

Neither of the two "major" contending working class tendencies, Stalinism and Trotskyism, are in a position to establish their unchallenged hegemony over the movement. The organized Social Democrats remain outside and hostile. It is this "stalemate" which permits accidental figures with little or no organization following or support to play so prominent a part in the leadership of the movement. What is amazing about this patchwork formation is that it is held together at all. I believe that the SWP-YSA can claim a large part of the credit for this achievement. For despite the meagerness of our forces, our influence has exercised an important and often a decisive role in holding it together. And I speak of our influence not only in the organization but in the political sense, which is testimony to the correctness of our general line, both as regards slogans advanced, single issue character, and thrust toward massive national demonstration actions in the streets.

And so far as tactics are concerned, it is *our* concept of the united front tactic that has prevailed, as against those who sought to narrow and cripple the movement by imposing a programmatic character upon it. For when it comes to *that* question there is no one with whom we can come to agreement outside of a narrow circle of our sympathizers and supporters. The correctness of our line has been abundantly confirmed by experience. There is no reason to alter it in any of its basic essentials—let alone throwing it overboard as our philological critic exhorts us to do. And I have not a single doubt that we will have the necessary tactical flexibility to meet whatever exigencies may arise in the future.

New York City
OCTOBER 16, 1967

6. THE FIGHT AGAINST THE VIETNAM WAR

The following resolution, reprinted from *SWP Discussion Bulletin*, Volume 27, No. 2, published in June 1969, was adopted by the September 1969 convention of the Socialist Workers Party.

PART I: THE CURRENT STAGE OF THE STRUGGLE AGAINST THE IMPERIALIST WAR IN VIETNAM

A. The Present Stage of the War

The war in Vietnam is the central issue in world and national politics today, as it has been since 1965 when American imperialism massively escalated its intervention. This war is a key part of American imperialism's offensive against the world revolution, whose axis during the past two decades has been in the colonial areas. The goals of U.S. imperialism in Vietnam are to crush the national liberation struggle and, if possible, overturn the North Vietnamese workers state, thus dealing fatal blows to the socialist revolution in all Southeast Asia. Additional aims include establishing a strong beachhead in this area, the better to take over the former holdings of the French, the British and the Dutch imperialists and to mount heavy military pressure against China. Washington will continue to seek these strategic aims no matter what tactical shifts may be necessitated by the worsening situation.

To pursue its objectives Washington has poured more than a half million troops, the most modern instruments of destruction, and billions of dollars into the adventure in Vietnam. But because of the heroic resistance of the workers and peasants, the U.S. has not been able to crush the Vietnamese revolution.

U.S. intervention in Vietnam began as a relatively limited "police" action. When the Vietnamese rebels came close to defeating the Saigon regime, Johnson "escalated" U.S. intervention in 1965, widening the scope of military action until it developed into one of the major wars in U.S. history—one that already has surpassed the Korean war in American dead and wounded.

Because of its international repercussions, the war became the central confrontation on a world scale between the forces of revolution and the counterrevolutionary power of American imperialism. American imperialism hoped to make Vietnam an object lesson which would serve to intimidate the revolutionary forces throughout the world. But Washington's intent now threatens to rebound against itself. The determined struggle of the Vietnamese has touched off a sympathetic response throughout the world, not only in the colonial world but also in the advanced capitalist countries and, to a lesser degree, in the workers states. A definitive victory for the Vietnamese revolution would impart to the world socialist revolution a fresh inspiration whose effects would be felt for years to come.

The Moscow bureaucrats have defaulted in their international obligation to defend the Vietnamese revolution. U.S. imperialism's initial military strategy in Vietnam was to undertake a step-by-step escalation, probing at each stage to see what the Soviet response would be before going ahead further. The Soviet bureaucrats retreated in the face of Washington's aggressive advances. To save face they have given minimal military and diplomatic aid to the Vietnamese while evincing a readiness to sacrifice the revolutionary movement for the Stalinist utopian strategy of peaceful coexistence with imperialism.

This capitulatory policy is reflected in the attitude and conduct of the pro-Moscow parties which have generally abstained from initiating or organizing mass opposition to the war in Vietnam—a compounded crime in those countries where the Communist parties have a mass following.

While primary responsibility for deterring Washington's aggression lies with Moscow, Peking has also defaulted in its obligation to defend Vietnam. Despite the immediate danger posed by the Vietnam war to the Chinese revolution and the security of their country, the Peking bureaucrats have persisted in their sectarian refusal to press for a united front with other workers states in defense of the Vietnamese revolution. Many pro-Peking parties have reflected this attitude by sectarian abstention from participating in united actions against the war and by belittling the importance of such efforts.

Only Cuba and, to a lesser extent, North Korea among the workers states have maintained a principled internationalist line in defense of the Vietnamese revolution.

The Social Democratic organizations, with a few exceptions such as in Japan, have either abstained from the struggle against the Vietnam war or have actually taken part in their own capitalist governments' complicity with U.S. imperialism's war effort. Wilson's Labour Party is the most shameful example.

As a result, the international antiwar movement has developed independently of the Stalinist and Social-Democratic parties and to the left of them. The antiwar movement has been marked by its youth, militancy, spirit of internationalism, and engendering of anticapitalist consciousness.

From the outset the scope of American opposition to involvement in the civil war in Vietnam was broad. This opposition has grown and intensified since 1965 until it now extends to a majority of the population and has come to involve hundreds of thousands in antiwar actions. The international antiwar opposition and the sharpening of social tensions at home owing to the war are important factors in limiting the ability of the American ruling class to continue the war as they would like.

For all its wealth and power, the American capitalist class has found it increasingly difficult to carry on a major war in Vietnam, simultaneously finance an expanded nuclear arms race, prop up and defend the rest of the capitalist world, and allocate sufficient resources to attempt to allay domestic unrest. The consequences of the war in Vietnam have shown that the basic relationship of class forces on a world scale is less and less favorable to imperialism.

It is the effect on its strategic interests that makes U.S. imperialism balk at withdrawing from Vietnam in humiliating defeat at the hands of the people of a small colonial nation. Yet the longer withdrawal is postponed, the worse the problem Washington faces in Vietnam becomes. If it is not possible at this time to roll back the revolutions in North Vietnam and China, Nixon, like Johnson before him, must at least try for an outcome like the one in Korea. If it is not possible to win by military means, other means must be sought.

The Tet offensive in 1968 provided dramatic proof of the difficulty U.S. imperialism faces in its efforts to "pacify" Vietnam, giving the lie to the boasts of the generals about military "progress" and about winning political support for the puppet Saigon regime. Within the United States, the actions of the antiwar movement reached extraordinary heights. Hundreds of thousands demonstrated against the war on April 15, 1967, October 21, 1967, and April 27, 1968. Almost a million students participated in the largest student strike in U.S. history on April 26, 1968. These mass actions reflected the underlying antiwar sentiment of tens of millions.

Washington's difficulties in Vietnam have sharpened the divisions within the ruling class itself. These differences are over the tactical implementation of American imperialism's basic counterrevolutionary strategy under current conditions. The differences concern the size of U.S. involvement in Southeast Asia; the danger of the war leading to a conflict with China, a "pre-emptive" nuclear strike and World War III; the relative importance and "price" of a temporary arms limitation agreement with the Soviet Union; how much money to pour into the war in Vietnam; the price of the war in terms of domestic social unrest. The American ruling class has also found it increasingly difficult to win support for its war from the capitalist governments of other countries. These differences have left considerable room for the growth of the antiwar opposition of the masses.

Under pressure of these mounting problems, Washington has altered its tactics, placing greater emphasis on the diplomatic front. This started with the Paris talks and Johnson's withdrawal from the presidential race in 1968. The bombing "halt" in the north was featured as part of the shift, although the "pause" was utilized to transfer troops elsewhere and orders were issued to maintain "maximum military pressure on the enemy." Nixon has continued this policy. Washington seeks to win at the negotiating table what it has been unable to exact on the battlefield—the derailment of the Vietnamese revolution. The objective is to try and impose a Korea-type settlement which will preserve a capitalist South Vietnam as an Asian base for U.S. imperialism.

Nixon, like Johnson, hopes to obtain the aid of the Soviet bureaucrats in bringing the Vietnamese revolutionaries to terms. Although this possibility cannot be excluded, the Soviet bureaucrats are far less able now than in parallel situations in earlier years to force the Vietnamese revolutionaries to submit to a capitulating compromise. The struggle in Vietnam has developed independently of Moscow and Peking; its leaders have learned bitter lessons from the experiences that followed 1954; and its militants are more determined than ever to reverse the colonial puppet status of South Vietnam.

The pause in the bombing of North Vietnam and Nixon's ballyhooed peace propaganda and token withdrawal of troops have not been accompanied by any reduction in the scale of U.S. military operations in Vietnam. The level of bombing, the number of casualties, and the flood of money pouring into the war remain as before. Moreover, forays into Laos and Cambodia have been stepped up, a fact that Washington has finally been compelled to admit.

The central problem facing U.S. imperialism in attempting to win the kind of settlement it wants is control of the state power in Vietnam, which depends in the last analysis on force of arms. Without the massive military might of U.S. imperialism, the Saigon regime would rapidly collapse. This fact shows the fraudulent nature of all the well-publicized Washington schemes for a settlement: the scheme of turning the war over to Saigon; the scheme of a coalition government; the scheme of elections under the Saigon administration. So long as the Vietnamese revolutionaries refuse to give up their arms and continue to carry on the fight a U.S. withdrawal will lead to rapid victory over the Saigon regime. Under these conditions, a "compromise" formula that does not settle the question of state power will remain illusory. The war can end only when one side is defeated; and until that happens, either on the battlefield or at the negotiating table, the war will go on.

While attempting to gain a negotiated political victory, Washington above all needs time. But here it faces the problem of domestic opposition to the war and the growth of social unrest on numerous fronts. So long as the war continues, so long as there are mass antiwar actions, the climate of protest will continue to intensify. Washington's capacity to achieve its war aims is limited by the need to deal with unrest at home or risk an intolerable growth of class conflict. "Pacifying" the antiwar opposition in the United States has become a prime necessity for the ruling class to gain the time they must have to try to "pacify" the Vietnamese.

Thus a second and extremely important side to Washington's maneuvers is its propaganda offensive aimed at allaying public aversion to the war. If the ruling class cannot now secure majority support for its war of aggression, it hopes at least to win acquiescence in its diplomatic offensive as a credible means to peace. This was the primary aim in Johnson's withdrawal from the 1968 presidential race, the initiation of the Paris talks, the bombing pause in North Vietnam, the election of Nixon as an apparent alternative to Johnson, and his war policies, and Nixon's token withdrawal of troops.

From the outset, the Nixon administration has attempted to convey the impression that its policies are not the same as Johnson's. However, the hints about secret talks and secret progress, the talk of "turning over" the bulk of the fighting to the Saigon regime, of expanded social legislation when the war is over, merely continue Johnson's line. Under increasing pressure to offer tangible evidence of de-escalation, Nixon finally began token withdrawals of troops. But this was already contemplated by the Johnson administration upon the Pentagon's assurance that it would not lower the current level of the war.

The time that Nixon seeks can only be purchased at a high price. In attempting to allay public opposition to the war, Nixon's peace propaganda raises the American people's anticipation and desire for a speedy end to hostilities.

Antiwar sentiment has grown considerably since the initiation of the Paris talks, and will continue to do so. This includes American GIs who find it increasingly difficult to see why they should risk their lives to save the Saigon regime.

Under these circumstances, the ruling class cannot hope to diminish mass sentiment for peace but only to deflect and disarm it. The propaganda maneuvers are meant to serve as a tranquilizer. But the effect can only be temporary. As the war goes on, the killing will continue. To scale down the fighting in the absence of a military victory or stalemate does not conform with the strategic objectives of U.S. imperialism. As the costs of the dirty war continue to affect the lives of the American people, the waves of indignation and protest will mount. Already the April 5–6 antiwar demonstrations revealed the beginning of massive disillusionment with Nixon's play for time. The new president thus faces the perspective of ending up as hated as Johnson, if not more so.

U.S. imperialism's increasingly grave difficulties in Vietnam and at home offer big opportunities and responsibilities for the antiwar movement. The task is to prevent the ruling class from gaining the time for maneuver that it so desperately needs. A new wave of massive antiwar demonstrations is called for to expose the deceit of the ruling class and to bring mass consciousness of the meaning of the war to a still higher level.

The demand for immediate withdrawal of U.S. troops from Vietnam has gained added urgency and importance. By giving fresh impetus to the demand to bring all the GIs home now, the antiwar movement can undercut the lie of the ruling class that its Paris talks are the avenue to peace.

B. The Present Stage of the Antiwar Movement

Washington's propaganda offensive temporarily dampened the explosive potential of antiwar sentiment in the United States. Although the desire for peace continued to grow among the mass of the American people, the sharpness of this sentiment was blunted by illusions regarding the Paris talks. In addition, part of the antiwar coalition was diverted into bourgeois electoral politics in the illusory hope of advancing the cause of peace by this means. The Nixon administration, upon assuming office, was granted the customary period of little or no criticism. Thus the lull in massive national antiwar demonstrations lasted almost a year, although there were large demonstrations in a few local areas and a marked increase in actions by antiwar GIs.

The organized antiwar movement suffered numerous defections in the months prior to the elections and afterwards in the immediate post-election period. The McCarthy campaign and a series of bourgeois "peace" candidates drew the class collaborationist wing of the antiwar movement away from mass action, a trend buttressed by illusions in the Paris talks. In many local areas, the antiwar coalitions eroded or collapsed entirely.

Owing to these defections, the National Mobilization Committee, which was formed for the purpose of organizing major national antiwar demonstrations, tended to lose its broad coalition character. This trend was reinforced by sectarian and exclusionary measures directed against the vanguard which favored mass actions around the slogan of immediate withdrawal. As a result, ultraleftism came to predominate in the apparatus of the NMC. The NMC adopted the line of confrontation tactics by a few as a substitute for organizing militant antiwar action by hundreds of thousands. The NMC placed more importance on adventurist tactics than on an independent antiwar political line. The disorienting character of this NMC line was shown at the Democratic Party national convention in Chicago where the demonstration organized by the NMC objectively favored McCarthy's bid for the Democratic nomination. Adventurist tactics subjected hundreds of antiwar youth to needless brutalization in a demonstration that, despite the great publicity it secured, was relatively small for a national action.

The continuation of the ultraleftist, sectarian course set the stamp of a single antiwar tendency upon the NMC, assuring its demise as an antiwar action coalition. The unpostponable next step for the antiwar forces is to build a new national antiwar coalition and to strengthen or rebuild the local antiwar coalitions for the purpose of organizing larger mass demonstrations.

The differences over perspective in the antiwar movement were also reflected in the Student Mobilization Committee, the principal organization of antiwar youth as well as the militant spearhead of the broader antiwar movement centered around the slogan of withdrawing the troops now. Immediately after the SMC's tremendously successful student strike in April 1968, a coalition of Communist Party and pacifist elements initiated a split in the SMC, breaking with the perspective of mass antiwar demonstrations. In the course of that fight, they attempted to jettison the non-exclusionary basis of the organization. Unable to capture the SMC, they withdrew from it.

Throughout the past year we supported all attempts to organize mass antiwar demonstrations, and through them recement the badly divided antiwar organizations. The Student Mobilization Committee played an essential role in taking the initiative in calling demonstrations and prodding other sectors into action. It called for antiwar demonstrations in August 1968, prior to the elections in October, and initiated the conference which called for the April 5–6, 1969 demonstrations. Though the first two of these actions were not as large as previous demonstrations, they maintained the perspective of massive action. The growth of antiwar activity by GIs was a major new development and an important factor in inspiring the antiwar demonstrations that did occur.

The scope and size of the April 5–6 1969 demonstrations signified that much of the disorientation within the antiwar movement had dissipated. The mounting casualties in Vietnam made it clear to many that Nixon was continuing Johnson's fundamental policies in Vietnam and served to stir hundreds of thousands back into the streets to protest the war. In view of the turnout of April 5–6, the fresh organizational impetus derived from it, and the shifts in the objective situation, the time is ripe for another series of major antiwar demonstrations.

As support for the April 5–6 demonstrations gathered momentum, these became the focal point around which many of the local antiwar coalitions were rebuilt. This advance has laid the groundwork for rebuilding the antiwar coalition nationally. The Student Mobilization Committee, still weakened organizationally prior to April 5–6, has since emerged as the authoritative national organization of antiwar youth and the major organizer of demonstrations on a national scale.

The importance of the Student Mobilization Committee within the broader antiwar movement was confirmed by the April 5–6 demonstrations. From the inception of the antiwar movement the youth have been the main initiators and most active participants in the mass mobilizations. Time and again it has been the left-wing youth who have kept the antiwar movement in the streets, refusing to be drawn into class-collaborationist gimmicks. They have provided the bulk of the activists and have continually pressured the more conservative elements into support for the militant mass actions. They have been the main force in fighting to win the antiwar movement to the demand for immediate withdrawal of U.S. troops from Vietnam. Repelled by any signs of a return to the norms of the Joe McCarthy era, the youth have been the key element in helping to maintain the nonexclusive character of the antiwar movement.

The April 5–6 demonstrations involved a higher percentage of youth than ever before, showing a marked increase in the numbers of high-school youth. The spring months of 1969 saw an unprecedented upsurge on the high-school and college campuses with the war in Vietnam and the black liberation struggle being the central issues.

On the college campuses, the issue of campus complicity in the war sparked a wave of protests against ROTC, against recruitment for the armed forces and the war industries, and against university war-related research. In some cases the student strikes involved the vast majority of students. These actions show how favorable the situation is for organizing against the war on the campuses. Such campus actions help to create a favorable atmosphere for street demonstrations, and vice versa, and are certain to remain a major feature of the SMC's antiwar activities.

The depth of antiwar sentiment on the campuses makes militancy and audacity appropriate in a situation where the antiwar students represent an overwhelming majority. In some cases, however, campus protests have suffered setbacks due to adventurism and organizational sectarianism, especially where SDS has initiated such actions.

The SMC has an important task to perform in educating large numbers of students on how to build the most effective struggles. The SMC's experience in organizing militant mass actions and its nonexclusionary organizational procedures are a necessary antidote to the organizational sectarianism and adventurism imposed by SDS elements on the campuses.

The possibilities for organizing high-school antiwar actions are extremely favorable. The present generation of high-school youth has grown to political consciousness in an atmosphere dominated by a war which they have rejected out of hand. The SMC has registered its greatest recent gains in this area. The potential for organizing the SMC in the high schools is enhanced by the absence of serious competition from other tendencies. One important feature of high-school antiwar activity is the fight for civil liberties against the arbitrary prohibitions against political activity by the school authorities.

In the past year there has been a decided increase in antiwar activity by GIs. Washington's peace propaganda and the opening of the Paris talks heightened the antiwar sentiments of the GIs; fresh force was given to their objections to fighting and dying in an unjust war which the government admitted it was not winning militarily. The growth of GI antiwar protests adds formidable new social weight to the antiwar movement and will be a permanent feature of antiwar protests from now on.

Important milestones in the past year were: (1) the nationwide antiwar demonstrations in October 1968; local antiwar demonstrations such as that in Seattle February 16, 1969; and, most important, the nationwide antiwar demonstrations April 5–6, 1969. More GIs participated in these demonstrations than ever before. (2) The proliferation of GI antiwar newspapers, published locally by GIs and distributed at the local bases. (3) The fights for GI rights waged at Ft. Jackson and Ft. Bragg.

These developments all reflected the widespread antiwar mood within the army. From the beginning, our political tendency was the only one to consistently point to the potential for GI antiwar activity. We have been the most insistent that the antiwar movement adopt a political approach to win the GIs as an ally. Our opponents, along with many antiwar activists in the past, have taken a moralistic attitude, encouraging individual noncompliance with the draft and blaming individual GIs for being somehow in complicity with the imperialist aggression in Vietnam. Their belittling of the potential for winning GIs to antiwar activity made them blindly reject a political approach to the GIs. However, with the growth of GI antiwar protests, our position has been confirmed in practice and is now accepted by large numbers of antiwar activists. But deep differences exist within the antiwar movement in evaluating the importance of the GI antiwar developments and how to approach them.

Our position is based on the mass character of the army. The ranks of the armed forces are composed of draftees or men who enlisted under pressure of the draft. As such, the army tends to reflect a cross-section of the youth in society, and the development of political consciousness in the army parallels that in the civilian population. The present army tends to incorporate much of the political ferment that exists among the youth and to bring antiwar sentiment to an acute pitch. In addition, the discriminatory nature of the draft system means that there is a disproportionate percentage of black and brown youth in the army, a percentage that is even more pronounced at the front lines.

Sentiment against the war is widespread among GIs, as it is among civilian youth. But because of the restrictive nature of the military, antiwar actions by GIs are still in their initial stages. Objective developments indicate that the pace of GI antiwar protests can be expected to increase rapidly, especially as they become more and more linked up with the mass civilian protests. The development of truly massive protests and a massive radicalization in the army could only occur interlinked with a similar mood in the civilian population and its readiness to support and defend the antiwar GIs. Our perspective is that of a parallel and interrelated development of GI and civilian antiwar protests.

In this light, we view the GIs as an important component of the antiwar movement, but not as a substitute for it. The axis of the antiwar movement remains mass mobilizations against the war, including GIs and civilians.

The fight for democratic rights is of special importance to GIs opposed to the war. It links up with civilian antiwar sentiment and the need for collective action as the most effective way to struggle against the war. There are three aspects to this approach:

(1) For open, collective action against the war rather than isolated individual actions or "underground" organizing.

Desertion, refusal to obey orders, or other individual actions are not acceptable to the majority of GIs. Those who take this course will be open to easy victimization from the brass without any corresponding gains. Such isolated acts may salve the consciences of individuals but are not an effective means of political opposition to the war. The political climate favors open, collective antiwar activity rather than "underground" organizing, which is many times more difficult and foolish when unnecessary.

(2) For the concept of the GI as a citizen-soldier. A GI is a citizen temporarily in uniform and therefore retains all his constitutional rights as a citizen, including the rights of free speech and free assembly. The full utilization of democratic rights is a powerful tool in the hands of the majority—and that is whom the antiwar GIs speak for. The brass, who want to use the army against the wishes of the soldiers, fear simple democracy; but to the GIs it is a powerful and necessary part of the struggle. Despite attempts by the brass to restrict the exercise of constitutional and democratic rights, these rights can be fought for and won in the army.

(3) For concentrating on the Vietnam war as the issue of main concern to the GIs.

The army being what it is, GIs have legitimate grievances on many different issues. But the greatest unity can be built around opposition to the war in Vietnam. It is the issue on which GIs can gain the maximum amount of civilian support and protection against the brass' attempts at victimization and restriction of constitutional rights.

Unlike coalitions formed for specific mass demonstrations ongoing antiwar activity by GIs cannot be effectively organized if it includes other approaches on a coalition basis. The continual possibility of victimization by the brass necessitates strict adherence to these three points. Experience has shown that on this threefold approach GIs can effectively oppose the war, minimize chances of victimization, and counter any victimizations inflicted on them.

Because of the depth of antiwar sentiment inside and outside the ranks of the armed forces, the brass has had to proceed cautiously and even retreat in many instances rather than deal too summarily with dissenters. The retreats by the brass encourage other GIs into activity.

The right of GIs to participate in demonstrations while *off base and out of uniform* has been established. Although the brass has attempted to inhibit the exercise of this right—by restricting GIs to base on the days of demonstrations, for example—the right has been conceded by the Pentagon. Where punitive measures have been taken, they have usually been for some other officially-stated cause, for demonstrating while in uniform or for allegedly being AWOL. The establishment of the right to demonstrate opens the door to an effective campaign to build GI participation in antiwar demonstrations.

The developments at Ft. Jackson and Ft. Bragg, initiated by GIs United, are among the most important antiwar and civil-liberties struggles that have taken place. For the first time the central question was raised of the right to protest the war while *on base and in uniform*. This is a higher level of the fight for GI rights. The brass' retreat from their intended victimization of the Ft. Jackson GIs was a major victory for the antiwar movement. It showed the importance of effective tactics in mobilizing extensive civilian support. It is to be expected that there will be continuing fights for the on-base, in-uniform rights of GIs. The most effective will have to be carried out with all the indigenous support and careful legal and political groundwork that attended the Ft. Jackson case.

Publicity about the lessons of the Ft. Jackson case will be an important aid in explaining the nature of GI antiwar activity. GIs United illustrates that the ongoing antiwar activities of GIs can best be organized, not from outside the military by civilians, but by the GIs themselves on their base along the lines of the threefold approach outlined above. Organized antiwar GIs can become a component part of the general antiwar action coalitions , working with other forces to build the mass demonstrations, yet retaining a distinctly GI form based on a specific political approach for GI antiwar activity, in much the same manner in which the student antiwar committees function in relation to the general antiwar coalitions.

Our central activity in relation to the antiwar activities of GIs will pivot around three points: (1) building GI participation in antiwar demonstrations; (2) publicity about GIs United; (3) the distribution of GI newspapers.

The primary manifestation of labor's resistance to the war has been its refusal to sacrifice for the war and the growth of union struggles in the midst of war. There has been a sharp increase in the number of strikes as workers have attempted to maintain their standard of living and job conditions in the face of mounting inflation and ruling-class pressure for sacrifice. The antiwar movement has been a factor in helping to spur these struggles. The divisions in the organized labor movement, which have produced an open breach within the trade-union bureaucracy, partially reflect the growing militancy observable among the ranks.

As antiwar sentiment and general social struggles continue to mount, it becomes more difficult for the official union leaderships to stand apart from the antiwar protests. Some local unions have gone on record in opposition to the war and lent their support to the antiwar demonstrations. This can now become more extensive. The antiwar movement has the opportunity and obligation to encourage this process and to involve the trade-union movement in the antiwar protests wherever possible. Lower levels of the trade-union officialdom can be won to the antiwar movement as it presently exists, opening up expanded opportunities to reach the ranks of the working class more easily.

In adapting to the antiwar pressures, some sections of the trade-union bureaucracy, especially on the higher levels, will undoubtedly bring great pressure to bear for exclusionary measures against the militants, for a negotiations line rather than withdrawal, and for support to capitalist politicians. All of these moves must be fought. But the negative pressures that may arise from the bureaucrats can be offset by the added social weight of the trade unions and the opportunity to involve the mass of the working class more easily.

The growth of the antiwar movement has been paralleled by the upsurge of the black masses and is related to it. Identification with the struggle of the nonwhite Vietnamese and the colonial revolution in general has been an important help in generating the new mood of militancy. The costs of the war have made it difficult for the ruling class to grant concessions to the black masses and for the Uncle Toms to put a damper on the growing struggle.

There has been a significant increase in antiwar sentiment among Afro-Americans, especially among the youth. This sentiment has been reflected to some extent in greater black participation in the antiwar demonstrations.

Almost every black organization has come out against the war, many of them in solidarity with the Vietnamese revolution. Some of the black organizations have participated in antiwar coalitions for the purpose of building mass demonstrations, most consistently on the high-school and college campuses. Many of the demands raised in the black student struggles have been specifically directed against U.S. imperialism's use of the high schools and colleges for the war in Vietnam. Within the army, black GIs have been central to many of the GI antiwar protests.

Both the working class and the black population bring great social weight to bear in the struggle to end the war in Vietnam. The antiwar movement must continue to conduct its actions in such a way as to earn their support and solidarity.

C. A Revolutionary Socialist Strategy against the War in Vietnam

The mass antiwar movement is unique in American history. It has grown and intensified even as the shooting war has taken place. Developing prior to a general radicalization of labor and in the absence of a mass working-class political party, the antiwar movement has organized large street demonstrations as the chief means of independently manifesting and organizing the antiwar sentiment of the American masses. These demonstrations have been far more than symbolic shows of protest. They have been the main factor in preventing a climate of social peace from being established for the duration of the war. The continued and growing involvement of masses in antiwar protests is a key factor in limiting the ability of American imperialism to press on with the war in Vietnam and to contemplate other wars like it.

The past few years, marked by the Vietnam war and its domestic repercussions, have seen the intensification of social conflict on numerous fronts. The antiwar movement has been a critical factor in the growth of these social conflicts, for the mass character of the antiwar actions enables them to affect broad layers of the masses and spur protests among youth, GIs, labor, and the black movement.

The political independence of the periodic mass demonstrations has helped prevent the permanent diversion of antiwar sentiment into class-collaborationist channels. That would have blunted its effect. The actions of the antiwar movement have helped legitimatize a general climate of protest, preventing the development of a wartime hysteria and helping to roll back most of the vestiges of McCarthyism that existed a few years ago. By virtue of the antiwar movement's example, the right of the people to oppose the government's policy has been reaffirmed in the midst of war and represents an implicit challenge to the rule of the capitalist class.

To ever-increasing numbers, the war in Vietnam and the mass opposition to it have laid bare the undemocratic and reactionary nature of American capitalism, producing a new wave of radicalization, especially among the youth. This has opened up expanded opportunities for recruitment to the Socialist Workers Party.

Antiwar coalitions have been the principal organizational vehicle for building the mass demonstrations against the war. Such coalitions are a particular form of the tactic of the united front. They correspond to the present situation which is marked by the absence of mass working-class political parties and the political bankruptcy of the official trade-union leadership. Of central importance has been the nonexclusionary character of these coalitions, enabling revolutionary socialists to participate in them while maintaining their own independent political positions. This has been a major factor in strengthening the left wing of the antiwar movement and in maintaining the independent mass-action axis of the antiwar protests.

The coalitions have proven to be unstable and shifting in composition, loosely composed of antiwar organizations, individuals, and political tendencies. The single issue that has united divergent tendencies in the antiwar coalitions has been the organization of mass demonstrations against the war. The antiwar movement is so heterogeneous politically and in composition that it cannot serve as a basis for a coalition around a general political program. But united in action, the different components of the antiwar movement have been able to organize demonstrations in the streets which are objectively anti-imperialist in character, whatever the varying and opposing views on other matters of the individual participants and organizations.

Within the broader coalitions we have sought to build the left wing on the basis of the demand for immediate withdrawal of U.S. troops from Vietnam. In contrast to all versions of the negotiations demand, the demand for immediate withdrawal is the only principled way of supporting the right of the Vietnamese to self-determination. It links up support for that right with the interests and antiwar sentiments of the GIs and the working class.

The history of the antiwar movement has been a history of continual struggle over its line, its course and its perspective. The antiwar movement has been subjected to tremendous pressures to divert it from an independent, anti-imperialist axis of mass action. The two central threats to this perspective have been: (1) being drawn into class-collaborationist politics and (2) being diverted into individual acts and adventures that would isolate the vanguard and steer the thrust of the antiwar struggle away from the masses.

Both of these threats have been quite strong on occasion, though never strong enough to permanently change the mass-action orientation of the antiwar movement. Other differences in the antiwar movement have generally derived from these. The participation of the Socialist Workers Party and Young Socialist Alliance has been an indispensable factor in maintaining the mass-action orientation of the antiwar movement.

The fundamental problem of policy facing the antiwar movement has been how to counter the threat of class collaboration. The Communist Party and bourgeois liberals have sought to use the antiwar movement as a means of pressure within the

Democratic Party. This current made the greatest headway during the 1968 elections.

The McCarthy campaign, with its stated goal of getting the antiwar movement "off the streets," succeeded in drawing many of these class collaborationists away from building mass demonstrations. Other variants of class-collaborationist electoral politics have been the various third-ticket "peace and freedom" campaigns directed at disorienting the more militant wing of the antiwar movement which could not be drawn directly into the Democratic Party.

Because there is no mass working-class political party to counterpose to these procapitalist candidates, we have sought to keep the antiwar movement from participating as a movement in electoral politics, advocating instead that it continue on its course of building mass antiwar demonstrations during the election season. Wherever possible we have run our own socialist election campaigns to win over the most revolutionary-minded forces within the antiwar movement.

A variant of the class-collaborationist approach in the antiwar movement has been the line of "multi-issue" organizing. Reformists of all stripes have advocated that the antiwar forces unite around a general political program in contrast to the single issue of joint action against the war. Given the class composition, political line, and heterogeneity of the groups involved in the antiwar movement, such a multi-issue program could only be a liberal-reformist one. It would function as a bridge to class-collaborationist electoral politics and divert concentration upon demonstrations against the war.

As a result of the growing youth radicalization this argument has been updated with left verbiage about transforming the antiwar movement with its mass actions into a general anti-imperialist movement. But such a coalition, ostensibly organized to fight against imperialism in general, would be a fraud. That task requires a revolutionary-socialist party and program to lead the struggle for the socialist revolution. The antiwar movement is anti-imperialist in its actions, not in the program of all its participants. The real function of this multi-issue line would be to build a verbally radical but nonetheless reformist organization as a substitute for organizing mass demonstrations against the war.

Our line in the antiwar movement has been to show the intimate relation between the Vietnam war and the rise in social tensions in the United States promoted by racism, antilabor legislation, inflation, taxes, cutbacks in social-welfare legislation, etc. By exposing the connection of these issues to the Vietnam war, the antiwar movement can enhance its ability to reach out to the working class and the black liberation movement and draw more powerful forces into the struggle against the war. To the newly-radicalized forces moving in a revolutionary direction we present, not a coalition program with liberals and reformists, but the revolutionary-socialist program of the Socialist Workers Party.

Another variant of the reformist approach in the antiwar movement has been to seek to limit actions to a local or "community" level and organize them around immediate issues. This line has usually been counterposed to the line of building mass antiwar demonstrations. Its proponents seek to substitute the struggle around immediate social-welfare issues for a frontal attack on the major issue of the war in Vietnam. Our position has been to link up the local and immediate struggles of the working-class and black masses with the mass demonstrations against the war, not to counterpose one to the other. In practice, the mass actions of the antiwar movement have helped to stimulate struggles on these other issues.

While less serious a problem in the long run, the threat to divert the antiwar struggle in an adventuristic direction and thus isolate it from the mass antiwar sentiment has been considerable in the past year. The standard pacifist line of civil disobedience through acts of "individual conscience" and the adventurist line of small-scale pseudo-confrontation tactics are equally unconcerned with winning over the broad masses and the working class. The most pernicious feature of the line of small confrontations is its substitution of super-militant tactics and their effects on a few participants for a political line aimed at bringing masses into action.

The source of this ultraleft line is frustration with the continuation of the war despite the mass opposition to it. Seeing a growing radicalization but not yet a mass working-class radicalization, the ultralefts aim at shortcuts which avoid the more difficult, prolonged, but indispensable task of bringing the working class into action. In that sense ultraleftism is merely the obverse of opportunism, which seeks its shortcut in supporting capitalist politicians. These two sides of the ultraleftist approach were clearly evidenced in the character of the demonstration at the Democratic Party convention, which combined aggressive tactics with an opportunist political line of backing McCarthy. Without a working-class political perspective, today's ultraleftists can easily turn into tomorrow's opportunists.

We differentiate between the organized ultraleftist groups which must be fought every step of the way and the newly radicalized youth who want to fight against capitalism but through impatience and inexperience may temporarily get sucked into adventurist gimmicks. We must patiently explain that militant antiwar actions which are massive in size and which aim at winning over the mass of the working class, GIs, and Afro-Americans are the politically effective actions to project. Confrontation with the ruling class is basically a political confrontation, not simply a series of tactical encounters.

As the political disorientation resulting from the Paris talks continues to dissipate and mass antiwar demonstrations become increasingly feasible, it is absolutely essential that the antiwar movement draw a clear line demarcating itself from the various ultraleftist and adventurist approaches. Otherwise it risks isolation from the prevailing mass antiwar sentiment.

The same twofold challenge to the axis of mass action is reflected in different approaches to the draft. We are opposed to capitalist conscription, to the discriminatory nature of the draft, and to the use of the schools by the ruling class to enforce it. We are for mass actions against the draft, tied in with the Vietnam war issue and politically directed towards winning the support of the draftees and enlistees. We do not advocate individual noncompliance with the draft but support the constitutional rights of GIs to oppose the war.

Two other lines have been counterposed to this Marxist policy: (1) The liberal antidraft line oriented toward lobbying Congress to modify or abolish the draft. This line has not had any serious impact in the antiwar movement. (2) The line of individual acts of non-compliance with the draft.

The draft-resistance approach has been declining in influence as GI antiwar actions have developed. At present the overwhelming majority of youth are not engaging in draft refusal. Individual draft refusal is ineffective because it easily victimizes those who engage in it and isolates them from the mass of young workers and other youth. Moreover, the draft refusal line cannot win the support of the GIs who view it as an inadmissible means of individual escape from the Army.

The history of the antiwar movement has been marked by a continual struggle for adherence to the demand for the immediate withdrawal of U.S. troops from Vietnam, as counterposed to various formulations for a negotiated peace or for demands falling short of immediate withdrawal. We have fought for the immediate withdrawal demand within the antiwar movement as the way of supporting the right of the Vietnamese to self-determination. The left wing of the antiwar movement has been organized around the immediate withdrawal demand and has been able to make it the major theme of the mass antiwar demonstrations.

In the context of the Paris talks and various ruling class maneuvers to disarm the antiwar movement, there are likely to be renewed pressures from the class collaborationists to take these maneuvers for good coin and demand less than the immediate withdrawal of all U.S. troops from Vietnam. Another pressure towards the negotiations demand has been the proposal by sections of the American antiwar movement to support the ten-point program of the National Liberation Front or the 12-point program of the Provisional Revolutionary Government. This proposal is a retreat from support to Vietnamese self-determination and a back-door concession to the right of the U.S. to negotiate Vietnam's future. It would also be a political trap for the antiwar movement to counterpose a propaganda stand of support to the NLF or PRG to Washington's peace propaganda and token troop withdrawal. It would play into the Nixon administration's hands as they attempt to put themselves forward as the ones who want to withdraw the troops! We will continue to fight for the antiwar movement to raise as its central slogan,

"Bring *All* the GIs Home *Now*!"

The continuing fight over whether or not to engage in mass antiwar demonstrations has been closely linked with the fight to maintain the nonexclusive character of the coalitions. The class-collaborationist forces have continually attempted to impose a reformist political program on them. The ultraleftists have tried to limit them only to those who would accept their tactics and verbal radicalism. On occasion both of these trends have attempted to scuttle the non-exclusionary foundations of the antiwar organizations. It has been a continual fight to maintain nonexclusion and unity around the single issue of antiwar action in the streets. The Socialist Workers Party has played a central role in welding together diverse tendencies for this sole purpose. We have supported and built the militant left-wing formations as part of the broader coalitions.

The antiwar movement has offered a major challenge to all the working-class tendencies in the United States. It has tested their ability to recognize and respond to the central issue in world and national politics; their ability and willingness to defend the revolutionary struggle of the Vietnamese; their ability to intervene with their political line and apply it to the immediate political issues; their ability to train their cadres to function in the living mass movement; and their ability to win recruits from among the thousands of youth who have been radicalized by the war in Vietnam. The Socialist Workers Party's participation in the antiwar movement stands in sharp contrast to that of our political opponents.

The organized and semiorganized Social Democrats have been largely bypassed by the antiwar movement ever since the 1965 SDS march on Washington, when they could no longer impose exclusionary measures. Mired in cold-war anti-Communist ideology, the Socialist Party has denounced the nonexclusive, mass-action antiwar movement and the slogan of immediate withdrawal of U.S. troops. Its efforts have been limited to electioneering for liberal capitalist politicians or pressuring them through such efforts as petition campaigns in favor of negotiations. The Socialist Party, which had considerable influence in the peace movement of the early 1960s, has stagnated in face of the growth of the mass movement against the war in Vietnam. The loosely-organized "third camp" Social Democrats have intervened in the antiwar movement to only a limited extent and made only minimal gains.

The Maoist Progressive Labor Party has pursued a sectarian and abstentionist policy towards the antiwar movement. At the inception of the antiwar movement, PL operated through the May 2nd Committee, which proclaimed itself as the exclusive organization for all antiwar actions but which was never able to organize mass demonstrations or willing to involve other tendencies. PL's refusal to participate in the united-action coalitions led it to abstain almost totally from the growing antiwar movement. PL dissolved the May 2nd Committee when it entered SDS at a time when SDS had retreated from the struggle against the war. Although PL has made gains from its entry tactic in SDS, it has cut itself off from the bulk of the radicalizing youth around the antiwar movement. Its political gains within the general youth radicalization have been meager.

The Communist Party has intervened in the antiwar movement intermittently, not on a consistent basis. The CP's basic line has been to seek to utilize the antiwar actions and organizations as a means of pressuring the Democratic Party. It has advanced its class-collaborationist line in all important disputes within the antiwar movement. It has remained hostile to the left-wing, immediate-withdrawal-based antiwar committees, viewing them as competitors to its youth organization and to the various liberal peace committees in which it operates.

Nevertheless, because of the mass character of the antiwar demonstrations, the CP has been forced to enter united-action coalitions, where it meets our direct competition. The result has been a relative weakening of the CP in comparison to the SWP, especially in regard to youth cadre. This changed relationship of forces is one of the most important byproducts of the antiwar movement for the revolutionary vanguard.

The organized ultraleft groupings have remained relatively ineffectual. Some, such as the Spartacist League and the Workers League, have abstained almost entirely from the antiwar movement. Those which have intervened, such as Workers World-Youth Against War and Fascism, have not built the mass demonstrations, but attempted to initiate adventuristic actions subsidiary to them or entirely isolated from them. Despite the militancy and inexperience of unaffiliated radicalizing youth, the organized ultraleft grouplets have not made significant gains, either in numbers or direct organizational influence.

Students for a Democratic Society is not a tendency in the working-class movement but a loosely organized amalgamation of competing tendencies and unorganized radicals. As a national organization, SDS retreated from the struggle against the war after its march on Washington in 1965. While SDS has experienced considerable numerical growth, its national weight within the organized antiwar movement has been minimal due to its abstentionist policy. Local SDS chapters have participated in the antiwar movement, not through national SDS, but through the antiwar organizations as they exist, primarily the Student Mobilization Committee.

The maturing political differentiations within SDS have further paralyzed its ability to act as a national organization. This opens the door for: (1) the Student Mobilization Committee to gain greater authority as an organizer of antiwar youth, including among most SDS members; (2) the Young Socialist Alliance and Socialist Workers Party to recruit more of the healthiest revolutionary-minded SDS members.

The Socialist Workers Party is the only working-class tendency that has from the first recognized the central political importance of the struggle against the Vietnam war and has met its obligation to defend the Vietnamese revolution. We have made the antiwar struggle the major arena of our work and have intervened in it on a number of levels. We have been the most consistent fighters for the central line of mass antiwar demonstrations and for the political demand for immediate withdrawal of U.S. troops from Vietnam. The support we have won for our political line and the consistent work we have done to implement it in building the antiwar actions have enabled us to exert a decisive influence in the leadership of the mass movement itself, as it presently exists.

The Vietnam war has been a major factor in generating a new wave of radicalization in the United States, opening up expanded opportunities for building the revolutionary party. As the revolutionary socialist wing of the antiwar movement, we have been able to reach the bulk of the radicalizing youth, gain a hearing for our political program, and add significantly to our forces. The majority of new recruits to the Socialist Workers Party in the past few years have come directly out of the antiwar movement. The combination of our political weight in the antiwar movement and our expanded recruitment have changed the relationship of forces within the working class vanguard significantly in favor of the Socialist Workers Party as compared to our opponents.

The antiwar movement has been an important training ground for the new cadres of the Socialist Workers Party, giving them valuable experience in applying the transitional program in the mass movement, and enabling them to learn in practice how to be tactically flexible while politically firm. Tested against opponent tendencies, the Socialist Workers Party has been able to deal them heavy blows and minimize their gains. This development is most important in relation to the Communist Party which remains the major long-term competitor of the revolutionary Marxists for leadership of the working-class vanguard. The political struggles that have taken place in the antiwar movement are part of the preparation for the struggles for the leadership of the general working-class radicalization which is to come and which will determine the future of the American socialist revolution.

Our central tasks in the antiwar movement are to continue to build the mass antiwar demonstrations that are dealing hammer blows to American imperialism and to recruit from the growing numbers that have begun to move in a radical direction as a result.

PART II: THE SWP APPROACH TO MILITARY POLICY AND ITS EVOLUTION SINCE 1940

Military policy is an essential part of any transitional program of the revolutionary party in the imperialist epoch with its monstrous growth of capitalist militarism. The naive outlook of the early socialist movement which disregarded the military aspects of the class struggle has long since become outmoded. The actual relations between nations, peoples and classes compel every political tendency to take a position and work out a policy toward both imperialist and class warfare.

The position of the SWP in this field as in others has been derived from Marxist principles and the methods and traditions of Bolshevism as interpreted and applied by the Fourth International. This general line has been consistently followed from the beginning of our movement in this country. But since 1940 the tactical application of this course has twice been modified because of changes in objective circumstances.

In 1940, on the eve of the impending World War II, the SWP set forth its revolutionary socialist antiwar program in the form of the proletarian military policy. This represented a specific application of the methods of the transitional program adopted in 1938 to the working-class psychology and political conditions of the time.

The program was based on the following concepts. (1) It continued our irreconcilable opposition to imperialist war and the capitalist system which breeds it. (2) It projected the perspective of a struggle to win leadership of the working class in order to carry through a fight for state power and establish a socialist society. (3) It laid stress on the need to build a Leninist-type party to fulfill these objectives.

Our approach was categorically counterposed to the misleading ideas and political confusion sowed by the professional pacifists and the Stalinists and Social Democrats on the issues of militarism.

The pacifists proceed on the utopian premise that the laws of the class struggle and capitalist competition can be nullified by the cooperation of people of goodwill who can prevail upon the imperialists to refrain from warmaking. Pacifists oppose the development of the class struggle in favor of class peace at almost any price.

From their moral and religious opposition to violence as such, and not simply to reactionary violence, flows a rejection of the right of armed self-defense. They substitute the individual "witness" for organized collective action. Their conscientious objection to military conscription and training leads to draft evasion or victimization by imprisonment which further isolates antiwar elements from the masses.

Pacifist ideology is as pernicious and prostrating under wartime conditions as in times of sharp class conflict. It demoralizes and disorients antiwar activists and movements, deters mass mobilizations, and plays into the hands of the imperialists.

Pacifism as a policy may look plausible so long as peaceful relations prevail but it collapses like a pricked balloon as soon as hostilities are declared. In previous periods many professional pacifists have turned into fanatical war supporters once the ruling class has plunged the nation into battle.

Marxists, on the other hand, have always recognized that under military conditions a military policy is mandatory.

In addition to their false line of class collaboration and supporting "peace" candidates who surrender to the warmongers, the Stalinists and Social Democrats take positions which are not essentially different from the simple antimilitarist attitudes of the pure pacifists and which prove to be equally impotent in the struggle against capitalism and its wars. Historically, they, too, have capitulated to the warring state power after war has broken out, or else they have refrained from advancing or acting upon a program of struggle to take state power from the capitalist rulers, the only way that capitalist militarism and imperialist wars can be abolished.

The military policy adopted in 1940 was a revolutionary line designed to promote the anticapitalist struggles of the workers under the given wartime conditions.

It was anticipated that proletarian revolutions would emerge in the advanced capitalist countries directly out of the consequences of World War II and that the worker masses in the giant conscript armies would play the decisive role in them.

The transitional measures proposed in the program were to be a bridge from the revolutionary vanguard to the young worker-soldiers drafted into the U.S. armed forces, who were imbued with a mixture of anti-Hitler, antifascist, defensist, democratic and patriotic sentiments. They aimed to develop an assertion of their class independence within the capitalist military machine so that it would be possible to proceed step by step toward winning ideological and political hegemony among them in preparation for the anticipated revolutionary upsurge.

This undertaking was politically prepared and reinforced by the party's public opposition to the imperialist war dramatized by the 1941 Smith Act trial and its documentation.

As part of its program, the party continued its unconditional opposition to capitalist conscription. At the same time it took cognizance of the fact that the antifascist and patriotic sentiments of the workers led them to favor compulsory military service. It therefore counterposed the concept of conscription by the workers' organizations to the capitalist military draft. It advocated military training under trade-union control, financed by the capitalist government.

These proposals aimed to build class-conscious workers' military formations capable of defending labor's interests under conditions of capitalist militarism, imperialist war and the threat of fascist counterrevolution.

Party members called up for military service submitted, as individuals, to capitalist conscription. In the armed forces they lent themselves to learning military skills and sought to win the political confidence of their fellow soldiers. Their participation as socialists in the military machine was viewed as a prerequisite for revolutionary action if a favorable turn of events made it possible to gain a majority to the idea of transforming the imperialist war into a struggle for workers power and socialism.

This set of measures, presented in propaganda form at the outset of the war, did not become the basis for any substantial action during the conflict because the actual pattern of events took a different turn which did not coincide with our expectations.

The most radical development which took place in the army was the "I want to go home" movement of the GIs at the end of the war in the Pacific which upset the plans of the Pentagon strategists by weakening their armed forces.

Although revolutionary situations erupted in Western Europe, no victorious revolutions occurred in the advanced capitalist countries. The axis of the world revolution shifted to the colonial world.

These postwar conditions created a world situation which was qualitatively different from that of the 1941–45 period. However important interimperialist rivalries remain, they have been subordinated to imperialism's cold war against the workers states and its military interventions against the colonial revolutions. The U.S. armed forces have become the principal instrument of world imperialist aggression.

These global developments have generated marked changes in the views of the American people toward the issues posed by Washington's armed interventions. U.S. involvement in World War II was almost unanimously accepted under the illusion that it was a progressive war waged against fascism.

While a noticeable and a significant decline in patriotic fervor was registered during the Korean war of the early 1950s, active and overt opposition was pretty much confined to circles on the left which were then on the decline.

Vietnam has brought about a decisive shift in popular attitudes toward imperialist war. An unprecedented antiwar movement has emerged which continues to win more and more supporters in the midst of a shooting war. It is led by insurgent youth who belong to the post-witchhunt generation and who have been radicalized by the colonial revolution and the black liberation struggle.

Instead of urging on the government to victory at all costs, defeatist moods have been gaining ground among large sections of the population since 1965. This resistance to the imperialists expresses itself directly in sympathy for the Vietnamese revolution and indirectly through condemnation of the war as illegal, immoral and unjust and in the reluctance of the organized workers and blacks to make any material sacrifices for the war effort.

This country's ruling class is having to pay the toll of its function as the chief guardian of world capitalism. In becoming the top dog of the imperialist pack, it has fallen prey to all the basic contradictions of international capitalism in its death agony. Washington is obliged to finance and provide the main military means required for increasingly massive measures to stem the tide of the anti-imperialist and anticapitalist mass struggles throughout the world.

The heavy costs of this course are being levied upon the people in the form of conscription and sizable military casualties; mounting taxes and inflationary pressures on real wages; and gross neglect of urgent social needs. These consequences of imperialist militarism have caused more and more Americans to question the Vietnam conflict and the official rationale for its prosecution. The official demagogy and barefaced deceit employed by the government to justify U.S. intervention have generated widespread suspicion. The growing criticism of imperialist policy and resentment against the war keeps adding to the number of Americans who want to bring it to a speedy halt.

The pacifist sentiments of the masses have a different significance than the ideology and policies of the professional pacifists. They grow out of distrust of the foreign policy imposed by the monopolists and militarists and revulsion against their aggression which have a revolutionary potential. If these healthy instincts can be deepened, politically developed and properly directed, they can become the basis and point of departure for the creation of a mass anticapitalist consciousness which can pass beyond the narrow political limits set by the professional pacifists and their fellow class collaborationists who have dominated previous "peace" movements.

The task of our party is to direct this antiwar protest into class-struggle channels. To make its military policy fit the new international and domestic conditions, the party has introduced the following changes in its tactics.

The slogan of military training under trade-union control has been laid aside along with the advocacy of conscription into workers' military organizations.

More emphasis is placed upon opposing capitalist conscription which is becoming increasingly unpopular.

As in the past, party members called up for military service submit to the draft.

In doing so, they refuse to sign the unconstitutional loyalty oath now made part of the conscription procedure.

Although the main weight of the antiwar movement continues to center in the civilian population, the opposition to the war which has developed within the present conscript army has added a new and extremely important political dimension to the forces involved in the fight against the imperialist warmakers. Revolutionary socialists within the armed forces focus their political activity on the assertion and defense of their constitutional right to express their views as citizens upon the war and other issues of government policy, using sound tactical judgment in exercising that right and avoiding disciplinary hangups and penalties over routine military matters and orders.

The basic aim of our current transitional approach is the same as its predecessor. It seeks to promote a struggle for power and socialism by the workers and their allies and to build a strong, democratically disciplined combat party capable of leading that struggle to the end.

PART II

Revolutionary Antiwar Policy and Practice

1. SOCIALISTS AND THE ANTIWAR MOVEMENT: A HISTORY, 1965/69

By Gus Horowitz

The following report by Gus Horowitz was adopted by the September, 1969 SWP convention. It is reprinted from the October 10, 1969 issue of *The Militant.*

In subsequent months, the antiwar movement acquired truly mammoth proportions. On October 15, 1969, National Vietnam Moratorium Day, antiwar activities involving several million people occurred in almost every locality in the U. S. On November 15, more than 750,000 people marched against the war in Washington, D. C. and San Francisco, the largest demonstration ever seen in the U. S. up to that time. These actions further intensified mass antiwar sentiment.

The history of the antiwar movement has been not only one of demonstrations, teach-ins, rallies and hundreds of other actions, it has also been a history of continual and turbulent internal struggle over political line—over how and for what purpose to mobilize the mass sentiment against the war in Vietnam.

The Communist Party and the liberals have persistently tried to draw the antiwar movement into class-collaborationist politics, to use it as a means of pressure within the Democratic party. At the same time, various pacifists and ultralefts have tried to divert the movement into ineffectual acts of individual witness and small adventurist actions which would isolate it from masses of people.

In contrast, the Socialist Workers Party has consistently fought for massive demonstrations, politically independent of the ruling class, which could express the sentiment of the tens of millions of people who are opposed to the war. Within the broader antiwar movement we have built the militant left wing, centered on the demand for immediate and unconditional withdrawal of all U. S. troops from Vietnam.

Although the antiwar movement has suffered many temporary setbacks in its history, the policy we projected has been able to win decisive influence over the long run. Opposing lines have been strong on occasion, but never strong enough to divert the antiwar movement permanently from its independent axis of mass action.

The basic character of the antiwar movement did not emerge fully developed. It was won in struggle, in large part due to the efforts of the revolutionary party. In this room are seated not only organizers, builders, activists and participants in the antiwar movement, but also—and most important—its conscious political leadership.

At each stage in the development of the antiwar movement, it has required the conscious intervention of the revolutionary party to win a course that would indeed deal blows to the imperialists. Although we are small in numbers, our conscious leadership has been required to move the struggle forward, to project each succeeding series of actions and to drive back threats to anti-imperialist mass action as the axis of the struggle.

To see how much has been accomplished, we need only contrast the present movement against the Vietnam war to the old peace movement of the early 1960s. *The Militant,* in April 1963, described a typical Easter peace march in Chicago, where a few students—among them, YSAers—carried signs against the war in Vietnam:

"Some self-appointed 'officials' tried to have these signs removed. But the Northwestern students insisted on carrying them. One argued, 'If you are not against the Vietnam war, you are not for peace.'

"A leaflet distributed by the Young Socialist Alliance called for nonexclusive picket lines. It also explained the socialist position that capitalism causes war."

That was a peace movement in which we had to fight to carry signs against the shooting war in Vietnam. And, excluded from the meetings which planned the demonstrations, we had to argue for political nonexclusion by distributing leaflets to the demonstrators.

The new antiwar movement was born in a break with the policy of the old peace movement. This was most evident in the first national demonstration against the war in Vietnam, the April 17, 1965, mass march on Washington called by SDS. In calling the march, a section of the SDS leadership broke with the League for Industrial Democracy, a social-democratic relic which at that time was the official parent organization of SDS.

The march was not for "peace" in the abstract; rather, it was directed against the specific war in Vietnam. In a break with cold-war liberalism, it characterized the Vietnam war as a civil war and called for self-determination for the Vietnamese people. The march was organized on a nonexclusionary basis; in particular, the SWP and YSA were welcomed to participate on the ground floor. And finally, the nature of the action was that of a militant, mass demonstration. It was independent and did not support any capitalist politicians.

The social democrats and sections of the old peace movement waged a bitter struggle against that march on Washington. They exerted all the pressure they could to tone down its political line and impose the old exclusionary anticommunist norms. They demanded complete bureaucratic control over the action and, failing to achieve that, they even tried to have it called off. On the eve of the demonstration they issued a public statement denouncing it.

But the march occurred. Some 20,000 came to Washington—more than twice as many as had participated in any of the old peace demonstrations—which proved the feasibility of organizing militant mass actions against the war.

It was this demonstration that established many of the basic political characteristics of the then new antiwar movement that remain to this day: nonexclusion; self-determination; and mass action.

The SWP and YSA played a large part in the struggle for the march on Washington. The issue was settled, not simply in meetings between SDS and the cold-war social democrats, but in battle—in actually building the march on the basis on which it had been conceived.

We recognized that this demonstration was a test. It was a means of establishing the new antiwar movement along the lines that we had fought for earlier. And so we plunged into the work of insuring its success.

The YSA endorsed the march. We sent speakers touring the country to build it and distributed literature on a far wider scale than had ever been done before. We took the lead—much more so than SDS itself—in establishing nonexclusive, ad hoc committees to build the march, to explain why it was important, and to argue for the policy of self-determination for the Vietnamese.

By getting the ball rolling, by convincing the activists, it was assured that the march would occur. That was how the issue was ultimately decided. So that when Bayard Rustin, the social democrat, demanded that SDS call off the march, they had to answer in effect: "We can't. It has wide support. The Trotskyists are going ahead and building it. And they'll carry it off without us."

Following the march on Washington, two aspects of the present antiwar movement remained to be established: (1) a national coalition to coordinate the much more massive actions that were to come; (2) popularization of the demand for immediate withdrawal of U. S. troops from Vietnam.

The next stage of struggle in the antiwar movement took place over these questions.

In 1965, hundreds of teach-ins and antiwar demonstrations occurred all over the country. They were organized primarily by ad hoc, nonexclusive, campus Committees to End the War In Vietnam (CEWVs). High points included a national teach-in in Washington which was broadcast to 100,000 students on more than 100 campuses; a 34-hour marathon teach-in in Berkeley, attended by 15,000; and local demonstrations on the International Days of Protest in October, which involved many tens of thousands.

A new challenge was thus posed to all tendencies in the antiwar movement. How would they orient to these action committees to end the war? This really boiled down to the root questions of independent mass action and withdrawal.

From the first, the SWP and YSA helped to build these CEWVs in a totally nonsectarian way. We sought to bring together all political tendencies opposed to the war around the single issue of action in the streets. At the same time, we argued for immediate withdrawal and were able to convince many antiwar committees of this perspective. This left wing formed the backbone of the antiwar movement.

The leadership of SDS drew back from the antiwar movement almost immediately after the successful march on Washington. And that has remained the policy of SDS nationally to this day. Needless to say, SDS turned its back on the CEWVs and counterposed itself and its line to them.

The Maoist Progressive Labor Party was, in its own way, equally sectarian. Wielding control over a group called the May 2nd Committee, PL proclaimed it to be the exclusive agency through which all antiwar actions must be channeled. This factional, ultimatistic policy did not work. Isolated from the real, rapidly growing antiwar movement, PL dissolved the May 2nd Committee to enter SDS, an SDS that had also abandoned the struggle against the war.

Shake-ups occurred in the old peace movement. These groups faced the alternative of cooperating with the CEWVs or standing aloof and trying to organize the old-style peace actions, a perspective that was none too promising, given the temper of the new militants. Under pressure of the mass actions, many groups in the old peace movement felt compelled to align themselves with the new antiwar committees. This laid the basis for the broad, mass-action coalitions that were to develop later.

The Communist Party's basic line was essentially the same then as it is today. The CP has supported the mass actions only intermittently and always with the intent of using them as a means to draw antiwar activists into capitalist electoral politics. To avoid collision with liberal capitalist politicians, the CP pushed a negotiations line and opposed withdrawal. The CP persistently counterposed a "respectable," multi-issue program of social reform and community electoral organizing to nationally coordinated antiwar demonstrations.

The mass action and withdrawal perspective of many CEWVs hampered the CP's ability to implement its popular-front line. Accordingly, the CP took a hostile and sectarian attitude to the antiwar committees and worked mainly through the old, "broader" peace groups which supported negotiations. Among the students, they tried unsuccessfully to counterpose the DuBois Clubs to the CEWVs.

The struggle between these contending political lines reached its first climax at the convention of the National Coordinating Committee to End the War in Vietnam (NCC) attended by 1,500 in November 1965. There the CP and SWP positions met in head-on collision, the first of a series of national political encounters which were decisive in determining the future course of the antiwar movement and in helping to change the relationship of forces on the left.

At the NCC conference, the central battle over mass action and withdrawal took an organizational form. We argued for a national organization of CEWVs based around the withdrawal demand, to be a part of a broader coalition to organize national mass actions. The supporters of negotiations, with the CP in the lead, tried to block this perspective. We were in a minority. The relationship of forces was still unfavorable, and it wasn't until a year later that these organizational forms would arise.

But the vigorous struggle we waged was crucial in preventing the CP's multi-issue, antiwithdrawal line from dominating the broad movement, even though they held decisive influence over the NCC's apparatus. Under pressure of the political battle, the CP was reluctant to try and block a call for the next mass action. A second International Days of Protest was set for March 1966. In these demonstrations the battle was joined once again.

The withdrawal-based, NCC convention minority formed a caucus and published the *Bring the Troops Home Now Newsletter.* This grouping of CEWVs, with our aid and support, took the fight to the ranks of the antiwar movement and waged an intensive and successful educational campaign. By the March demonstrations, the central demand was "Bring the GIs Home Now," and that has been the norm ever since. Most of the original opponents of withdrawal have in the meantime changed their position.

The NCC's political perspective, set by the pro-CP elements in its leadership, was not geared to organizing the March mass action. So we threw forces into that task as well. Travelers toured the country to build the action. Literature was published in quantity. In every city the militant CEWVs, mostly student based, spearheaded the action. These CEWVs eventually became a key ingredient in the formation of the Student Mobilization Committee. Then, as now, the militant, withdrawal-based youth section of the antiwar movement has been the decisive factor in pushing the other sections of the movement along.

Thanks to this effort, the NCC was unable to divert the whole movement away from militant mass action. Although some antiwar committees destroyed themselves trying to carry out the NCC line, others switched their course. The majority of the antiwar movement was won to the line we fought for.

But the antiwar movement lost precious time because the first attempt at forming a national coalition was aborted. A gap existed between the objective possibilities of the antiwar struggle and the formal organization needed for it.

While the NCC declined in 1966, the process of building antiwar actions led to the creation of broad-based, local antiwar coalitions on a fairly permanent basis. The most important of these was the New York Fifth Avenue Vietnam Peace Parade Committee, which brought hundreds of organizations together for the demonstrations it organized.

The Parade Committee was central to uniting the forces that eventually formed the new national antiwar coalition. Smaller demonstrations in August and November 1966 set the stage for the conference which called the huge April 15 demonstrations in New York and San Francisco and formed what was to become the National Mobilization Committee, the national antiwar coalition for the next period.

The Student Mobilization Committee was formed soon after—at a conference which was to be the second round in the series of confrontations between the SWP and CP in the antiwar movement. It was initially a narrow conference called and controlled top to bottom by the CP. But we had won enough support for our line to be able to turn it around and form a united front of students, based on the withdrawal demand.

With that, the line we had fought for at the NCC convention a year before had won out. The relationship of forces in the antiwar movement had been reversed.

The political struggles of 1965–1966 were necessary to organize the great mass demonstrations of 1967 and 1968.

On April 15, 1967, a half-million people marched in the streets of New York and San Francisco. On Oct. 21, 1967, 150,000 marched on Washington in a direct political confrontation with Johnson's war policy. And on April 26, 1968, the SMC organized a remarkably successful nationwide student strike. With close to a million participants it was larger than any of the student antiwar strikes of the 1930s. The following day, mass demonstrations were held in cities all over the country, the largest—in New York—some 200,000 strong.

These historic actions illustrate the power of the tactic of the united front and its particular application in the form of the antiwar coalitions. No single group acting alone could have organized such large and militant demonstrations. In those united fronts, the left wing, the SMC, was the best builder and the militant spearhead of the actions.

These actions also helped solidify the international antiwar movement, which also developed independently of the Stalinist and social democratic parties and to the left of them. This had been a key factor in developing a renewed spirit of internationalism, militancy and anticapitalist consciousness, especially among the youth. This shakeup and realignment of class forces has in turn opened expanded opportunities for building the Fourth International.

But the struggle for our antiwar line was far from over. The most recent period has seen the continuation of the struggle—in slightly different form and under slightly different conditions, but showing the same basic characteristics.

American imperialism faces a dilemma in Vietnam. Its central strategic objectives remain the same. It still aims to crush the national liberation struggle in South Vietnam and deal a major setback to the socialist revolution in southeast Asia.

For the imperialists to withdraw from Vietnam

in defeat would contradict this strategic goal. The struggle of the Vietnamese has already given great impetus to revolutionary developments in other countries. A definitive revolutionary victory would magnify that impact manyfold.

But two factors have caused the American ruling class to adjust its tactics.

The first is the fact that the U. S. has so far been unable to win an outright military victory in Vietnam despite a massive effort. Though imperialism has by no means been totally defeated, its inability to win a victory is in itself a tremendous setback.

The second factor compelling a tactical shift by the U. S. ruling class is the growth of the worldwide opposition to the war, in particular the mounting protests in the U. S. itself. For to carry on the war in Vietnam, the American ruling class needs social peace at home. Unable to win wide support for the war, it needs at the very least a disoriented and disarmed opposition.

For this reason, the mass mobilizations strike blows at the ability of the ruling class to wage the war. The capitalists face the threat of an intolerable growth of class conflict as the mood of protest and opposition spills over and exacerbates social tensions on all fronts.

In 1968, Washington responded to this threat with a major diplomatic and propaganda offensive.

First, the talks were set up in Paris. Washington's aim in these negotiations is at minimum a Korea-type settlement that would mean the derailment of the Vietnamese revolution. As we know, the Paris talks did not signal a significant slowdown of the war or a genuine move towards peace. While there was a pause in the bombing of the North, the same high level of bombing continues, all of it now concentrated in the South. Orders to the Pentagon called for bringing maximum military pressure on the liberation fighters, and the level of fighting stays high as they try to force the Vietnamese to capitulate.

At the same time a slick propaganda offensive was mounted to dissipate the antiwar sentiment of the American masses. The Paris talks and the pause in the bombing of the North were demagogically portrayed as steps towards a speedy peace. The token troop withdrawals are just the latest such maneuver.

The hated President Johnson withdrew as a candidate for reelection. Nixon, portraying himself as an alternative, won a temporary respite from the wrath of millions of people. This was all compounded in 1968, when the McCarthy campaign was mounted with the stated goal of getting the antiwar movement off the streets.

But although the mass antiwar sentiment was temporarily diverted and confused, the ruling class had also paid a price. All the talk about deescalation raised the anticipation and desire of the masses of people for a quick end to the war. Antiwar sentiment grew considerably. It was only a matter of time before there would be another wave of indignation and hundreds of thousands would once again take to the streets and tear away the facade of lie and illusion.

The propaganda maneuvers of the ruling class posed another major test for all tendencies in the antiwar movement. How to respond? American imperialism was in deep trouble, and the situation cried out for keeping on the course that had put it there.

The class collaborationists, full of illusions about the Paris talks, abandoned mass action. They turned to the elections, with the aim of using their influence in the antiwar movement to drum up support for McCarthy and the procapitalist peace candidates.

As a result of these defections, many of the local antiwar coalitions tended to fall apart. On a national level, National Mobe lost its broad coalition character. The old Mobe's apparatus came to be dominated by frustrated ultralefts who saw no future in mass action. And in the spring of 1968, the Communist Party and pacifists in the Student Mobilization Committee split from the organization, in retreat from mass antiwar action.

In contrast to every other political tendency, the SWP and YSA put forward a line that encouraged the independence of the antiwar movement from the capitalist parties in the elections. It was a line designed to maintain the perspective of reaching out and drawing larger numbers into action. It was designed to maintain the position of immediate withdrawal and to puncture the illusions about the Paris talks. And it was designed to lay the groundwork for building even larger mass mobilizations than those which had already occurred.

That is what we argued for, and—most important—that is what we were able to carry out in action.

The SWP's approach to the 1968 elections differed from the class collaborationists in two important ways.

First, we ran our own candidates. We did not abandon the field to the procapitalist candidates, but counterposed our revolutionary socialist program to them. By waging an all-out campaign effort, we were able to win considerable support from antiwar militants.

But that was only one side of our approach. Our policy in the antiwar movement was completely nonsectarian. The supporters of Halstead and Boutelle continued building demonstrations during the election period. We did not make the mistake of withdrawing from the antiwar movement in the illusion that we could then allot added forces to make greater gains for our campaign. On the contrary—revolutionaries always gain when the mass movement is built effectively.

One of the precedents that we had fought for previously—in particular, during the 1966 elections—was that the antiwar movement, as a movement, should not get involved in electoral politics, but should rather continue to unite everyone possible, regardless of divergent political views, for antiwar actions during the election periods. That precedent made it exceedingly difficult for the class collaborationists to scuttle the antiwar movement in 1968.

And we stuck to that policy. Even in those antiwar organizations where our campaign had considerable support, we resisted attempts to put them on record for the Halstead-Boutelle campaign. There were many antiwar activists who did not agree with the program of the SWP, but wanted to engage in antiwar actions, as we did. It would have narrowed the scope of the antiwar movement to make agreement with any full political program the basis for antiwar action.

The antiwar movement did suffer a setback in the 1968 election period and immediately afterwards. But it was a *temporary* setback. The movement was not scuttled. A series of demonstrations—even though they were generally smaller than before—continued the mass-action perspective that we had fought for.

In that period ultraleftist adventurism also exerted considerable influence over many antiwar militants. Frustrated because the war continues despite the mass opposition to it, the ultralefts aim at shortcuts through the isolated acts and adventures of a few, which renders impossible the arduous but solely effective path of winning over the masses of the people. The actions of the old National Mobe, SDS and some smaller groups tended to project this disorienting line.

In recent months the ultralefts have had less influence, but they continue to pose a problem for the antiwar movement. Some of them have even degenerated to the extent of introducing hooligan methods into the movement. The low point was reached in New York when a small group was able to take over the rally platform on Aug. 9.

The key to combating ultraleft adventures lies in the scope of the actions themselves. In the recent past smaller antiwar mobilizations gave the hardened ultralefts the opportunity to exert disproportionate influence over impatient and inexperienced activists. Now, however, the possibility exists to mobilize hundreds of thousands. A political line geared to involve such numbers of people will be the single greatest deterrent to isolated adventures. They tend to become simply lost in the crowd.

In addition, we must wage an educational campaign in the antiwar movement to explain the need for preventing hooligan disruption of the demonstrations. It will then be possible to organize adequate marshalling to insure that the decisions of the antiwar coalitions are carried out.

This is particularly important because of the GIs. Once Washington launched its propaganda offensive, with its continual talk of peace, the average GI naturally questioned the need to continue to risk his life, especially in a war which he was most likely opposed to or had serious doubts about. As a result, there has been a big increase in GI antiwar activity, and this will be a permanent feature of the antiwar movement from now on.

The importance of, and potential for, reaching GIs is something we have long emphasized. We pointed to the powerful social weight that the GIs would bring into the antiwar movement—our basic Marxist approach has always stressed reaching the socially decisive sectors of society.

In 1965, we published our pamphlet on the Bring the Troops Home Movement of World War II. In 1966, we went on a campaign to defend the Fort Hood Three and publicize the case to the movement. In 1967, defense of Howard Petrick was an important model in the fight for GI rights.

In 1968 and 1969, the vindication of our line was apparent in the wide circulation of GI papers, the big jump in GI participation in the demonstrations, and in the unprecedented fights for GI rights, particularly those of GIs United at Fts. Jackson and Bragg.

It is not surprising that the political differences that exist in the antiwar movement extend to its GI sector. Most other tendencies project a line which would be ineffective or lead to defeats. Such proposals include individual "acts of conscience," such as draft resistance or desertion; underground organizing; and GI union organizing which emphasizes issues other than the war in Vietnam.

The threefold approach to GI work which we have supported has proved most effective. It may be summarized: 1) for collective action, rather than isolated individual acts of conscience; 2) emphasis on the legal rights of GIs as citizen-soldiers; 3) opposition to the Vietnam war as the central issue of concern to GIs and around which they are utilizing their civil liberties.

The past period, to repeat, posed a major challenge to the antiwar movement. To counter the maneuvers of the ruling class required the conscious leadership of the revolutionary party. We were the ones who fought for continuing on a course of effective action that could mobilize masses in independent antiwar struggle.

The key to this fight was the Student Mobilization Committee. It was the militant, withdrawal-based, student wing of the antiwar movement that backed the perspective of mass antiwar mobilizations.

As always, it took a political struggle, and there was a major fight in the SMC over this perspective. The CP and pacifist section walked out. In so doing, they tried to brand the SMC as an impotent, paper organization, containing no one besides the SWP and YSA. They were proven dead wrong.

We had—and have—no interest in paper organizations or in capturing ourselves. To the contrary, our approach has always been one of building broad united fronts for mass action. Those who quit the SMC were splitting from this line, from what the SMC had stood for all along, and from what it stands for now.

The needs of the antiwar movement required the maintenance of the perspective of mass action. The SMC stood for that, and we backed it to the hilt. The SMC called for antiwar demonstrations in August 1968, and October 1968, and it initiated the conference that called the demonstrations on April 5 and 6, 1969. These demonstrations laid the groundwork for remobilizing the entire antiwar movement.

Even though there were considerable difficulties in convincing others to act in that period, we avoided any temptation to go it alone by substituting the vanguard of the struggle for the movement as a whole. We sought to find every conceivable way to involve other groups in united fronts for the mass actions.

The payoff came with the April 5–6 demonstrations.

The second Tet offensive in Vietnam and the high rate of battle casualties began to destroy the illusion that the war was coming to an end. There was a shift in mass consciousness. The April 5–6 demonstrations, organized by united fronts, were able to mobilize tens of thousands across the country—100,000 in New York alone—with a larger turnout of GIs than ever before.

The SMC seized the opportunity offered by April 5–6 to emerge as the authoritative national organizer of the antiwar youth. In many local areas, the April 5–6 demonstrations also enabled us to rebuild the antiwar coalitions. This set the stage for calling the next national demonstration, one with a potential of being more massive than any previous one, at a time when that is of central political importance.

All that was needed was the conference to call it and a new national coalition to organize it. And that occurred on July 4 in Cleveland, when the national antiwar conference called the Nov. 15 march on Washington.

Here again, the SWP and YSA played a central role in insuring that the antiwar movement would take the next necessary steps forward. It took a political struggle to win the conference, and it took a political struggle at the conference to win the call to the demonstration.

The key again was the SMC. The SMC took the call to the conference and publicized it far and wide. The SMC pushed and prodded others to come along (and more than a few came, somewhat reluctantly at first). The SMC made the conference a representative gathering of the antiwar movement with the authority to call the march on Washington. After a thorough political debate, there was a highly favorable response to the idea of Nov. 15, and a new national coalition was set up to organize it. The next day, an SMC conference called for a student strike on Nov. 14, which can involve hundreds of thousands and build wide support for the march on Washington.

We must see the importance of the Nov. 15 demonstration in the context of the overall political situation. American imperialism is in deep trouble in Vietnam. It hasn't been able to win. And its strategic goals make it shy away from withdrawing in defeat. It hopes to force the Vietnamese to capitulate in Paris. But that is a questionable proposition at best. And it needs time for that anyway. It needs time above all.

But the U. S. is running out of time.

The crux of the matter is this: The strategic objectives of American imperialism do not allow it to scale down the fighting to any significant degree. Their Achilles heel is that as the war continues, the death toll mounts. More and more people will see through their lies and duplicity, be outraged and demand a halt.

And now is the time that they can be brought to Washington to say, "No! Stop it! Bring *all* of the GIs home *now*!"

All indications, including the polls, show that there is deep and growing impatience with Nixon's war in Vietnam. The demonstration Nov. 15 can be both massive in size and devastating in its political impact. The antiwar movement must set itself the task of preventing American imperialism from gaining the time for maneuver that it so desperately needs.

The Nov. 15 demonstration must aim to involve new sectors of the population. Last April 5–6, significant numbers of GIs and high school students demonstrated. Their numbers can be increased. Now, there are new opportunities to draw in sections of the trade-union and black and brown movements. Every effort must be taken to make this potential a reality.

Make no mistake about it. The main spokesmen for the ruling class are worried. Just listen to what James Reston had to say in his *New York Times* column Aug. 27, shortly after the protests by the GIs of Company A who refused to obey battle orders:

"For the more the President says he's for peace, the more troops he withdraws from Vietnam and Thailand, the more he concedes that Southeast Asia is not really vital to the security of the United States, the harder it is to ask for the lives of the men of Company A.

"They may not be typical, but they are a symbol of his coming dilemma. He wants out on the installment plan, but the weekly installments are the lives of one or two hundred American soldiers, and he cannot get away from the insistent question: Why? To what purpose?

"The breaking point comes in politics as it came to Company A, and it is not far off."

Finally, if there is one point that should be emphasized, it is the importance of the Student Mobilization Committee. This fall, through its Nov. 14 student strike, the SMC will be the central organizer of the student antiwar upsurge that will surely take place.

The objective situation on the college campuses has never been more favorable. Antiwar sentiment is no mere majority view. It is overwhelming. The wave of protests against ROTC and campus complicity that shook the campuses last spring are but a preview to the action this fall.

The same holds true in the high schools. All indications point to a highly favorable objective situation, one in which the SMC has already registered impressive gains.

One of the most important features of the SMC's approach on the campuses will be its efforts to build united fronts to wage the most effective and militant struggles. This is particularly important in offering an alternative to SDS's political line and methods of organizing.

Last spring, SDS's sectarianism, exclusion, ultraleft formulations and adventurist tactics led to many a setback. But this fall, the faction-ridden SDS, continuing on its course of political degeneration, will find it increasingly difficult to win antiwar students to its insane adventures, and increasingly difficult to organize anything at all.

The SMC has a unique opportunity to win over, not only non-SDS antiwar activists, but also the many SDS members who are fed up with the SDS national office—either one. It can involve them in the student strike, in Nov. 15, and in all related antiwar actions.

Our perspective, in short, is one of expanded and powerful mass antiwar action. The march on Washington on Nov. 15 will deal another major blow to American imperialism's war in Vietnam.

Our role in the antiwar movement is a powerful example of what even a small party can do in taking our revolutionary program and applying it in life, in being able to gauge accurately the objective situation and pose the next necessary steps forward for the mass movement.

In the process we have grown, and the struggle for the international socialist revolution has taken steps forward.

As the resolution before this convention states: "Our central tasks in the antiwar movement are to continue to build the mass mobilizations that are dealing hammer blows to American imperialism and to recruit from the growing numbers that have begun to move in a radical direction as a result."

2. MAY 1970—A STUDENT UPSURGE WITHOUT PRECEDENT

On May 30, 1970, Nixon announced the invasion of Cambodia by U. S. troops, in an effort to prop up the recently-installed military dictatorship that was threatened by a popular uprising. The response to this new escalation was immediate—protests on campuses across the country. In one of these demonstrations four students at Kent State University in Ohio were murdered by the national guard. This sparked a national student strike and a wave of demonstrations that rocked the country and forced Nixon to withdraw U. S. troops from Cambodia.

a. The Impact on Capitalists, Unions, and Students

By Jack Barnes

"The Impact on Capitalists, Unions, and Students," by Jack Barnes, first appeared in the June 5, 1970 issue of *The Militant.*

The American events of May 1970 did not lead, as the French events of May 1968 did, to a general strike of the working class. Nevertheless the American events marked a new high point in antiwar consciousness and action by important sectors of the American people and may prove to have opened the door to the most decisive struggles yet waged against American imperialism's war in Southeast Asia.

Three events occurred in May that either were unique in the history of the antiwar movement or represented turning points both in the struggle against the war and the deepening radicalization in the United States:

- American students conducted the biggest student strike in the history of the world.
- Sections of the capitalist class split publicly not only over the war but over its effects on their ability to rule the United States.
- The first large layer of AFL-CIO unions and unionists publicly repudiated the line of support to the war that George Meany and his cohorts have developed in the name of organized labor for half a decade.

The strike that swept the nation's campuses in May revealed that the American students have a political potential and weight that they themselves had never suspected.

On a national scale, in educational institutions of every type and level, the strike demonstrated without question that the deeply felt hatred for the American imperialist war in Southeast Asia and the willingness to oppose it have passed far beyond a radical vanguard of the students. Virtually an entire generation is involved.

The May actions against the war were not limited to the campus organizations previously engaged in protest. A number of all-Black universities and colleges organized against the war—even before the Augusta and Jackson murders; at some all-women's schools newly formed women's liberation committees sparked the actions; high school and junior high students had large-scale strike actions with widespread participation by the Third World youth. Official student governments and faculty bodies joined in.

This massive response to the invasion of Cambodia and the murder of the Kent students marks a new stage in the American student movement.

For the first time, the students, on a broad scale, took a step beyond mass protest to winning control of some of the wide range of facilities of the American universities. These "antiwar universities" were used as a base from which to organize their actions and propaganda against the war and campus complicity with the war machine, and to reach out to other key sectors of the population—the GIs, the Third World communities, the labor movement—to involve them in the struggle to get the troops out of Southeast Asia.

On the campuses, as a result of these events, there is a new consciousness of what it is possible to accomplish. There has also been a favorable shift in the relationship of forces between the antiwar students and sympathetic faculty on one side, and the direct agents of capitalism—the administrators, trustees, and regents—on the other.

Under the impact of these events, the coming months will see continuing campus struggle—with a greater chance of success than ever. Struggles will be waged to eliminate restrictive rules regulating the social, political, and personal lives of the students and against every aspect of campus complicity with the war machine.

Attempts to turn the large and varied resources and the apparatus of the universities away from the projects and priorities of the ruling class, trustees, and administrators will increase. The orientation will be to turn the university resources toward the projects and priorities of the students in the struggle against the war, against repression and oppression of Third World people and women, against exploitation of resources and pollution of the environment by unfettered big business.

With the May events under their belts, the students will more frequently and in greater numbers use their newly won positions of strength on the campuses to link up with and organize support for the struggles of the working class, the oppressed nationalities, and women. More and more often, campus facilities will be opened to embattled forces off the campuses and experiences will be exchanged.

The degree of control over university resources and facilities will vary from campus to campus. But the basic strategic concept—winning and then using the vast resources of the American universities as a powerful base from which to link up with the coming mighty social struggles against American capitalism—has been given a trial run, its validity and the experience will not be forgotten. Another valuable addition to the capital of the entire movement has been the appearance on many campuses of broad strike councils. They implemented the tasks decided on in mass campus meetings, and represented the forces of the upsurge in a way no single organization could. This form will undoubtedly be refined, improved, and used on a broader scale at the next stage of the struggle. This kind of democratic leadership committee, which can unite forces in a large struggle and be viewed as the legitimate authority of a mass upsurge, is an important example for GIs, Third World communities, and the labor movement.

The May events open a new chapter for the growth of the Young Socialist Alliance in numbers, geographical extension, and political experience and influence. The need for and the role of a nationwide revolutionary socialist youth organization with a political program and strategy that links campus rebellion to the key political fight against American capitalism can be understood today by thousands of radical students who were not sure of this a month ago.

The May events detonated an open rift in the ruling class all the way up to the Nixon cabinet and precipitated a deep sense of crisis publicly expressed by a wide spectrum of spokesmen for the ruling class.

The difference in attitude from the time of the march on Washington in November 1969 is illustrated by the shift in even Nixon's public posture. In November he said protests could have no effect on his policy, and demonstratively let it be known that he was watching a football game on TV during the demonstration.

In May he conceded an area for the demonstrators near the White House where he "could hear the protest," told the nation he couldn't sleep a wink all night before the demonstration, and went out at dawn to "discuss" with some of the demonstrators.

What stunned even members of Nixon's own cabinet and drove them to public expressions of dismay was neither the Cambodian invasion nor the Kent massacre. It was the mass eruption of outraged protest against them, which they feared would completely discredit and permanently isolate the Nixon administration.

Similarly, spokesmen for the ruling class outside the Nixon administration expressed alarm not because of basic disagreement over imperialist foreign policy, but because the May events convinced them of the real possibility that social upheavals generated by the expansion of the war threaten the future of American capitalism.

Former Chief Justice Earl Warren gave the following estimate in a speech on May 15:

"We are, indeed, in a crisis. We have . . . a divisiveness in our society to a degree of intensity that has not been equaled in the past hundred years."

The day before, John W. Gardner, a Republican and former cabinet member of the Johnson administration, released to the national press a speech in which he said:

"And while each of us pursues his selfish interest and comforts himself by blaming others, the nation disintegrates. I use the phrase soberly: The nation disintegrates."

In the "extraordinary reaction" to Nixon's Cambodian invasion, Gardner saw evidence that a "crisis of confidence in our leadership" has been growing. "The seeming abrupt reversal of implied commitments deepened the question in the minds of millions of Americans as to whether they can believe the promises of their leaders."

James Reston, of *The New York Times,* writing from Washington two days later saw Nixon "in deep trouble" because, like Johnson, "he is increasingly up against the dilemma of getting out of Vietnam quicker than he planned or not being able to govern the country. . . . His advisers recognize the changed mood in the capital. They thought, when they came to power, that they were dealing with a foreign war, and they now see that they are dealing with a rebellion against that war, and maybe even with a revolution at home."

Another top figure of the Johnson administration, McGeorge Bundy, president of the Ford Foundation, warned on May 15: "Not only must there be no new incursion of Americans across the Cambodian border, but nothing that feels like that to the American public must happen again. . . . Any major action of this general sort, if undertaken in the same fashion as the Cambodian decision—now that the domestic effects of that decision are visible—would tear the country and the administration to pieces. At the very least the Congress would stop money for the war, and the chances of general domestic upheaval would be real."

Thus, while attempting to maintain the image of unity behind the myth that his "Vietnamization" policy was ending the war, Nixon has actually opened a credibility gap deeper than the Johnson administration ever faced. He has set into motion a greater public outpouring of opposition within his own class than that which forced his predecessor from office. This open rift in the ruling class, itself a consequence of the May events, creates the conditions for further and broader expressions of mass opposition to the war.

No powerful organization outside the government has supported the White House-Pentagon policies on the war throughout its entire escalation more fervently than the AFL-CIO bureaucracy headed by George Meany. This has effectively blocked the strongest social force in the country, the organized working class, from participating in the growing antiwar movement. But the May events opened a public fissure in this seeming monolith.

The example of the students and the pressure from workers, whose growing disenchantment with the war and its effects had found no expression in the top union bureaucracy, combined in May to explode the claim that Meany's prowar line represents the sentiments of a majority, let alone all, of American labor.

Three major developments highlight the breakup of this logjam:

Under the impact of the Kent killings and telegrams from locals around the country, on May 7 the national convention of the American Federation of State, County, and Municipal Employees (AFSCME) overwhelmingly passed a resolution demanding withdrawal of all American troops from Southeast Asia. AFSCME is the eighth largest union in the AFL-CIO and represents 490,000 workers.

In New York an important section of the union movement, including locals affiliated to the AFL-CIO, the Alliance for Labor Action and independent unions, for the first time called a street demonstration against the war. Some 25,000 New Yorkers were mobilized on May 21 in a common labor-student effort. The sponsors included New York unions with large Black and Puerto Rican memberships. The rally drew a larger percentage of Black and Puerto Rican participants than any previous antiwar action.

On May 18, 452 Bay Area elected union officials and shop stewards placed a full-page ad in the *San Francisco Examiner* differentiating themselves from Nixon's policies, asserting their disbelief and distrust in anything the government says about the war, and demanding that U. S. troops be brought home from Vietnam and Cambodia now.

These open breaks in the labor bureaucracies make it possible for opponents of the war inside the unions to effectively argue their view and mobilize the sentiment against the war that already exists among millions of American workers. They can realistically begin to translate that opposition into effective antiwar action.

The antiwar movement outside the unions now has a totally new opportunity to use the resolutions, endorsements, actions, and official statements of sections of the labor movement to solicit support, aid and participation in antiwar actions from other sections.

Now that the ice has been broken, a new problem for the capitalist rulers can materialize in the near future: When the next major actions of the antiwar struggle begin—that is, when the May events find their logical continuation—big sections of organized labor could be involved from the beginning. Both a qualitative change in the composition and character of street actions and the beginning of job actions against the war, loom as real possibilities.

Unlike France's May events of two years ago a revolutionary situation did not develop in May 1970 in the United States. But a preview could be seen of the forces that, if combined in mass political action against the policies of the American government, could shake capitalism to its foundations.

b. From 'After the May Upsurge: Young Socialists and the Student Movement'

The following is an analysis on the May, 1970 events from "After the May Upsurge: Young Socialists and Student Movement," the political resolution adopted by the Young Socialist Alliance convention in December, 1970. This excerpt is reprinted from *Young Socialist Discussion Bulletin* Volume 14, No. 4.

The 1970s will be a decade of profound crises for American capitalism and of unprecedented opportunities for revolutionary socialists. We in the YSA are optimistic about the prospects for organizing masses of people in struggle against the U. S. ruling class and its government in Washington. Our experience in 1970 has confirmed our view that the current radicalization, which began in the 1960s, can lead to the elimination of capitalism in the stronghold of world imperialism through a socialist revolution in the United States.

The May Upsurge

In May 1970, two government actions—the invasion of Cambodia and the massacre of students at Kent State—touched off the largest student general strike in history. The invasion of Cambodia by U. S. forces represented a decision by the Nixon administration to extend and intensify the war in Southeast Asia. The murder of the Kent students symbolized the attempts of the ruling class to silence one of the most dynamic and effective opponents of Washington's war plans, the student movement.

The combination of these two events, which were followed by the gunning down of Black youth in Augusta, Ga., and at Jackson State, in Mississippi, triggered a nationwide student upsurge which threw the entire country into a major social crisis, producing shock waves which have not yet subsided.

The size and scope of the campus actions were unparalleled. The Carnegie Commission on Higher Education, headed by Clark Kerr, reported on the extent of the May campus upsurge: major protests occurred on 1454 campuses (out of a total of 2551); and 550 campuses had strikes which completely halted the normal functioning of the schools.

One of the most significant features of the upheaval was the creation of new forms of struggle by the mobilized masses of students. For the first time in history, striking students "opened up" their schools as antiwar universities. Students began reconstituting their schools, turning them into instruments of struggle against the war. Taking control of the school facilities, students used them for reaching out to involve other sectors of the population in the antiwar movement. The process of attempting to reach out beyond the campus demonstrated an understanding by students of the need to link up with more powerful social layers in order to win their aims. This understanding represents a new advanced consciousness among thousands of students about the student movement's role in fighting for social change.

The form of organization which spontaneously emerged in the struggles of May was the broad-based, representative strike committee which called and presented proposals to mass meetings and coordinated strike activities. At many schools, these committees involved the entire university community and served to organize the new functions of the antiwar university.

These important new forms of struggle have become permanent acquisitions of the student movement because, while the strike was only temporary, it lasted long enough for the concept of the antiwar university and democratic strike councils to engrave itself in the consciousness of the millions of students who took part. Future upsurges will tend to follow the pattern established in May. In this sense we can say that May 1970 was the "1905 of the student movement"—new organizational forms of struggle emerged and were tested for the first time, just as the first soviets emerged and were tested in the 1905 Russian Revolution, and in 1917 became the organs of the new state power. Universities run by the strike committees will not become organs of state power, but they will emerge again to play a crucial role in helping to organize masses outside the campus into anticapitalist action.

The YSA learned important lessons in the May events. First, the events expressed the tremendous depth of the youth radicalization and revealed young people's increasing lack of confidence in the government's ability to solve the problems facing American society. While the radicalization is deepest among youth, the widespread sympathy and support for the students' objectives expressed in other sections of the population and the strike's impact on the rest of the country offered impressive testimony to the extent of the radicalization in society as a whole.

Second, the May events dramatically illustrated once more that the war in Indochina remains a central driving force in the radicalization and the central issue in U. S. politics. In spite of Nixon's elaborate schemes for "Vietnamization," U. S. imperialism is gripped more tightly than ever in the vise of trying to maintain its world domination on one side and trying to maintain social peace at home on the other. The war in Vietnam and the antiwar movement are the sharpest expression of the dilemma Nixon faces.

Third, the May strike revealed more clearly than ever before the increased social weight and power of the student movement in today's neocapitalist society. The impact of the students' actions, both directly on the government and through their influence on other social sectors, provided conclusive evidence of the decisive role students can play in detonating major social explosions. The May student strike stamped its impression on the entire society, serving notice to America's rulers that they must take account of the reaction of students in any of their future plans.

Fourth, the development of antiwar universities confirmed in action the YSA's strategy for the student movement, that is, the use of the university as a base to organize other sectors of the population into anticapitalist struggle. This proved to be an attractive idea to masses of students once they had gained a sense of their own power in the first days of the strike.

Finally, the student upsurge graphically illustrated the power of independent mass action. The student strike, which arose completely independently of the "dove" capitalist politicians, forced Nixon to adapt his plans and helped educate masses of people that they can succeed only by taking action on their own without relying on the capitalist politicians who pose as their leaders.

Another aspect of the strike as massive independent political action was the rejection, on the overwhelming majority of campuses, of any ultraleft actions or forms of organization which would narrow the base of the strike, such as limiting participation in the strike committee to the traditional campus radicals. This stands in sharp contrast to the SDS-led campus struggles of 1968–1969.

The YSA's understanding of these lessons enabled us to play a leading role in the May events. YSAers helped initiate and participated in strike committees on many campuses, working to mobilize students and to deepen their understanding of the antiwar university. Where it was possible, we helped organize citywide and regional coordination of the strike. We were the only group able to act as a national organization in our support of and participation in the upsurge. *The Militant*, to a limited extent, served the function of a national strike newspaper, giving the only national coverage and analysis of the events as they were happening.

We went on a campaign footing to build the strike and explain the concept of the antiwar university. At the same time, we reached the broadest possible layers of the population with the ideas of revolutionary socialism.

The pattern established in May illustrated the potential for the next upsurge to succeed in drawing in the participation of the organized working class, high school students, the Third World communities and masses of women. The May events produced the first significant break in the trade union bureaucracy's monolithic backing of Nixon's war policy, a break which expressed itself, for example, in the labor-student demonstration called in New York City at the initiative of trade union officials as a response to "hard hat" attacks on antiwar demonstrators. While the May strike fell short of touching off a generalized social upheaval, it came close enough to let the ruling class see the outlines of a social revolution in this country. The capitalists were so frightened by what they saw that the threat of another May has become a permanent factor for them to consider before making any major moves in their continuous campaign to crush the world revolution.

Nixon's Offensive

During May, the ruling class counterposed campaigns for capitalist "peace" candidates and doorbell-pushing for legislation such as the Cooper-Church and Hatfield-McGovern bills to the independent mass action organized by the students. In typical fashion, they attempted to disorient the mass movement and divert its independent struggle back into the arena of the Democratic and Republican parties. While the majority of students did not shed their illusions about the possibility of winning their demands through capitalist "peace" candidates, the attempt to divert their struggle met with little success during May.

Once the strike had been effectively ended by the pullback from Cambodia and the closing of the schools, the ruling class launched a two-pronged counterassault designed to eliminate the threat revealed in May. First, the U. S. rulers used the fake debates of the capitalist campaigns for the November elections to play down the issue of the war and to try to draw students back into "the system." Second, they conducted a propaganda campaign against "campus violence" and initiated a drive to restrict students' rights to organize political activity.

During every election campaign, the ruling class puts up "alternatives" to try to make the American people think they have a choice and to give them the illusion that they control the government. Maintaining these illusions is, of course, one of the primary functions of elections in a bourgeois democracy. Because of the deepgoing and widespread nature of such illusions among the masses of people and the resources the capitalists put behind their campaigns, election periods have always been difficult times for organizing mass independent political action. There was virtually no independent political action in 1964 when nearly everyone stampeded into supporting the "lesser evil" of Lyndon Johnson against Goldwater. The support of many antiwar activists for Congressional "doves" in the capitalist parties during the 1966 elections seriously hampered the development of the then new antiwar movement. In 1968, the Kennedy and McCarthy campaigns were successful in recruiting the energies of thousands of young people away from mass action into playing the two-party shell game.

Considering this pattern, the striking feature of the 1970 elections was not that they were able to dampen independent struggles but that *they were far less successful* than previous elections in this respect. There are three reasons for the relatively limited effects of the 1970 elections.

First, Nixon's phony gestures at "winding down" the war succeeded in silencing opposition among the "doves," who endorsed his maneuver with grotesque servility.

Second, virtually all of the liberal candidates caved in under Nixon's and Agnew's pressure and adopted a patriotic "law and order" pose, denouncing student "extremists."

Third, more young people than ever before have begun to see through the fraud of capitalist politics. These radicalizing young women and men perceive the futility of supporting a capitalist party "lesser evil" and look instead for ways to express their opposition independently.

Far from "swinging to the right," (as the bourgeois press reported in an orgy of wishful thinking), young people in fact rejected the real shift to the right by the capitalist candidates.

Combined with the effort to draw students into the elections has been the second prong of the capitalist counter-offensive. Nixon's drive to de-politicize the campuses is aimed at silencing the student movement, which has consistently opposed his administration and his continuing aggression in Southeast Asia. Nixon hopes to divide and disorient the student movement in order to prevent another May. He has employed several tactics in this drive.

First, Nixon has launched a general propaganda offensive to discredit student radicals in the eyes of the American people. Characterizing students as "bums" and "thugs," the capitalist politicians and the bourgeois press have tried to associate a few isolated incidents of terrorism with the mass movements on the campuses. Falsely pinning the blame for violence on students, they have attempted to whip up hysteria about student-inspired "anarchy."

Second, Nixon sent, along with his own covering letter, an "Open Letter to College Students" from J. Edgar Hoover to 900 college administrators. In his letter, Hoover calls the attention of the administrators to the "extremist" groups which are most dangerous, fingering the YSA and the Student Mobilization Committee as prime targets for administrators to attack.

Third, the Nixon administration initiated a set of unconstitutional political guidelines through the Internal Revenue Service, threatening universities and colleges with the loss of their tax-exempt status if they allow campus facilities to be used for "political" activity, such as support of candidates for public office. These guidelines are designed to give college administrations an excuse to crack down on the student movement. In accordance with the IRS-backed guidelines, most colleges have issued their own guidelines restricting the political rights of students. These range from prohibiting the use of student funds for the antiwar movement to proscribing the sale of radical literature on campus.

Fourth, the Ohio Grand Jury indicted the Kent 25 in the most blatant example of the attack on students, attempting to use the trial of these activists to whitewash the murder of four Kent students and intimidate the entire student movement.

The counteroffensive directed against the students in direct response to May has not succeeded in stifling struggles on the campus. In spite of the ruling class attempt to curb the radicalization, activity since May demonstrates clearly the potential for another upsurge in the near future.

3. DISPUTED ISSUES IN THE ANTIWAR MOVEMENT

The "Vietnamization" policy of limited withdrawals of U. S. troops from Vietnam and Nixon's profuse promises of approaching "peace" were a major challenge to the antiwar movement after May 1970. Massive antiwar protests continued despite the confusion caused by Nixon's demagogy, the biggest being in Washington, D. C. and San Francisco on April 24, 1971 in which more than 800,000 persons participated. On April 22, 1972, in the midst of the bombing of Hanoi, more than 100,000 demonstrated in New York City while tens of thousands protested in other cities. Nixon's December 1972–January 1973 bombing of North Vietnam, aimed at forcing more concessions from the Vietnamese at the bargaining table, sparked a new wave of protests, culminating in a march of more than 100,000 in Washington, D. C. on January 20, 1973, shortly before the accords were signed.

Within the local and national antiwar coalitions those who favored mass action and immediate U. S. withdrawal had to continually contend with (1) those who favored drawing the movement out of the streets and into support for liberal Democrats; and (2) those who favored diverting the movement into isolated individual acts and adventures. After May 1970 these differences were reflected in the emergence of two coalitions. One, the National Peace Action Coalition (NPAC), was supported by the mass action-immediate withdrawal wing. The second, the National Coalition Against War, Racism, and Repression (NCAWRR)—later renamed the People's Coalition for Peace and Justice (PCPJ)—stressed support to the position of the liberal Democrats, who called for a campaign in Congress to convince Nixon to "set the date" for withdrawal. The PCPJ also encompassed those who favored organizing small actions around a multitude of issues, and those who favored "disruptive" actions with the announced goal of "stopping the war machine." The SWP and YSA gave their support to NPAC, while the Communist Party, pacifists, and ultra-lefts backed PCPJ.

The Nixon-Brezhnev-Mao detente, the signing of the January 1973 accords, the end of U. S. bombing, and the withdrawal of U. S. troops (except for 20,000 "advisors") led to a general popular belief that "peace" had been achieved. This illusion was given additional credence when the North Vietnamese government and the leaders of the liberation movements in Indochina hailed the compromise settlement as an "epochal victory" that opened the door to "national reconciliation." As a result of all these factors, it became impossible to mobilize sizable demonstrations and the organized antiwar movement went into abeyance.

The articles reprinted below reflect a few of the key debates which occurred in the antiwar movement between May 1970 and the signing of the accords.

a. Mass Action vs. Calculated Confrontation

By Doug Jenness

From the April 30, 1971 issue of *The Militant*

The breadth of support from nearly every sector of American society for the massive antiwar actions in San Francisco and Washington, D. C., on April 24 is unprecedented. Never before in U. S. history has there been such broad domestic opposition to a war—while the capitalist government was actually waging it.

The April 24 demonstrations are the latest manifestation of the antiwar movement's sustained activity, the most recent of the periodic mass actions organized over the past six years. Such mobilizations are the greatest organized force the American people can bring against the Nixon administration at this time. For any person seriously interested in ending the Vietnam war, they are inspiring events.

Unfortunately, there are always some people who reject the power and significance of mass actions and think there may be some other means to force the government to end the war. Such is the case with a group that calls itself the May Day Tribe, headed by Rennie Davis, a former leader of the now defunct Students for a Democratic Society and the similarly defunct New Mobilization Committee.

A component of the heterogeneous People's Coalition for Peace and Justice (PCPJ), the May Day Tribe counterposed its own actions, scheduled for early May, to the April 24 demonstrations. Although it acceded to the PCPJ's decision to support April 24, in practice the May Day Tribe has done little but attack it.

Davis brought his proposals to the Jan. 8–10, 1971, conference of the National Coalition Against War, Racism and Repression (short-lived predecessor to the PCPJ), where they didn't receive much support.

He then took them to the Feb. 7–8 Ann Arbor "Student and Youth Conference on a People's Peace," called by the National Student Association, where they were adopted.

Originally, the conception was to have a series of activities the first week of May which would include, among other things, an auto stall-in on the bridge linking Washington to the Pentagon area of northern Virginia.

These activities are still planned and Davis and his followers have announced that they intend to support PCPJ activities beginning on April 25, hoping to convince some people to stay in Washington after the April 24 mass demonstration. In order to accommodate those they expect to stay over, they applied for permission to use Rock Creek Park as a camping site. When a permit was denied, Davis announced that they would use the park anyway, thus raising the specter of a confrontation with Washington cops.

'Stop the government'

At a Feb. 8 news conference in Washington, D. C., Davis explained the goals of the actions: "Unless Nixon commits himself to withdrawal by May 1—that is, if he won't stop the war—we intend to stop the government."

A resolution adopted at the Ann Arbor conference indicated how they hope to back up this ultimatum. "To be effective—i.e. to provide the spark that can coalesce people who oppose the war into activity—we must be willing to do more than march. . . . Civil disobedience will allow groups as diverse as church and youth groups to take part. It also means that people will be taking some risks, opening themselves to arrest. But mass arrest penalties for white people are still relatively light and the demonstration will not be Gandhi-like. People can and should defend themselves from attack."

In their *May Day Manual*, they add: "In brief, the aim of the May Day actions is to raise the social cost of the war to a level unacceptable to America's rulers. To do this, we seek to create the specter of social chaos while maintaining the support or at least the toleration of the broad masses of American people."

Their description of their own intentions, including the anticipation of arrests and physical attacks, could hardly be clearer.

Davis and his disciples are planning an action consciously intended *not to involve* large numbers of antiwar Americans. If the American people "tolerate" their action, it is sufficient for them.

Their reference to "penalties for white people" makes it clear that they don't expect many Blacks, Chicanos or Puerto Ricans to participate.

"We've all felt that it's a damn poor demonstration that can only boast a big body count for its accomplishments," states a recent (undated) May Day Tribe Leaflet. "No more demonstrations like November 15th [1969] or May 9th [1970]."

This is the heart of their political opposition to the April 24th demonstrations. They reject mass action, the most powerful form of political struggle that exists.

'Dumb sheep'

Not only do they attack mass action, but they have arrogant contempt for those that participate in such actions. "Nobody gives a damn," their leaflet states, "how many dumb sheep can flock to Washington demonstrations, which are dull ceremonies of dissent that won't stop the war."

Since these self-appointed shepherds aren't interested in appealing to millions of antiwar Americans and involving as many as possible in action directed against the government and its imperialist war policies, who then do they hope to attract to their more exciting and titillating activities? They don't explicitly say, but it's clearly a very thin stratum of already radicalized persons, frustrated by their limited political impact on the most powerful ruling class in history and looking for shortcut alternatives to the difficult task of organizing and building a mass movement.

Why do Davis and his cohorts think that actions carried out by a relatively small number of radicals organized around built-in confrontations with the cops are more effective than mass actions? They believe that confrontation with the cops serves to radicalize people. Furthermore, like children throwing tantrums, they think they will scare "old man" Nixon into setting a date for withdrawing U. S. troops from Indochina.

It's true that many people will be angered by unjust and savage police attacks on such actions and a few may even draw radical conclusions as a result. However, actions like these, which almost always are smashed or dispersed, fail to accomplish their objectives (they are hardly capable of "stopping the government"), and consequently they serve to demoralize, frustrate and victimize more people than they radicalize.

Government officials, rather than being frightened by ultimatums, defiance of the law, threats of social chaos, etc., use these acts and accompanying rhetoric to isolate and victimize groups like the May Day Tribe.

Davis told the press that if the May Day Tribe defied the ban on camping in Rock Creek Park it might result in a confrontation similar to what occurred in Chicago at the 1968 Democratic Party convention. He was one of the leaders of the 1968 Chicago demonstration and apparently considers it a model for effective action.

Chicago

The truth about the Chicago action is that it was one of the smallest antiwar actions organized by a national coalition in the history of the antiwar movement—no more than 7,000 were at its largest rally during a week of activities—even though it received more publicity than most national antiwar actions.

It was small because the clique within the leadership of the National Mobilization Committee that organized it publicly proposed to disrupt the Democratic Party convention, thus alienating many antiwar Americans. Many left-wing forces did not participate because, in the context of the Democratic Party convention, the action appeared to be backing Eugene McCarthy's bid for the presidential nomination. This was reinforced by the fact that at the final rally, where revolutionary socialists were barred from speaking, the platform and sound equipment were turned over to McCarthy.

Daley's cops viciously attacked the demonstrators throughout the entire week, and afterwards the leaders, including Rennie Davis, were indicted on trumped-up conspiracy charges. Although the police attack and the conspiracy indictments stirred nationwide outrage, no rational person would say that a smashed demonstration with many victims was a success or showed a serious political challenge to the government's war policy.

Davis and the other leaders knew full well that the action's small size and Daley's determination to prevent any disruption of the Democratic Party convention would result in arrests and injuries.

Like his irresponsible leadership role in the Chicago action, Davis and his supporters take a similar attitude toward those participating in the May Day activities. Although it mouths niceties about the nonviolent character of its plans, the May Day Tribe has been organizing its action in such a way as to almost guarantee a violent attack on the demonstrators. Davis and his clique acknowledge in advance that the participants will likely be arrested and possibly attacked physically. They even advise everyone to bring medical supplies to Washington.

For them, the people they hope to shepherd into their actions are only so many "dumb sheep" whose cracked skulls and fines are the necessary sacrifice for carrying out their confrontation tactics.

Although they attack the broad leadership of the coalition that organized April 24 as "movement generals" and "elite bureaucrats," they are in reality falsely projecting onto the April 24 leadership the only concept of political leadership that they themselves understand. Their arrogant elitism and contempt of the masses turns them into manipulators who play with the safety and lives of others.

Another aspect of the Chicago demonstration which is similar to the May Day plans is that it combined a liberal political line (implicit support to McCarthy) with ultraleft tactics. At the Ann Arbor conference where plans for the May Day action were made, it was agreed that on May 1 the demonstrators would present Nixon with the People's Peace Treaty. This is a document signed between Vietnamese and American students which includes among other points the liberal demand for *setting the date* for withdrawal as opposed to *immediate* withdrawal of U. S. troops from Southeast Asia. The treaty also enumerates conditions which the Vietnamese must live up to in return for withdrawal of troops. Rennie Davis' militancy seems to be more in his rhetoric and in his determination to have a confrontation than in his political line.

Another alleged virtue of the May Day action was offered by Stephen d'Arazien, in an April 15 *Village Voice* article. D'Arazien, the May Day Tribe's press secretary, writes: "What was needed, it was felt, was a tactic more militant than mere mass mobilization, one which could capture the energy of the young and keep them from dropping out of the struggle and 'going to the country,' but one which *might* have an effect." (Emphasis added.)

While admitting that the May Day Tribe's action may have no effect on Nixon's war policies, he justifies it for its "therapeutic" value on those participating. His neighborly concern for those droping out of political activity is very touching, but it doesn't help solve the political problem of how to build the most effective movement against the Vietnam war.

The history of the antiwar movement has demonstrated in practice that mass actions are the most effective form of struggle. They have made it progressively more difficult for the administration to continue the war and maintain the myth that it has the support of the majority of Americans.

This was clearly illustrated when the massive student strike and demonstrations of unprecedented size in May 1970 forced Nixon to withdraw U. S. troops from Cambodia. The fear of another May was the principal deterrent to the use of U. S. ground troops in Laos.

We have not yet succeeded in ending the war, but victories such as May 1970 were won without the mobilization of powerful social forces like the labor movement and the Black community.

The task facing those concerned with continuing the fight until the war is over, is to involve those sectors of the population which *can* have a decisive impact on the government. The course of the war itself, and the massive displays of opposition to it over the last six years, have combined to generate broader and broader support behind the antiwar movement's demand for immediate U. S. withdrawal from Southeast Asia. New social forces, more powerful than those previously involved in the antiwar struggle, have been mobilized to speak out and show their strength in Washington and San Francisco this spring. This is what April 24 is all about.

But April 24 is not the end. This is only the beginning of a new drive toward even greater mass mobilizations which have the potential power to finally end the war in Southeast Asia.

b. Mass Action vs. 'Multi-issue' Reformism

By Larry Seigle

From the April 16, 1971 issue of *The Militant*

The debate over what political course the antiwar movement should follow has been going on ever since the movement began. One of the central issues in the debate has been the repeated attempts to convert the antiwar movement into a "multi-issue" movement. Those who have raised this perspective disparage a movement that is "only" against the war, and counterpose to it a movement that would organize around a multiplicity of political and social issues.

The latest group to champion this proposal is the People's Coalition for Peace and Justice. In a recent statement entitled "Building United Mass Action in the Spring, 1971," the People's Coalition indicates that it views this question as being at the heart of the differences between it and the National Peace Action Coalition. In explaining why it has abandoned the perspective of mobilizing people on the basis of opposition to the war, the People's Coalition says, "We realized that we could no longer separate the question of the war in Indochina from the domestic oppression of nonwhite America; from the political repression by the government, and from the need to change the structure of American society so that the Pentagon was no longer the strongest single force in our society."

Because of these "realizations," the leaders of the People's Coalition decided to create "an entirely new coalition, one that would seek to bring the peace movement, the youth, the poor, the nonwhites, women, and all repressed peoples together in a single coalition aimed at ending the war and rebuilding our society."

Thus, the People's Coalition adds itself to the long list of organizations and would-be movements which have rejected the course of building the mass movement against the war and opted in favor of a coalition around a multi-issue program. This list includes such groups as the National Conference on New Politics, the Radical Organizing Committee (a short-lived split-off from the Student Mobilization Committee), and the Peace and Freedom Party. These groups, all now defunct or virtually so, have been generally supported by the Communist Party.

What's really behind this question of multi-issuism? Why does it keep recurring? And why doesn't it ever work?

A misleading dichotomy

The formulation of the question as a "single-issue approach" versus a "multi-issue approach" is misleading because it implies that groups like the Socialist Workers Party and the Young Socialist Alliance, which are in favor of building a mass movement around the single question of the war, are "single-issue" organizations. Nothing could be further from the truth.

The war in Indochina has cut deeply into this society, raising and accentuating a number of questions about racism, sexism, unemployment, inflation, political repression, etc. The war and its effects on the United States have exposed the true nature of this capitalist system for millions to see. Revolutionary socialists of the SWP and the YSA are the first to point out that opposition to the war is only the first step. It is necessary to draw some conclusions about this society, and to realize that there will be an endless series of Indochinas unless capitalism is wiped off the face of the earth and replaced with socialism.

It is the growing acceptance of this fact that has led many young activists to join the YSA—people who first became politically active around the war and then came to see the need for a fundamental change in this society and decided to join an organization that has a program for and participates actively in the movements of all the oppressed sectors of this society.

So having a multi-issue program for changing society and for relating the war to the other evils of capitalism is quite a different thing from advocating that the antiwar movement become a multi-issue movement.

Subordination to liberals

Once this smokescreen has been cleared away, the essence of "multi-issuism" can be examined: it is an attempt to subordinate the antiwar movement to reformist politics and to the liberal Democratic Party politicians in particular.

This debate, like all the other major disputes within the antiwar movement, is based on the contradiction between the objectively anti-imperialist and independent thrust of the movement and the pressures toward liberal and reformist politics constantly being exerted on the movement.

This becomes clear as soon as one asks the advocates of a new "multi-issue" movement, What would be the *program* of such a movement? What would its position be on key questions such as nationalism, women's liberation, civil liberties, electoral politics, etc.? Were the response to be, "Why, we would adopt a revolutionary-socialist program, like the program of the SWP," it would immediately be clear that the proposal is absurd. To impose the entire program of the SWP on the antiwar movement would immediately eliminate everyone except revolutionary socialists from the antiwar movement.

But, of course, the program proposed for this "new" coalition is not a revolutionary program at all. Rather, it is a liberal program, one which dovetails with the program of the "progressive" Democratic Party politicians.

For example, the People's Coalition, in the best tradition of mealy-mouthed reformism, speaks in the statement quoted above of "changing the structure of American society so that the Pentagon is no longer the strongest single force in our society." Not a word about the capitalist system, about the need for a socialist revolution, about the necessity for anticapitalist action. And, of course, not a word about breaking from the Democratic Party!

It is no coincidence that the call for "multi-issuism" is almost always raised in the same breath as other attacks on the politics of the antiwar movement, such as the call to substitute "set the date" for the demand for immediate and unconditional withdrawal. It is the "set the date" demand that has become the rallying point for the doves in Congress.

Reformist perspective

This reformism in the antiwar movement comes from two sources. First are those individuals and groupings who have no organization of their own other than the antiwar movement and want to establish a political base for themselves by converting the antiwar movement into a support group for their particular brand of reformist politics.

Second are the reformist organizations, chief of which is the Communist Party, whose sole perspective for the antiwar movement is to use it as a pressure group, a "lobby" that can be turned over to the "progressive" candidates of the Democratic Party in the 1972 election campaigns.

But, once having answered the question of why the People's Coalition multi-issue perspective leads only to reformist politics, the question is raised of why this approach has so consistently failed to establish a viable organization or movement. Certainly their orientation towards the Democratic Party coincides with the level of understanding of millions of Americans who are against the war but who have not yet reached the stage of a conscious break with capitalist politics. Why do the advocates of this perspective seem to behave like a dog chasing its own tail, running faster and faster, without getting any closer to their goal?

Why, after years of campaigning for multi-issuism, are they still confined to the relatively narrow political base of the People's Coalition? The answer lies in three basic political errors of the People's Coalition.

Political errors

First, their "multi-issuism" is used to cover up their subordination of the war issue to other questions. They ignore and try to obscure the centrality of the fight against the war in Indochina to all social layers and movements in this country. Part of their attack on the "single-issue" perspective stems from the fact that they *do not agree* that the war in Indochina is the single most important political question facing the American people, a question that is of burning relevance to the struggles of the oppressed nationalities, to the women's liberation movement, to the students, workers, GIs, and other sectors of society. This stems from their attempt to avoid a direct political confrontation with the ruling class and its political representatives. By submerging the question of the war, they ignore the one question that, in this period, can unite in action all of the growing movements for social change.

Their second error is to attempt to organize their coalition by trying to hide the real political differences that exist between the various components of the People's Coalition. To cover for their lack of agreement on a political program, they issue vaguely formulated statements of support for all sorts of struggles. Yet, by trying to hide these differences, they do not make them go away. It is precisely these political differences that are always forced to the surface, embarrassing and dividing the coalition, at key political junctures. (This is why the coalition is forced to change its name as quickly as most people change a pair of socks, and almost as frequently.)

For example, the People's Coalition encompasses individuals and groups who are opposed to participating in electoral politics along with those who are openly supporters of the Democratic Party; people who are pacifists as a matter of moral principle along with those who believe in disruption through "mobile tactics"; supporters of the women's liberation movement along with those who believe that feminism "divides" the working class; and supporters of nationalism of oppressed nationalities along with those who believe nationalism is only "racism in reverse." This type of coalition can be maintained if it confines itself to mobilizing people in action against the war. But once it projects itself as a political movement with a broad social program, it can only be a short while until the inevitable internal divisions spring to the surface.

The third mistake made by the leaders of the People's Coalition is the failure to comprehend the united-front nature of the antiwar movement. One of the key aspects of the antiwar movement is that it has been independent of control or domination by any of the existing political forces. The antiwar movement is far bigger than all of the radical political tendencies put together. And the only times that the different radical and socialist organizations have been able to play a leading role in the antiwar movement is when they have agreed to unite around an action against the war. When the leaders of the People's Coalition think they can use their political authority as leaders of the antiwar movement to construct a "multi-issue" formation and abandon the road of mass action against the war, they find themselves cut off from the mass movement and rapidly fall into a decline marked by internal divisions and factionalism.

Does this mean, as the People's Coalition has charged, that the perspective of mass action against the war excludes relating the war to other issues and movements? Not at all. One need only point to the success of the United Women's Contingent, the Third World Task Force, the Gay Task Force, and the involvement of labor officials in building the April 24 demonstrations to show that it is precisely through the perspective of independent mass actions against the war that the different movements and social forces can be united around fighting against the war, which affects all of them.

It is such a perspective that can best mobilize the American people against this war and can do the most to defeat Nixon and his plans for an indefinite continuation of the slaughter in Indochina.

c. The Communist Party and the April 24, 1971 Demonstration

by Larry Seigle

From the June 4, 1971 issue of *The Militant*

If your only source of information about what's going on in this country were the *Daily World*, the newspaper reflecting the views of the U.S. Communist Party, you would have a very strange view of the April 24 antiwar actions in Washington and San Francisco. You would not have learned of the projected actions until three months after they were called; then you would have received the impression the CP was going all out in support of April 24; and then the enthusiastic articles about "A New Force for Progress" and how "The Majority Marches On," would have left you with the impression that the CP had been among the best builders of April 24 from the beginning.

But this was not the case. Since the CP is hardly in a position to accurately assess its role in the action, we will attempt to set the record straight.

The attitude of the CP toward the antiwar movement, like its attitude toward all the other mass movements, is determined by its support for liberal capitalist politicians in general and the Democratic Party in particular. For example, one of the central reasons the *Daily World* supports the demand for Nixon to "set the date for withdrawal" as opposed to the demand for immediate withdrawal from Indochina is because "set the date" has become the rallying cry for the liberals in Congress.

This stance toward the Democratic Party does not mean that the CP opposes all mass demonstrations against the war. (Neither do the more astute Democratic and Republican party politicians.) There are times when mass demonstrations are seen as useful by these people because they help create an atmosphere and political climate of support for liberal "peace" candidates.

However, *every* mass demonstration directed against the policies of the government is an example of independent political action insofar as it is organized independently of the capitalist political parties. For large numbers of people, mass demonstrations against the war strengthen the concept of action going beyond the limits of capitalist politics, and operate against the continued subordination of masses of people to the capitalist political parties.

It is for these reasons that the CP has always maintained an ambivalent attitude toward mass antiwar actions, and even when participating in them has done everything possible to keep them restricted to terms agreeable to the liberal Democrats. This is especially true at election time.

April 24 was one of the largest political demonstrations ever organized in the U.S. and it was directed squarely against the government *right in the midst of a shooting war being waged by that government.* Coming at a time when a big campaign was being waged by the government and the press to convince everyone that the antiwar movement was dead, that the students were "cooling off," it definitely proved that not only was the antiwar movement alive but it was growing and reaching out to significant social forces in addition to the student movement.

And yet the incontrovertible fact is that the Communist Party *actively opposed* this demonstration for three full months after it was initially called. Only when it became clear to the entire world that the demonstration was going to be a major event did the CP decide to go along with it, and even then it refused to join the National Peace Action Coalition, which was organizing April 24.

To many who marched on April 24 this may come as a surprise. The CP may be wrong on a lot of questions, but can they be so far off the beam as to place themselves in opposition to the mass movement against U.S. aggression in Indochina? The record is clear. It needs only to be set down in writing.

Action called

April 24 was called at a national antiwar conference of 1,500 people, sponsored by the National Peace Action Coalition on Dec. 4–6, 1970, in Chicago. The conference was open to all antiwar groups and individuals, and many forces attended who had previously not participated in NPAC.

The CP declined to attend or participate. A representative of the CP did join a committee from the National Coalition Against War, Racism and Repression (precursor to the People's Coalition for Peace and Justice), which tried to convince the leaders of NPAC that it would be preferable if the convention did not issue a call for an antiwar action. The NCAWRR delegation at first indicated that they were considering calling an action in May and didn't want NPAC to set a competing date. When the leaders of NPAC expressed a willingness to set the date for the spring action on May 8, a day that had been mentioned as a possibility by the NCAWRR leaders, the committee from NCAWRR rejected the idea. This response made it clear that what was involved was not a disagreement over a date but a conflict over whether or not there should be a massive antiwar action at all.

The *Daily World* carried *not one* word about the NPAC convention or its decision. This news blackout on April 24 was not merely a temporary embargo, but lasted for *three months*, during which time the hard work of obtaining initial support, publicity and financial backing for the 24th was done against the opposition of the CP.

At a conference in late January, NCAWRR rejected the idea of organizing a mass, legal and peaceful demonstration for the immediate withdrawal of troops from Vietnam. Its successor, the People's Coalition, in a statement dated Feb. 5, 1971, explicitly rejected the idea of demonstrations on the central issue of the war as "one-sided" and proclaimed the determination of the PCPJ to "advance beyond marches and rallies" to "sustained nonviolent direct action and civil disobedience." On the basis of this approach, the PCPJ outlined plans for a week of activities beginning on May 2, which were directly counterposed to April 24.

Momentum builds

But the momentum building up around April 24 by this time was exerting tremendous pressure on the PCPJ and on the CP. The response to the call for a mass protest around the demand "Out Now" obviously surpassed what the CP had anticipated. For example, on Sunday, Feb. 14, an ad appeared in the *New York Times* expressing support for April 24, signed by a very broad list of labor officials, antiwar movement leaders, artists and intellectuals, and by eight members of Congress.

It began to be clear to many forces in the PCPJ that their opposition to the 24th was not going to prevent masses of people from joining it, nor were they going to be able to force NPAC to call off the action.

On the weekend of Feb. 20–21, the national convention of the Student Mobilization Committee, attended by more than 2,000 student antiwar activists, voted overwhelmingly and enthusiastically to support and help build April 24. At the conference, the Young Workers Liberation League and CP representatives continued to argue against April 24. But, rather than stating their political objections to it, the CP instead supported a motion asking that the 24th be canceled (!) on the grounds that the "new" situation (this was during a time of major escalation including the invasion of Laos) meant that we couldn't wait until April 24 for a demonstration and had to call an emergency action.

The majority of the SMC conference correctly viewed this move as a maneuver to trick the SMC into rejecting April 24 in favor of an action of unspecified character to be organized by some unspecified group on an unspecified date. The conference participants concluded that the best way to respond to the new escalation was to *intensify* the organizing campaign for April 24, not to call it off.

This growing enthusiasm for April 24 among wide sectors of the American antiwar movement was complemented by a statement issued by Xuan Thuy, ambassador to the Paris peace talks from the Democratic Republic of Vietnam. Realizing the power that a big antiwar demonstration could have in tying Nixon's hands in Indochina, Xuan Thuy appealed for unity in action among the different U.S. antiwar organizations around the question of the war.

Xuan Thuy's statement was published in part in the March 2 *Daily World*: "Facing the serious situation as it presents now, I call upon the progressive American people and all antiwar organizations in the United States to unite closely, to associate all forces and strata of the population irrespective of their skin color, religion and political trend, thus making a wide and strong movement so as to curb in time new military adventures by the U.S. administration, to demand an end to their war of aggression in South Vietnam, Laos and Cambodia, to demand the withdrawal of all American troops from Indochina and let the Indochinese people settle their own internal affairs.

"Such is the way beneficial to the peoples of Vietnam and Indochina, beneficial to the American people, beneficial to peace in the world."

The *Daily World* commented that the message was "expected to have a persuasive effect in unifying the plans for a spring peace offensive by various sections of the U.S. antiwar movement."

24th endorsed

The effect of all these developments was to drive home to the leaders of the PCPJ the fact that a continuation of their boycott of April 24 would so isolate them as to drastically limit their influence and reputation within the antiwar movement both in the U.S. and internationally. It was because of this fact, not because the PCPJ or CP had changed their political views about the effectiveness of mass action against the war, that they finally decided at the end of February to reverse their position and endorse the April 24 actions.

The NPAC leadership quite correctly welcomed their endorsement as a genuine step forward for the antiwar movement and continued NPAC's policy of doing everything possible to facilitate collaboration between NPAC and PCPJ.

After PCPJ endorsed, the *Daily World* began to cover plans for April 24, usually avoiding mention of NPAC. Reading only the *DW*, one would think that the CP was actively building April 24. In fact the CP and PCPJ did almost nothing for April 24. This contrast can only lead one to believe that the CP used the *DW*'s show of support as cover, to avoid having to explain why it didn't play a major role in a historic action. The *DW* will still find it hard to explain the history of the 24th. So hard that it may not even try.

The great majority of participants were enthused by April 24 and want to plan continuing action. To this end, NPAC is holding an open convention in New York July 2–4 to set an action date and plan antiwar activities. One hopes the CP will attend the conference and the *Daily World* won't wait three months to report its decisions.

d. The Communist Party's Peace Policy

by Dave Frankel

From the April 21, 1973 issue of *The Militant*

Differences within the antiwar movement on questions of tactics, slogans, and even the nature of the movement itself are nothing new to the activists who participate in it. Nevertheless, many antiwar activists have been shocked by the continued refusal of the People's Coalition for Peace and Justice (PCPJ) and many of the organizations associated with it to join with the National Peace Action Coalition (NPAC) in a nationwide effort to help mobilize people for the April 22 demonstrations in New York and Los Angeles.

PCPJ's intransigence is all the more shameful in the face of the intense combat now taking place throughout Vietnam and the significant escalation of the bombing by the U.S. government. The administration's concern with how the American people react to its moves in Indochina has been stressed in news coverage of the Vietnamese offensive. The response of the antiwar movement to the increased bombings and the possibility of further escalation will be a major factor in Nixon's calculations on how far he can go in propping up the Thieu dictatorship in Saigon.

At the heart of the differences between NPAC and PCPJ is disagreement on the type of movement each is trying to build. NPAC is simply an antiwar coalition. It attempts to mobilize the largest possible numbers of people in opposition to the war in Indochina and its effects, regardless of their views on other issues.

This approach makes it possible to unite in action socialists, who want to see U.S. troops withdrawn from Indochina because they favor the victory of the Vietnamese revolution; pacifists, who oppose the U.S. presence in Indochina because they oppose all violence; and those who vote for Democratic or Republican candidates. It unites women, Blacks, Chicanos, unionists, GIs, veterans, students, and others in common action against capitalist war policy. The different components of NPAC continue to express their positions on other issues while acting together on their point of agreement—opposition to the imperialist war in Indochina.

PCPJ, in contrast, seeks to involve people around a general program for social reform in which the war in Indochina is one of many concerns. The best-known, best-organized, and largest group supporting the PCPJ perspective is the Communist Party (CP), which finds PCPJ's approach complementary to its own electoral perspective. The CP, according to an article by Gus Hall (CP 1972 presidential candidate) in the March 4 *Daily World*, wants to "turn the country towards an anti-monopoly course of peace, economic security and a wider based democracy, to bring about the crystallization of a broad people's coalition of the anti-monopoly, anti-war, anti-racist, anti-fascist, pro-labor forces in the United States."

Jarvis Tyner, the CP's vice-presidential candidate, characterizes his party's program as one which "though short of socialism . . . provides for the building of an anti-monopoly coalition which will nationalize many industries and place them under democratic control." (*Daily World*, March 1.)

The CP's dream is to construct a broad coalition such as the one led by Allende in Chile. Such a coalition, in the CP's view, would include socialists, Communists, and politicians from the "progressive" wing of the capitalist class. However, to remain acceptable to the capitalist politicians, its program would not call for socialism.

Because the CP wants a coalition that involves the liberal politicians, it sees the Democratic Party as its main arena of electoral activity at this time. As Tim Wheeler warns in the Jan. 11 *Daily World*,

"'Go-it-alone' formations such as 'new' parties, have tended to cut activists off from mass struggles inside the Democratic Party. . . ."

Peggy Dennis, in setting forth the CP's electoral approach in the December 1971 issue of *Political Affairs,* refers with pride to "the recent electoral victories of Congressman Ron Dellums (Calif.), Congresswomen Shirley Chisholm and Bella Abzug (New York), the growing number of Black mayors around the country, and the mounting influence of the Black Caucus in Washington, D.C.

"But oddly, few in the Left refer to the fact that practically all of these people's victories were the result of militant *merging* and *unity* of the radical movement outside the two-party system with the hundreds of thousands inside those parties who were given an opportunity to support and actively campaign for these militant candidates within the framework of the two-party system in which they battled and won the party designation." (Emphasis in original.)

Dennis calls for merging the mass movements outside of the Democratic Party, such as the antiwar movement, with the electoral campaigns of the liberals within the Democratic Party.

When PCPJ's open letter to NPAC (published in the April issue of its newsletter, *Movin' Together*) talks about the need to "bring together blacks, Chicanos, Puerto Ricans and whites, workers and intellectuals, the religious community, small businessmen, women—all of these forces—into a coalition that becomes, in effect, an American Left," the CP sees the same type of liberal-reformist coalition that it longs for.

The role the CP envisions for PCPJ is reflected in an article by Donna Ristorucci in the April 1 *Daily World.* Reporting on a discussion with a PCPJ staff member, Ristorucci stresses that "The peace movement attaches great importance to the 1972 elections" and to "the effort by local PCPJ chapters and affiliates to influence state primaries."

This means that local PCPJ chapters will be working to turn out votes for the two parties that initiated the war in Indochina and continue to prosecute it.

Ristorucci explains the "Citizens Action Pledge," one of the mechanisms designed to rope people into campaigns for Democratic Party "peace candidates." "One part of the pledge is to be used to sign up candidates during the election campaign. . . ." she says. "The other part is to be signed by citizens pledging that they will not support a candidate who does not support the three points."

The three points are: stop the air war, set the date for total withdrawal of all personnel and matériel, and end support for the Thieu regime. Many liberal politicians have come out in favor of these demands. The task facing the antiwar movement, however, is to build a mass movement so powerful that the U.S. rulers are forced to end the war no matter who is in office. Such a movement cannot rely on election promises to set some future date for withdrawal, thus violating the Vietnamese people's right to self-determination. It must depend on its own ability to mobilize masses in the streets.

The differences within the antiwar movement have sharpened with the approach of the 1972 elections. The CP's evaluation, set forth by Gus Hall, is that "Because of the extreme reactionary nature of the Nixon challenge, the opportunities for the crystallization of a broad people's anti-war, anti-racist, pro-labor and democratic coalition is a real possibility. But it must have a base in the cities and Congressional Districts." (*Daily World,* March 4.)

The CP would like to have the antiwar movement serve as part of the "base in the cities and the Congressional Districts." As Hall sees it, "The forces of reaction are out to destroy any candidate or elected official who does not have such a mass base."

When the CP favors mass actions, it wants them subordinated to this scheme. Such actions would then serve to win people to groups taking this electoral approach, to expand their authority and make them known. They would give the liberal capitalist politicians leading such a movement added weight and room to maneuver, while putting pressure on the less responsive elements within the Democratic Party.

As a perspective to transform this society, this view must be rejected. Its stated objective is limited to reforming capitalism rather than organizing the masses of the American working people to take power and establish a socialist society.

As a strategy for building the antiwar movement it is ineffective. By subordinating the need to unite the largest number of people in action against the war to its concept of an "American Left," PCPJ restricts whom it will unite with. It can only include those groups and individuals willing to accept PCPJ's reformist social program. On this basis it excludes revolutionaries. It excludes Black nationalists who do not agree with its program on how to fight racism.

PCPJ's insistence that it will unite with others only on the basis of *its* program for ending repression, *its* program for welfare reform, *its* program on the war, flows from putting its social reform program before the need for a united antiwar movement. That is why PCPJ refuses to put real effort into the April 22 antiwar demonstrations.

Both the CP and PCPJ are doing a disservice to the U.S. antiwar movement and to the Vietnamese revolution. All the justifications they manufacture can't cover up the fact that they prefer the prospect of organizing support for Democratic Party hacks to unity with the thousands of antiwar activists who will be demonstrating in the streets April 22 for the immediate withdrawal of all U.S. forces from Indochina.

e. Why Moscow and Peking Favor the 'Sign Now' Demand

By Barry Sheppard

From the January 19, 1973 issue of *The Militant*

In last week's *Militant* I explained why it would be wrong for the antiwar movement and revolutionary socialists to demand that Nixon "Sign Now" the nine-point draft accord released by Hanoi in October. In this article, I want to discuss the role of Moscow and Peking, and explain why they, and those in the U.S. who support their line, insist on the "Sign Now" slogan.

Before proceeding, let me summarize some of the points made last week:

1) The principle involved is the right of Vietnam to self-determination. The "Out Now" slogan, which means the complete, immediate, and unconditional U.S. withdrawal from Southeast Asia, is a concrete expression of that principle in a form that can educate and mobilize masses of Americans.

2) Washington's military pressure has compelled the Vietnamese to negotiate, and they have every right to do so. But for the antiwar movement here to raise the "Sign Now" slogan concedes that the U.S. has a right to negotiate about the future of Vietnam.

3) If the antiwar movement, which is not being forced by Nixon's bombs to make concessions, were to give up the "Out Now" demand in favor of "Sign Now," this could only imply to the American people that the antiwar movement supports the provisions of the nine-point accord. While some of the provisions can be supported, such as the stopping of the bombing and withdrawal of U.S. soldiers from South Vietnam, other provisions should be opposed.

For instance, under the nine points, U.S. bombers and troops would remain in Thailand, off the coast of Vietnam, and elsewhere in Asia, ready to intervene at any moment. Also, the Thieu regime would be maintained, bolstered by U.S. bases and armor that would be turned over to it, and supported by thousands of U.S. "civilian advisers."

4) Contrary to the claims of many supporters of the "Sign Now" slogan, Nixon's signing of the nine points would not mean a victory for the liberation forces, nor does it represent a "face-saving" cover for U.S. withdrawal.

The nine points recognize two governments and two armies in South Vietnam, one representing the workers and peasants, and the other representing the regime of the landlords and capitalists. There can be no compromise on which side rules. The outcome of this inherently unstable situation would be decided by the relationship of forces and the intentions of both sides.

The conditions Washington insisted must be included in the nine points prove that Washington intends to continue to intervene to protect the Saigon regime, with or without an accord. Any illusions on this score should have been eliminated by the latest terror bombing of Hanoi and Haiphong, *a military operation carried out from bases that would be completely unaffected if the nine points were signed.*

Concessions demanded

Nixon has so far refused to sign the nine-point accords. He is insisting on further concessions from the Vietnamese, including implicit recognition of the Saigon regime as the legitimate government throughout Vietnam. This would make it "illegal" for North Vietnamese troops to remain in the South and would take away the legality of the Provisional Revolutionary Government.

Advocates of the "Sign Now" position are currently arguing that since the October accords would contain fewer conditions than what Nixon is now demanding, the antiwar movement should demand that the U.S. accept the nine points.

It is certainly true that the nine points contain fewer concessions from the Vietnamese than what Nixon now thinks he can get. But to conclude from that fact that we should endorse the nine points is faulty logic. Such reasoning allows Nixon to put the antiwar movement in the position of applauding concessions already wrung from the Vietnamese, merely by upping the ante and demanding "More!"

This, in fact, is what has happened to some groups in the antiwar movement. Many who today support the nine-point draft as a "just and honorable" settlement were, only a few months ago, supporting the PRG "seven-point program," which was the temporary negotiating position of the Vietnamese. The seven points also contained concessions that infringed upon the sovereignty of Vietnam, but not as many as are in the nine points.

For example, the seven-point plan insisted that the Thieu regime be dumped. The nine points guarantee that Thieu will not be dumped. As recently as Sept. 13, an editorial in the *Guardian* (which currently supports the nine points), called for "new educational offensives" to explain the issues in the war to the American people and to rally support for the seven-point plan. The most important point was that "Americans must be made aware of the key importance of scrapping the Thieu regime."

Thus, those who formerly supported the seven points are today supporting, and appealing to the American people to accept, conditions they were opposed to yesterday.

What if, under the impact of the bombing, the Vietnamese are compelled to make even further concessions? This certainly is possible. The logic of the "Sign Now" position will lead its adherents to support these conditions, too.

Why does Nixon believe he can get away with continuing to increase the pressure on the Vietnamese? The answer to this question sheds light on the motivation of many who support the "Sign Now" position.

Nixon has obviously calculated that the Soviet Union and China will do nothing effective to counter his aggression. Unfortunately, he has solid grounds for this assumption.

The entire history of the Vietnam war has been the history of the failure of the bureaucracies in Moscow and Peking to come to the defense of Vietnam.

At each critical juncture in Washington's step-by-step escalation of the war, the Soviet Union and China have failed to take effective countermeasures, thus emboldening the imperialists to press further. The aid given to the liberation fighters in Vietnam has been completely inadequate to meet the massive U.S. aggression. Particularly criminal has been the refusal to provide the Vietnamese with defensive weapons that could make Washington's air war too costly to continue. Moscow, because of its vast military resources, is primarily to blame for this.

Moscow and Peking have failed to form a united front on the governmental level against Washington's aggression. Moreover, they have refused to promote the formation of united action fronts throughout the world against the U.S. aggression. Neither has even mobilized the Communist parties and other groups that look to them for leadership.

The Soviet and Chinese bureaucracies took a qualitatively new step last year in their rapprochement with Washington, epitomized by Nixon's visits to Moscow and Peking. This new "friendship" was purchased at the expense of the Vietnamese, who are now paying for it with their own blood.

The trip to Peking, and the prospect of improved relations between the U.S. and China, secured Peking's acquiescence in pressuring the Vietnamese to make a settlement acceptable to the U.S. This set the stage for Nixon's Moscow visit, undercutting any possible criticism of it by the Maoist regime.

The North Vietnamese launched a major offensive last spring, after Nixon had been to Peking and prior to his visit to Moscow. Under the blows of the offensive, Thieu's forces began to crumble. Nixon answered with massive bombing and by mining North Vietnam's ports. This was a direct challenge to the Soviet Union and China, particularly the former, since much of its supplies to North Vietnam are sent by sea.

In response to the new situation, antiwar forces began to mobilize with renewed energy in the U.S. and around the world.

Then, Moscow agreed to proceed with the scheduled Nixon visit and, except for a few routine phrases of "solidarity" with the Vietnamese, Moscow did exactly nothing. This cut the ground out from under the antiwar movement. Masses of people believed that the war would soon be ended, with the "assistance" of Moscow and Peking. Nixon was thus able to defuse the potentially massive antiwar response to his unprecedented escalation of the bombing.

We don't know what secret agreements Mao and Brezhnev reached with Nixon. But their public statements and actions make clear that they agreed to put the pressure on the Vietnamese to accept a "settlement" with Washington.

It is within this framework of betrayal by Moscow and Peking and intensified military pressure from the U.S. that the Vietnamese have been forced to make further concessions.

Again, in the latest terror bombing of North Vietnam, Moscow and Peking countered with—words. And the content of those words was to plead with Nixon to avoid endangering improved relations with Moscow or Peking.

With world opinion overwhelmingly opposed to Nixon's latest bombing, Moscow could not have asked for a more propitious time to come to North Vietnam's defense and put a stop to Nixon's criminal attack. That would have done more for peace in Vietnam and throughout the world than all the agreements carrying Nixon's worthless signature negotiated in Moscow last May.

But neither Moscow nor Peking answered Nixon's aggression. They breathed a sigh of relief audible throughout the world when there was promise of more negotiations, and we can be certain that they are right now twisting the arms of the Vietnamese a little more.

This is why both Moscow and Peking are so hot for "Sign Now," and why they hail the October accords, or any accords, as a "victory"—they want to cover up their betrayal. For if a "victory" can be negotiated with Washington, it is obvious that there was no betrayal at all—no need for more aid, no lasting negative results from the bombing, mining, etc.

This obscene spectacle is rounded out with the American Communist Party echoing Moscow's "Sign Now" line, like the toadies they are.

And the *Guardian*, which has evidently decided to build a "base" in this country by serving up weekly apologies for Peking, finds itself in the same position. It has become one of the shrillest proponents of the "Sign Now" slogan.

Instead of hailing a "victory" that has not occurred, revolutionary socialists should be demanding increased aid for Vietnam from Moscow and Peking. The antiwar movement must expose every fraud and every trick of Kissinger and Nixon, including the concessions they are trying to extract by force from the Vietnamese.

The most powerful and effective way to fight against the war is to join in building a worldwide movement, united in action, to demand the immediate and unconditional withdrawal of U.S. forces from all of Southeast Asia.

Appendix

INTRODUCTORY NOTE

This appendix contains documents, articles, and transcripts of speeches dealing with questions of principle and tactics that confronted revolutionists in applying the Marxist position of opposition to imperialist wars during World War I and World War II.

The first part of this appendix contains three items written by Lenin. These were not agitational articles aimed at a wide working class audience. They were written as programmatic statements on issues in dispute in the international socialist movement. Through such statements, Lenin sought to sharply differentiate the revolutionary socialist opponents of imperialist war from the right wing Social Democrats who avidly supported "their imperialists" in the war, from the centrists like Kautsky who took a position which boiled down to apologizing for the crudest social patriotism, and from professional pacifists who claimed to oppose all wars but usually lined up with one or another gang of imperialists once the shooting started.

Slogans put forward by Lenin in these articles like "conversion of the present imperialist war into a civil war" were meant as guidelines to provide strategic direction for the work of revolutionary socialists, rather than as popular slogans of agitation directed at the masses. The heart of Lenin's approach was an irreconcilable opposition to class peace with the imperialist rulers and defense of a revolutionary working class perspective in wartime as in times of peace.

Lenin did not view the approach he outlined as providing automatic answers to all tactical problems that might arise or as a license for adventurist tactics that would isolate revolutionists from the masses. Writing of his policy of revolutionary defeatism, Lenin stated, "note that this does not mean 'blowing up bridges,' organising unsuccessful strikes in the war industries, and in general helping the government defeat the revolutionaries." ("The Defeat of One's Own Government in the Imperialist War," in *Collected Works*, Volume 21, Progress Publishers, Moscow, 1964.)

An example of the slogans used by Lenin and the Bolsheviks during the Russian Revolution to build mass opposition to imperialist war and support for proletarian revolution among the working masses was "Bread, Peace, Land!"

"The Conference of the R.S.D.L.P. (Russian Social Democratic Labor Party) Groups Abroad" and "The Question of Peace" are reprinted from Volume 21 of Lenin's *Collected Works* (op cit.). "The Military Programme of the Proletarian Revolution" is from Volume 23 of the same edition.

The second part of this appendix deals with the application of the Leninist position by the Socialist Workers Party in World War II. This approach, called the "proletarian military policy," was developed in collaboration with Leon Trotsky. It aimed at combining irreconcilable opposition to the imperialist war with slogans and tactics that would strengthen the class struggle and deepen class consciousness during the war. In addition, this strategy sought to prevent the isolation of revolutionary socialists from the working class masses who accepted, and even strongly supported, World War II.

The first three items were products of the September 27–29, 1940 combined plenum-conference of the SWP held in Chicago. The "Resolution on Proletarian Military Policy," adopted at the conference, is reprinted from the October 5 issue of the *Socialist Appeal,* which was at that time the weekly organ of the SWP. Cannon's main speech to the conference, "The Military Policy of the Proletariat" is reprinted from the October 5, 1940 issue of *Socialist Appeal*. The excerpts from the summary speech by Cannon are reprinted from the October 26, 1940 issue of *Socialist Appeal*. "Militarism and Workers Rights," by James P. Cannon, appeared in the November 30, 1940 issue of the *Socialist Appeal*.

Examples of the popular application of this political approach in revolutionary socialist propaganda during the war can be found in *Socialism on Trial* (Pathfinder Press, 1973), the transcript of Cannon's testimony in the trial of eighteen Trotskyist leaders, including Cannon himself, on frameup Smith Act charges stemming from their opposition to the war, and in "How to Fight Imperialist War," a radio talk given by Cannon in 1942, which appears in *Speeches for Socialism* (Pathfinder Press, 1971).

An explanation of the modifications that were made in the SWP's proletarian military policy during the Vietnam war can be found in the discussion in the SWP Political Committee on June 25, 1965 and in the SWP's 1969 resolution on the fight against the Vietnam war. Both documents are published in the first part of this bulletin.

The third part of this appendix takes up the mass movement of GIs that brought about the demobilization of the U.S. army after World War II. "A Hidden Chapter on the Fight Against War: The Going Home Movement," by Mary-Alice Waters first appeared in the November–December 1965 issue of the *Young Socialist,* published by the Young Socialist Alliance. It subsequently appeared in the Pathfinder Press pamphlet, *GIs and the Fight Against War.*

I. REVOLUTIONARY STRATEGY IN WORLD WAR I: THREE ARTICLES BY LENIN

1. The Conference of the Russian Social Democratic Labor Party Abroad

The following article is reprinted from Lenin, *Collected Works*, Progress Publishers, Moscow, 1964, Volume 21, pp. 158–164.

Held in Switzerland, a conference of the R.S.D.L.P. groups whose members are resident abroad concluded its work several days ago. Besides discussing purely foreign affairs, which we shall try briefly to comment on in the next issues of the Central Organ, the conference framed resolutions on the important and burning question of the war. We are publishing these resolutions forthwith, in the hope that they will prove of use to all Social-Democrats who are earnestly seeking the way towards live work from the present-day welter of opinions which boil down to an acknowledgement of internationalism in word, and an urge to come to terms at any cost with social-chauvinism in deed. We might add that, on the question of the "United States of Europe" slogan, the discussion was purely political, it being decided that the question be deferred pending a discussion, in the press, of the *economic* aspect of the matter.

The Conference's Resolutions

The conference, which stands on the basis of the Central Committee's Manifesto, as published in No. 33, lays down the following principles designed to bring system into propaganda:

On The Character Of The War

The present war is imperialist in character. This war is the outcome of conditions in an epoch in which capitalism has reached the highest stage in its development; in which the greatest significance attaches, not only to the export of commodities, but also to the export of capital; an epoch in which the cartelisation of production and the internationalisation of economic life have assumed impressive proportions, colonial policies have brought about the almost complete partition of the globe, world capitalism's productive forces have outgrown the limited boundaries of national and state divisions, and the objective conditions are perfectly ripe for socialism to be achieved.

The 'Defence Of The Fatherland' Slogan

The present war is, in substance, a struggle between Britain, France and Germany for the partition of colonies and for the plunder of rival countries; on the part of tsarism and the ruling classes of Russia, it is an attempt to seize Persia, Mongolia, Turkey in Asia, Constantinople, Galicia, etc. The national element in the Austro-Serbian war is an entirely secondary consideration and does not affect the general imperialist character of the war.

The entire economic and diplomatic history of the last few decades shows that both groups of belligerent nations were systematically preparing the very kind of war such as the present. The question of which group dealt the first military blow or first declared war is immaterial in any determination of the tactics of socialists. Both sides' phrases on the defence of the fatherland, resistance to enemy invasion, a war of defence, etc., are nothing but deception of the people.

At the bottom of genuinely national wars, such as took place especially between 1789 and 1871, was a long process of mass national movements, of a struggle against absolutism and feudalism, the overthrow of national oppression, and the formation of states on a national basis, as a prerequisite of capitalist development.

The national ideology created by that epoch left

a deep impress on the mass of the petty bourgeoisie and a section of the proletariat. This is now being utilised in a totally different and imperialist epoch by the sophists of the bourgeoisie, and by the traitors to socialism who are following in their wake, so as to split the workers, and divert them from their class aims and from the revolutionary struggle against the bourgeoisie.

The words in the *Communist Manifesto* that "the workingmen have no country" are today truer than ever before. Only the proletariat's international struggle against the bourgeoisie can preserve what it has won, and open to the oppressed masses the road to a better future.

The Slogans Of The Revolutionary Social-Democrats

"The conversion of the present imperialist war into a civil war is the only correct proletarian slogan, one that follows from the experience of the Commune, and outlined in the Basle resolution (1912); it has been dictated by all the conditions of an imperialist war between highly developed bourgeois countries."

Civil war, for which revolutionary Social-Democracy today calls, is an armed struggle of the proletariat against the bourgeoisie, for the expropriation of the capitalist class in the advanced capitalist countries, and for a democratic revolution in Russia (a democratic republic, an eight-hour working day, the confiscation of the landowners' estates), for a republic to be formed in the backward monarchist countries in general, etc.

The appalling misery of the masses, which has been created by the war, cannot fail to evoke revolutionary sentiments and movements. The civil war slogan must serve to co-ordinate and direct such sentiments and movements.

The organisation of the working class has been badly damaged. Nevertheless, a revolutionary crisis is maturing. After the war, the ruling classes of all countries will make a still greater effort to throw the proletariat's emancipation movement back for decades. The task of the revolutionary Social-Democrats—both in the event of a rapid revolutionary development and in that of a protracted crisis, will not consist in renouncing lengthy and day-by-day work, or in discarding any of the old methods of the class struggle. To direct both the parliamentary and the economic struggle against opportunism, in the spirit of revolutionary struggle of the masses—such will be the task.

The following should be indicated as the first steps towards converting the present imperialist war into a civil war: (1) an absolute refusal to vote for war credits, and resignation from bourgeois governments; (2) a complete break with the policy of a class truce (*bloc national, Burgfrieden*); (3) formation of an underground organisation wherever the governments and the bourgeoisie abolish constitutional liberties by introducing martial law; (4) support for fraternisation between soldiers of the belligerent nations, in the trenches and on battlefields in general; (5) support for every kind of revolutionary mass action by the proletariat in general.

Opportunism And The Collapse Of The Second International

The collapse of the Second International is the collapse of socialist opportunism. The latter has grown as a product of the preceding "peaceful" period in the development of the labour movement. That period taught the working class to utilise such important means of struggle as parliamentarianism and all legal opportunities, create mass economic and political organisations, a widespread labour press, etc.; on the other hand, the period engendered a tendency to repudiate the class struggle and to preach a class truce, repudiate the socialist revolution, repudiate the very principle of illegal organisations, recognise bourgeois patriotism, etc. Certain strata of the working class (the bureaucracy of the labour movement and the labour aristocracy, who get a fraction of the profits from the exploitation of the colonies and from the privileged position of their "fatherlands" in the world market), as well as petty-bourgeois sympathisers within the socialist parties, have proved the social mainstay of these tendencies, and channels of bourgeois influence over the proletariat.

The baneful influence of opportunism has made itself felt most strongly in the policies of most of the official Social-Democratic parties of the Second International during the war. Voting for war credits, participation in governments, the policy of a class truce, the repudiation of an illegal organisation when legality has been rescinded—all this is a violation of the International's most important decisions, and a downright betrayal of socialism.

The Third International

The war-created crisis has exposed the real essence of opportunism as the bourgeoisie's accomplice against the proletariat. The so-called Social-Democratic "Centre", headed by Kautsky, has in practice completely slid into opportunism, behind a cover of exceedingly harmful and hypocritical phrases and a Marxism falsified to resemble imperialism. Experience shows that in Germany, for instance, a defence of the socialist standpoint has been possible only by resolute opposition to the will of the majority of the Party leadership. It would be a harmful illusion to hope that a genuinely socialist International can be restored without a full organisational severance from the opportunists.

The Russian Social-Democratic Labour Party must support all and every international and revolutionary mass action by the proletariat, and strive to bring together all anti-chauvinist elements in the International.

Pacifism And The Peace Slogan

Pacifism, the preaching of peace in the abstract, is one of the means of duping the working class. Under capitalism, particularly in its imperialist stage, wars are inevitable. On the other hand, however, Social-Democrats cannot overlook the positive significance of revolutionary wars, i.e., not imperialist wars, but such as were fought, for instance, between 1789 and 1871, with the aim of doing away with national oppression, and creating national capitalist states out of the feudal decentralised states, or such wars that may be waged to defend the conquests of the proletariat victorious in its struggle against the bourgeoisie.

At the present time, the propaganda of peace unaccompanied by a call for revolutionary mass action can only sow illusions and demoralise the proletariat, for it makes the proletariat believe that the bourgeoisie is humane, and turns it into a plaything in the hands of the secret diplomacy of the belligerent countries. In particular, the idea of a so-called democratic peace being possible without a series of revolutions is profoundly erroneous.

The Defeat Of The Tsarist Monarchy

In each country, the struggle against a government that is waging an imperialist war should not falter at the possibility of that country's defeat as a result of revolutionary propaganda. The defeat of the government's army weakens the government, promotes the liberation of the nationalities it oppresses, and facilitates civil war against the ruling classes.

This holds particularly true in respect of Russia. A victory for Russia will bring in its train a strengthening of reaction, both throughout the world and within the country, and will be accompanied by the complete enslavement of the peoples living in areas already seized. In view of this, we consider the defeat of Russia the lesser evil in all conditions.

The Attitude Towards Other Parties And Groups

The war, which has engendered a spate of chauvinism, has revealed that the democratic (Narodnik) intelligentsia, the party of the Socialist-Revolutionaries (with complete instability of the oppositional trend, which is centred in *Mysl*), and the main group of liquidators (*Nasha Zarya*) which is supported by Plekhanov, are all in the grip of chauvinism. In practice, the Organising Committee is also on the side of chauvinism, beginning with Larin and Martov's camouflaged support of chauvinism and ending with Axelrod's defence of the principle of patriotism; so is the Bund, in which a Germanophile chauvinism prevails. The Brussels bloc (of July 3, 1914) has disintegrated, while the elements that are grouped around *Nashe Slovo* are vacillating between a Platonic sympathy with internationalism and a striving for unity, at any price, with *Nasha Zarya* and the Organising Committee. The same vacillation is manifest in Chkheidze's Social-Democratic group. The latter has, on the one hand, expelled the Plekhanovite, i.e., the chauvinist, Mankov; on the other hand, it wishes to cover up, by all possible means, the chauvinism of Plekhanov, *Nasha Zarya*, Axelrod, the Bund, etc.

It is the task of the Social-Democratic Labour Party in Russia to consolidate the proletarian unity created in 1912–14, mainly by *Pravda*, to re-establish the Social-Democratic Party organisations of the working class, on the basis of a decisive organisational break with the social-chauvinists. Temporary agreements are possible only with those Social-Democrats who stand for a decisive organisational rupture with the Organising Committee, *Nasha Zarya* and the Bund.

Written not later than February 19 (March 4), 1915. Published on March 29, 1915 in *Sotsial-Demokrat* No. 40. Published according to the text in *Sotsial-Demokrat*.

2. The Question of Peace

The following is reprinted from Lenin, *Collected Works*, Progress Publishers, Moscow, 1964, Vol. 21 pp. 290–294.

The question of peace as an immediate programme of action for the socialists, and in this connection the question of peace terms, presents a universal interest. One can only be grateful to *Berner Tagwacht* for its efforts to pose the question, not from the usual petty-bourgeois national angle, but from one that is genuinely proletarian and internationalist. The editorial note in No. 73 ("*Friedenssehnsucht*"), that the German Social-Democrats who wish for peace must break (*sich lossagen*) with the policies of the Junker government, was excellent. Also excellent was Comrade A. P.'s attack (Nos. 73 and 75) on the "pompous airs of impotent phrasemongers" (*Wichtigtuerei machtloser Schönredner*), who are vainly attempting to solve the peace question from the petty-bourgeois point of view.

Let us see how this question should be posed by socialists.

The peace slogan can be advanced either in connection with definite peace terms, or without any conditions at all, as a struggle, not for a definite kind of peace, but for peace in general (*Frieden ohne weiters*). In the latter case, we obviously have a slogan that is not only non-socialist but entirely devoid of meaning and content. Most people are definitely in favour of peace in general, including even Kitchener, Joffre, Hindenburg, and Nicholas the Bloodstained, for *each* of them wants an end to the war. The trouble is that every one of them advances peace terms that are imperialist (i.e., predatory and oppressive, towards other peoples), and to the advantage of his "own" nation. Slogans must be brought forward so as to enable the masses, through propaganda and agitation, to see the unbridgeable distinction between socialism and capitalism (imperialism), and *not* for the purpose of *reconciling* two hostile classes and two hostile political lines, with the aid of a formula that "unites" the most different things.

To continue: can the socialists of different countries be united on definite *terms* of peace? If so, such terms must undoubtedly include the recognition of the right to self-determination for all nations, and also renunciation of all "annexations", i.e., infringements of that right. If, however, that right is recognised only for *some* nations, then you are defending the *privileges* of certain nations, i.e., you are a nationalist and imperialist, not a socialist. If, however, that right is recognised for *all* nations, then you cannot single out Belgium alone, for instance; you must take *all* the oppressed peoples, both in Europe (the Irish in Britain, the Italians in Nice, the Danes in Germany, fifty-seven per cent of Russia's population, etc.) *and outside of Europe*, i.e., all colonies. Comrade A.P. has done well to remind us of them. Britain, France, and Germany have a total population of some one hundred and fifty million, whereas the populations they oppress in the colonies number over four hundred million! The essence of the imperialist war, i.e., a war waged for the interests of the capitalists, consists, not only in the war being waged with the aim of oppressing new nations, of carving up the colonies, but also in its being waged primarily by the advanced nations, which *oppress* a number of other peoples comprising the *majority* of the earth's population.

The German Social-Democrats, who justify the seizure of Belgium or reconcile themselves to it, are actually imperialists and nationalists, not Social-Democrats, since they defend the "right" of the German bourgeoisie (partly also of the German workers) to oppress the Belgians, the Alsatians, the Danes, the Poles, the Negroes in Africa, etc. They are not socialists, but *menials* to the German bourgeoisie, whom they are aiding to rob other nations. The Belgian socialists who demand the liberation and indemnification of Belgium *alone* are also actually defending a demand of the Belgian bourgeoisie, who would go on plundering the 15,000,000 Congolese population and obtaining concessions and privileges in other countries. The Belgian bourgeoisie's foreign investments amount to something like three thousand million francs. Safeguarding the profits from these investments by using every kind of fraud and machinations is the *real* "national interest" of "gallant Belgium". The same applies in a still greater degree to Russia, Britain, France and Japan.

It follows that if the demand for the freedom of nations is not to be a false phrase covering up the imperialism and the nationalism of *certain individual countries*, it must be extended to *all* peoples and to *all* colonies. Such a demand, however, is obviously meaningless *unless* it is accompanied by a series of revolutions in *all* the advanced countries. Moreover, it cannot be accomplished without a successful *socialist* revolution.

Should this be taken to mean that socialists can remain indifferent to the peace demand that is coming from ever greater masses of the people? By no means. The slogans of the workers' class-conscious vanguard are one thing, while the spontaneous demands of the masses are something quite different. The yearning for peace is one of the most important *symptoms* revealing the beginnings of *disappointment* in the bourgeois lie about a war of "liberation", the "defence of the fatherland", and similar falsehoods that the class of capitalists beguiles the mob with. This symptom should attract the closest attention from socialists. All efforts must be bent towards *utilising* the masses' desire for peace. But *how* is it to be utilised? To recognise the peace *slogan* and repeat it would mean encouraging "pompous airs of impotent [and frequently what is worse: *hypocritical*] phrase-mongers"; it would mean *deceiving* the people with illusion that the existing governments, the present-day master classes, are *capable*—without being "taught" a lesson (or rather without being eliminated) by a series of revolutions—of granting a peace in any way satisfactory to democracy and the working class. Nothing is more harmful than such deception. Nothing throws more dust in the eyes of the workers, nothing imbues them with a more deceptive idea about the *absence of deep* contradictions between capitalism and socialism, nothing *embellishes* capitalist slavery more than this deception does. No, we must make use of the desire for peace so as to explain to the masses that the benefits they expect from peace cannot be obtained without a series of revolutions.

An end to wars, peace among the nations, the cessation of pillaging and violence—such is our ideal, but only bourgeois sophists can seduce the masses with this ideal, if the latter is divorced from a direct and immediate call for revolutionary action. The ground for such propaganda is prepared; to practice that propaganda, one need only break with the opportunists, those allies of the bourgeoisie, who are hampering revolutionary work both directly (even to the extent of passing information to the authorities) and indirectly.

The slogan of self-determination of nations should also be advanced *in connection* with the imperialist era of capitalism. We do not stand for the *status quo*, or for the philistine Utopia of *standing aside* in great wars. We stand for a revolutionary struggle against imperialism, i.e., capitalism. Imperialism consists in a striving of nations that oppress a number of other nations to extend and increase that oppression and to repartition the colonies. That is why the question of self-determination of nations today *hinges* on the conduct of socialists of the *oppressor* nations. A socialist of any of the *oppressor* nations (Britain, France, Germany, Japan, Russia, the United States of America, etc.) who does not recognise and does not struggle for the right of oppressed nations to self-determination (i.e., the right to secession) is in reality a chauvinist, not a socialist.

Only this point of view can lead to a sincere and consistent struggle against imperialism, to a proletarian, not a philistine approach (today) to the national question. Only this point of view can lead to a consistent application of the principle of combating any form of the oppression of nations; it removes mistrust among the proletarians of the oppressor and oppressed nations, makes for a united international struggle for the socialist revolution (i.e., for the only accomplishable regime of complete national equality), as distinct from the philistine Utopia of freedom for all small states in general, under capitalism.

This is the point of view adopted by our Party, i.e., by those Social-Democrats of Russia who have rallied around the Central Committee. This was the point of view adopted by Marx when he taught the proletariat that "no nation can be free if it oppresses other nations". It was from this point of view that Marx demanded the separation of Ireland from Britain, this in the interests of the freedom movement, not only of the Irish, but especially of the *British* workers.

If the socialists of Britain do not recognise and uphold Ireland's right to secession, if the French do not do the same for Italian Nice, the Germans for Alsace-Lorraine, Danish Schleswig, and Poland, the Russians for Poland, Finland, the Ukraine, etc., and the Poles for the Ukraine—if all the socialists of the "Great" Powers, i.e., the great robber powers, do not uphold that right in respect of the colonies, it is solely because they are in fact imperialists, not socialists. It is ridiculous to cherish illusions that people who do *not* fight for "the right to self-determination" of the oppressed nations, while they themselves belong to the oppressor nations, are capable of practising socialist policies.

Instead of leaving it to the hypocritical phrase-mongers to deceive the people by phrases and promises concerning the possibility of a democratic peace, socialists must explain to the masses the impossibility of anything resembling a democratic peace, unless there are a series of revolutions and unless a revolutionary struggle is waged in every country against the *respective* government. Instead of allowing the bourgeois politicians to deceive the peoples with talk about the freedom of nations, socialists must explain to the masses in the *oppressor* nations that they cannot hope for their liberation, as long as they help oppress other nations, and do not recognise and uphold the right of those nations to self-determination, i.e., the freedom to secede. That is the socialist, as distinct from the imperialist, policy to be applied to all countries, on the question of peace and the national question. True, this line is in most cases incompatible with the laws punishing high treason—but so is the Basle resolution, which has been so shamefully betrayed by almost all the socialists of the oppressor nations.

The choice is between socialism and submission to the laws of Joffre and Hindenburg, between revolutionary struggle and servility to imperialism. There is no middle course. The greatest harm is caused to the proletariat by the hypocritical (or obtuse) authors of the "middle-course" policy.

Written in July–August 1915. Signed: Lenin. First published unsigned in the magazine *Proletarskaya Revolutsia* No. 5 (28), 1924. Published according to the manuscript.

3. The Military Programme of the Proletariat

The following is reprinted from Lenin, *Collected Works*, Progress Publishers, Moscow, 1964, Volume 23, pp. 77–87.

Among the Dutch, Scandinavian and Swiss revolutionary Social-Democrats who are combating the social-chauvinist lies about "defence of the fatherland" in the present imperialist war, there have been voices in favour of replacing the old Social-Democratic minimum-programme demand for a "militia", or "the armed nation", by a new demand: "disarmament". The *Jugend-Internationale* has inaugurated a discussion on this issue and published, in No. 3, an editorial supporting disarmament. There is also, we regret to note, a concession to the "disarmament" idea in R. Grimm's latest theses. Discussions have been started in the periodicals *Neues Leben* and *Vorbote*.

Let us take a closer look at the position of the disarmament advocates.

I

Their principal argument is that the disarmament demand is the clearest, most decisive, most consistent expression of the struggle against all militarism and against all war.

But in this principal argument lies the disarmament advocates' principal error. Socialists cannot, without ceasing to be socialists, be opposed to all war.

Firstly, socialists have never been, nor can they ever be, opposed to revolutionary wars. The bourgeoisie of the imperialist "Great" Powers has become thoroughly reactionary, and the war *this* bourgeoisie is now waging we regard as a reactionary, slave-owners' and criminal war. But what about a war *against* this bourgeoisie? A war, for instance, waged by peoples oppressed by and dependent upon this bourgeoisie, or by colonial peoples, for liberation? In §5 of the *Internationale* group theses we read: "National wars are no longer possible in the era of this unbridled imperialism." That is obviously wrong.

The history of the twentieth century, this century of "unbridled imperialism", is replete with colonial wars. But what we Europeans, the imperialist oppressors of the majority of the world's peoples, with our habitual, despicable European chauvinism, call "colonial wars" are often national wars, or national rebellions of these oppressed peoples. One of the main features of imperialism is that it accelerates capitalist development in the most backward countries, and thereby extends and intensifies the struggle against national oppression. That is a fact, and from it inevitably follows that imperialism must often give rise to national wars. *Junius*, who defends the above-quoted "theses" in her pamphlet, says that in the imperialist era every national war against an imperialist Great Power leads to the intervention of a rival imperialist Great Power. Every national war is thus turned into an imperialist war. But that argument is wrong too. This *can* happen, but does not always happen. Many colonial wars between 1900 and 1914 did not follow that course. And it would be simply ridiculous to declare, for instance, that after the present war, if it ends in the utter exhaustion of all the belligerents, "there can be no" national, progressive, revolutionary wars "of any kind", waged, say, by China in alliance with India, Persia, Siam, etc., against the Great Powers.

To deny all possibility of national wars under imperialism is wrong in theory, obviously mistaken historically, and tantamount to European chauvinism in practice: we who belong to nations that oppress hundreds of millions in Europe, Africa, Asia, etc., are invited to tell the oppressed peoples that it is "impossible" for them to wage war against "our" nations!

Secondly, civil war is just as much a war as any other. He who accepts the class struggle cannot fail to accept civil wars, which in every class society are the natural, and under certain conditions inevitable, continuation, development and intensification of the class struggle. That has been confirmed by every great revolution. To repudiate civil war, or to forget about it, is to fall into extreme opportunism and renounce the socialist revolution.

Thirdly, the victory of socialism in one country does not at one stroke eliminate all war in general. On the contrary, it presupposes wars. The development of capitalism proceeds extremely unevenly in different countries. It cannot be otherwise under commodity production. From this it follows irrefutably that socialism cannot achieve victory simultaneously *in all* countries. It will achieve victory first in one or several countries, while the others will for some time remain bourgeois or pre-bourgeois. This is bound to create not only friction, but a direct attempt on the part of the bourgeoisie of other countries to crush the socialist state's victorious proletariat. In such cases a war on our part would be a legitimate and just war. It would be a war for socialism, for the liberation of other nations from the bourgeoisie. Engels was perfectly right when, in his letter to Kautsky of September 12, 1882, he clearly stated that it was possible for *already victorious* socialism to wage "defensive wars". What he had in mind was defence of the victorious proletariat against the bourgeoisie of other countries.

Only after we have overthrown, finally vanquished and expropriated the bourgeoisie of the whole world, and not merely of one country, will wars become impossible. And from a scientific point of view it would be utterly wrong—and utterly unrevolutionary—for us to evade or gloss over the most important thing: crushing the resistance of the bourgeoisie—the most difficult task, and one demanding the greatest amount of fighting, in the *transition* to socialism. The "social" parsons and opportunists are always ready to build dreams of future peaceful socialism. But the very thing that distinguishes them from revolutionary Social-Democrats is that they refuse to think about and reflect on the fierce class struggle and class *wars* needed to achieve that beautiful future.

We must not allow ourselves to be led astray by words. The term "defence of the fatherland", for instance, is hateful to many because both avowed opportunists and Kautskyites use it to cover up and gloss over the bourgeois lie about the *present* predatory war. This is a fact. But it does not follow that we must no longer see through to the meaning of political slogans. To accept "defence of the fatherland" in the present war is no more nor less than to accept it as a "just" war, a war in the interests of the proletariat—no more nor less, we repeat, because invasions may occur in any war. It would be sheer folly to repudiate "defence of the fatherland" *on the part* of oppressed nations in their wars *against* the imperialist Great Powers, or on the part of a victorious proletariat in *its* war against some Galliffet of a bourgeois state.

Theoretically, it would be absolutely wrong to forget that every war is but the continuation of policy by other means. The present imperialist war is the continuation of the imperialist policies of two groups of Great Powers, and these policies were engendered and fostered by the sum total of the relationships of the imperialist era. But this very era must also necessarily engender and foster policies of struggle against national oppression and of proletarian struggle against the bourgeoisie and, consequently, also the possibility and inevitability, first, of revolutionary national rebellions and wars; second, of proletarian wars and rebellions *against* the bourgeoisie; and, third, of a combination of both kinds of revolutionary war, etc.

II

To this must be added the following general consideration.

An oppressed class which does not strive to learn to use arms, to acquire arms, only deserves to be treated like slaves. We cannot, unless we have become bourgeois pacifists or opportunists forget that we are living in a class society from which there is no way out, nor can there be, save through the class struggle. In every class society, whether based on slavery, serfdom, or, as at present, on wage-labour, the oppressor class is always armed. Not only the modern standing army, but even the modern militia—and even in the most democratic bourgeois republics, Switzerland, for instance—represent the bourgeoisie armed *against* the proletariat. That is such an elementary truth that it is hardly necessary to dwell upon it. Suffice it to point to the use of troops against strikers in all capitalist countries.

A bourgeoisie armed against the proletariat is one of the biggest, fundamental and cardinal facts of modern capitalist society. And in face of this fact, revolutionary Social-Democrats are urged to "demand" "disarmament"! That is tantamount to complete abandonment of the class-struggle point of view, to renunciation of all thought of revolution. Our slogan must be: arming of the proletariat to defeat, expropriate and disarm the bourgeoisie. These are the only tactics possible for a revolutionary class, tactics that follow logically from, and are dictated by, the whole *objective development* of capitalist militarism. Only *after* the proletariat has disarmed the bourgeoisie will it be able, without betraying its world-historic mission, to consign all armaments to the scrap-heap. And the proletariat will undoubtedly do this, but *only when this condition has been fulfilled, certainly not before.*

If the present war rouses among the reactionary Christian socialists, among the whimpering petty bourgeoisie, *only* horror and fright, only aversion to all use of arms, to bloodshed, death, etc., then we must say: Capitalist society is and has always been *horror without end.* If this most reactionary of all wars is now preparing for that society an *end in horror,* we have no reason to fall into despair. But the disarmament "demand", or more correctly, the dream of disarmament, is, objectively, nothing but an expression of despair at a time when, as everyone can see, the bourgeoisie itself is paving the way for the only legitimate and revolutionary war—civil war against the imperialist bourgeoisie.

A lifeless theory, some might say, but we would remind them of two world-historical facts: the role of the trusts and the employment of women in industry, on the one hand, and the Paris Commune of 1871 and the December 1905 uprising in Russia, on the other.

The bourgeoisie makes it its business to promote trusts, drive women and children into the factories, subject them to corruption and suffering, condemn them to extreme poverty. We do not "demand" such development, we do not "support" it. We fight it. But *how* do we fight? We explain that trusts and the employment of women in industry are progressive. We do not want a return to the handicraft system, pre-monopoly capitalism, domestic drudgery for women. Forward through the trusts, etc., and beyond them to socialism!

With the necessary changes that argument is applicable also to the present militarisation of the population. Today the imperialist bourgeoisie militarises the youth as well as the adults; tomorrow, it may begin militarising the women. Our attitude should be: All the better! Full speed ahead! For the faster we move, the nearer shall we be to the armed uprising against capitalism. How can Social-Democrats give way to fear of the militarisation of the youth, etc., if they have not forgotten the example of the Paris Commune? This is not a "lifeless theory" or a dream. It is a fact. And it would be a sorry state of affairs indeed if, all the economic and political facts notwithstanding, Social-Democrats began to doubt that the imperialist era and imperialist wars must inevitably bring about a repetition of such facts.

A certain bourgeois observer of the Paris Commune, writing to an English newspaper in May 1871, said: "If the French nation consisted entirely of women, what a terrible nation it would be!" Women and teen-age children fought in the Paris Commune side by side with the men. It will be no different in the coming battles for the overthrow of the bourgeoisie. Proletarian women will not look on passively as poorly armed or unarmed workers are shot down by the well-armed forces of the bourgeoisie. They will take to arms, as they did in 1871, and from the cowed nations of today—or more correctly, from the present-day labour movement, disorganised more by the opportunists than by the governments—there will undoubtedly arise, sooner or later, but with absolute certainty, an international league of the "terrible nations" of the revolutionary proletariat.

The whole of social life is now being militarised. Imperialism is a fierce struggle of the Great Powers for the division and redivision of the world. It is therefore bound to lead to further militarisation in all countries, even in neutral and small ones. How will proletarian women oppose this? Only by cursing all war and everything military, only by demanding disarmament? The women of an oppressed and really revolutionary class will never accept that shameful role. They will say to their sons: "You will soon be grown up. You will be given a gun. Take it and learn the military art properly. The proletarians need this knowledge not to shoot your brothers, the workers of other countries, as is being done in the present war, and as the traitors to socialism are telling you to do. They need it to fight the bourgeoisie of their own country, to put an end to exploitation, poverty and war, and not by pious wishes, but by defeating and disarming the bourgeoisie."

If we are to shun such propaganda, precisely such propaganda, in connection with the present war, then we had better stop using fine words about international revolutionary Social-Democracy, the socialist revolution and war against war.

III

The disarmament advocates object to the "armed nation" clause in the programme also because it more easily leads, they allege, to concessions to opportunism. The cardinal point, namely, the relation of disarmament to the class struggle and to the social revolution, we have examined above. We shall now examine the relation between the disarmament demand and opportunism. One of the chief reasons why it is unacceptable is precisely that, together with the illusions it creates, it inevitably weakens and devitalises our struggle against opportunism.

Undoubtedly, this struggle is the main, immediate question now confronting the International. Struggle against imperialism that is not closely linked with the struggle against opportunism is either an empty phrase or a fraud. One of the main defects of Zimmerwald and Kienthal—one of the main reasons why these embryos of the Third International may possibly end in a fiasco—is that the question of fighting opportunism was not even raised openly, let alone solved in the sense of proclaiming the need to break with the opportunists. Opportunism has triumphed—temporarily—in the European labour movement. Its two main shades are apparent in all the big countries: first, the avowed, cynical, and therefore less dangerous social-imperialism of Messrs. Plekhanov, Scheidemann, Legien, Albert Thomas and Sembat, Vandervelde, Hyndman, Henderson, et al.; second, the concealed, Kautskyite opportunism: Kautsky-Haase and the Social-Democratic Labour Group in Germany; Longuet, Pressemane, Mayéras, et al., in France; Ramsay MacDonald and the other leaders of the Independent Labour Party in England; Martov, Chkheidze, et al., in Russia; Treves and the other so-called Left reformists in Italy.

Avowed opportunism is openly and directly opposed to revolution and to incipient revolutionary movements and outbursts. It is in direct alliance with the governments, varied as the forms of this alliance may be—from accepting ministerial posts to participation in the war industries committees (in Russia). The masked opportunists, the Kautskyites, are much more harmful and dangerous to the labour movement, because they hide their advocacy of alliance with the former under a cloak of plausible, pseudo-"Marxist" catchwords and pacifist slogans. The fight against both these forms of prevailing opportunism must be conducted in *all* fields of proletarian politics: parliament, the trade unions, strikes, the armed forces, etc. The main distinguishing feature of *both* these forms of prevailing opportunism is that the concrete question of the *connection between the present war and revolution, and the other concrete questions of revolution,* are hushed up, concealed, or treated with an eye to police prohibitions. And this despite the fact that before the war the connection between *this* impending war and the proletarian revolution was emphasised innumerable times, both unofficially, and officially in the Basle Manifesto. The main defect of the disarmament demand is its evasion of all the concrete questions of revolution. Or do the advocates of disarmament stand for an altogether new kind of revolution, unarmed revolution?

To proceed. We are by no means opposed to the fight for reforms. And we do not wish to ignore the sad possibility—if the worst comes to the worst—of mankind going through a second imperialist war, if revolution does not come out of the present war, in spite of the numerous outbursts of mass unrest and mass discontent and in spite of our efforts. We favour a programme of reforms directed *also* against the opportunists. They would be only too glad if we left the struggle for reforms entirely to them and sought escape from sad reality in a nebulous "disarmament" fantasy. "Disarmament" means simply running away from unpleasant reality, not fighting it.

In such a programme we would say something, like this: "To accept the defence of the fatherland slogan in the 1914–16 imperialist war is to corrupt the labour movement with the aid of a bourgeois lie." Such a concrete reply to a concrete question would be more correct theoretically, much more useful to the proletariat and more unbearable to the opportunists, than the disarmament demand and repudiation of "all and any" defence of the fatherland. And we could add: "The bourgeoisie of all the imperialist Great Powers—England, France, Germany, Austria, Russia, Italy, Japan, the United States—has become so reactionary and so intent on world domination, that *any* war waged by *the bourgeoisie of those* countries is bound to be reactionary. The proletariat must not only oppose all such wars, but must also wish for the defeat of its 'own' government in such wars and utilise its defeat for revolutionary insurrection, if an insurrection to prevent the war proves unsuccessful."

On the question of a militia, we should say: We are not in favour of a bourgeois militia: we are in favour only of a proletarian militia. Therefore, "not a penny, not a man", not only for a standing army, but even for a bourgeois militia, even in countries like the United States, or Switzerland, Norway, etc. The more so that in the freest republican countries (e.g., Switzerland) we see that the militia is being increasingly Prussianised, particularly in 1907 and 1911, and prostituted by being used against strikers. We can demand popular election of officers, abolition of all military law, equal rights for foreign and native-born workers (a point particularly important for those imperialist states which, like Switzerland, are more and more blatantly exploiting larger numbers of foreign workers, while denying them all rights). Further, we can demand the right of every hundred, say, inhabitants of a given country to form voluntary military-training associations, with free election of instructors paid by the state, etc. Only under these conditions could the proletariat acquire military training for *itself* and not for its slave-owners; and the need for such training is imperatively dictated by the interests of the proletariat. The Russian revolution showed that every success of the revolutionary movement, even a partial success like the seizure of a certain city, a certain factory town, or winning over a certain section of the army, inevitably *compels* the victorious proletariat to carry out just such a programme.

Lastly, it stands to reason that opportunism can never be defeated by mere programmes; it can only be defeated by deeds. The greatest, and fatal, error of the bankrupt Second International was that its words did not correspond to its deeds, that it cultivated the habit of hypocritical and unscrupulous revolutionary phrase-mongering (note the present attitude of Kautsky and Co. towards the Basle Manifesto). Disarmament as a social idea, i.e., an idea that springs from, and can affect, a certain social environment, and is not the invention of some crackpot, springs, evidently, from the peculiar "tranquil" conditions prevailing, by way of exception, in certain small states, which have for a fairly long time stood aside from the world's path of war and bloodshed, and hope to remain that way. To be convinced of this, we have only to consider the arguments advanced, for instance, by the Norwegian advocates of disarmament. "We are a small country," they say. "Our army is small; there is nothing we can do against the Great Powers [and, consequently, nothing we can do to resist forcible involvement in an imperialist *alliance* with one or the other Great-Power group]. . . . We want to be left in peace in our backwoods and continue our backwoods politics, demand disarmament, compulsory arbitration, permanent neutrality, etc." ("permanent" after the Belgian fashion, no doubt?).

The petty striving of petty states to hold aloof, the petty-bourgeois desire to keep as far away as possible from the great battles of world history, to take advantage of one's relatively monopolistic position in order to remain in hidebound passivity—this is the *objective* social environment which may ensure the disarmament idea a certain degree of success and a certain degree of popularity in some of the small states. That striving is, of course, reactionary and is based entirely on illusions, for, in one way or another, imperialism draws the small states into the vortex of world economy and world politics.

In Switzerland, for instance, the imperialist environment objectively prescribes *two* courses to the labour movement: the opportunists, in alliance with the bourgeoisie, are seeking to turn the country into a republican-democratic monopolistic federation that would thrive on profits from imperialist bourgeois tourists, and to make this "tranquil" monopolistic position as profitable and as tranquil as possible.

The genuine Swiss Social-Democrats are striving to use Switzerland's relative freedom and her "international" position to help the victory of the close alliance of the revolutionary elements in the European workers' parties. Switzerland, thank God, does not have "a separate language of her own", but uses three world languages, the three languages spoken in the adjacent belligerent countries.

If twenty thousand Swiss party members were to pay a weekly levy of two centimes as a sort of "extra war tax", we would have twenty thousand francs per annum, a sum more than sufficient periodically to publish in three languages and distribute among the workers and soldiers of the belligerent countries—in spite of the bans imposed by the general staffs—all the truthful evidence about the incipient revolt of the workers, their fraternising in the trenches, their hope that the weapons will be used for revolutionary struggle against the imperialist bourgeoisie of their "own" countries, etc.

That is not new. It is being done by the best papers, like *La Sentinelle, Volksrecht and the Berner Tagivacht,* although, unfortunately, on an inadequate scale. Only through such activity can the splendid decision of the Aarau Party Congress become something more than merely a splendid decision.

The question that interests us now is: Does the disarmament demand correspond to this revolutionary trend among the Swiss Social-Democrats? It obviously does not. Objectively, disarmament is an extremely national, a specifically national programme of small states. It is certainly not the international programme of international revolutionary Social-Democracy.

Written in September 1916. First published in the magazine *Jugend-Internationale* Nos. 9 and 10, September and October 1917. Signed: N. Lenin. First published in Russian in 1929 in the second and third editions of Lenin's *Collected Works,* Vol. XIX. Published according to the magazine text. Translated from the German.

II. PROLETARIAN MILITARY POLICY, BY JAMES P. CANNON

1. Resolution on Proletarian Military Policy

The following resolution, adopted by the September 27–29, 1940 plenum-conference of the SWP, is reprinted from the October 5, 1940 issue of *Socialist Appeal.*

1. Capitalism has plunged the world into a horrible vortex of war and militarism. This testifies not to the vitality of capitalism but to its fatal weakness, its incapacity to regain stability. The epoch of the death agony of capitalism and the beginning of social transformation is an epoch of universal militarism. It can be brought to an end only by the definitive victory of the proletariat. This is the essential feature of the present world situation.

2. The intervention of the United States in the present war, or its clash with a victorious Germany or Japan at a later date, is predetermined by all the circumstances. All the realistic leaders of American capitalism clearly understand this. Only a few pacifist fools have the slightest doubt about it. The two main groups in the camp of U.S. imperialism—interventionalist and so-called isolationists—differ only in regard to military strategy. Both are agreed on the policy of preparing to fight and grab. The stupendous arms program adopted by Congress has and can have only one meaning: military agression in the near future on a world scale.

The question of whether German imperialism, having conquered Europe, can or cannot "attack" the United States has nothing to do with the real issue. The very existence of one aggressive and expanding imperialist power in the modern world is an "attack" on the others. The United States, as an imperialist power having its foundations throughout the world, is "attacked" anywhere a rival power attempts to seize a market, a piece of territory, or a sphere of influence.

Whether the United States directly intervenes in the present European war or defers open military action for another point of attack is only a secondary consideration in evaluating the perspective. The real course is clear: U. S. imperialism is preparing with all possible speed to put its strength and its weakness to the test of war on a colossal scale.

3. In the epoch of militarism great questions can be decided only by military means—this is the fundamental lesson of the developments of the present war.

The agents and apologists of democratic imperialism—the social democrats, the centrists, the trade union reformists, and the pacifists—fill the air with lamentations over the smashing military victories of Hitler and spread the sentiments of pessimism and prostration.

We Fourth Internationalists thrust aside these traitors and panic mongers with hatred and contempt. Our task is to ascertain what has been destroyed and what has been proved by the momentous events in Europe and to draw the necessary conclusions for the future struggle.

In the first place the victories of the fascist war machine of Hitler have destroyed every plausible basis for the illusion that a serious struggle against fascism can be conducted under the leadership of a bourgeois democratic regime. The war in Europe, as previously in the Spanish rehearsal, has shown up the hollowness, the rottenness, and the contemptible cowardice and greed of the whole ruling stratum of the bourgeois democrats. They are unwilling to sacrifice anything but the lives of the duped masses. To save their personal lives and their property they were ready in one country after another to capitulate to fascism and seek its protection against the wrath of their own people.

No less complete and devastating has been

the destruction of the traditional reformist labor movement. At best, this traditional movement—the parties and the trade unions—was pacifist in character. That is, it was designed for peace, not for war. Parties which confined themselves to protests against the horrors of war and did not seriously conduct a struggle for power to end the system which causes war—such parties were completely helpless when submitted to the test of war. The same proved true of the outwardly imposing trade unions. All concepts of peaceful, gradual, reformist progress within the framework of capitalism, and all parties and organizations which represented these concepts in any degree, were smashed like a house of cards.

The war in Europe has once again, and more categorically than ever, posed the fundamental alternative of the epoch of wars and revolutions: either the dictatorship of fascist capitalism, or the dictatorship of the proletariat. The attempt of the European workers, under the influence of the reformist labor bureaucracies, to find in democratic capitalism a third alternative, led to catastrophe. The third alternative has been destroyed in blood and fire. But the program of the workers fight for power has not been destroyed. When the workers of Europe rise again—and rise they will—that program will be their banner. These are the fundamental lessons of the war.

4. Bolshevism alone, which aims to direct the workers movement to the seizure of political power by revolutionary means, stands up and gains strength under the test of the great new events. War and militarism which crush all other organizations and discredit all other programs, only provide a new verification of the premises of Bolshevism. The military epoch has room only for parties which inspire the workers to scorn all half measures, to stop at nothing, and to carry their struggle through to the very end. These are parties of a new type having nothing in common with the reformist-pacifist parties of the traditional labor movement. Such a party is the Socialist Workers Party. Its program can be described in one phrase: dictatorship of the proletariat.

5. The certainty that the United States also will be dominated by militarism confronts the party with the categoric necessity to purge itself of all remnants of liberal, petty-bourgeois pacifist tendencies and conceptions carried away from the past, in particular from the left social-democratic movement. Pacifism is a debilitating poison in the workers movement. Pacifism, in all its forms, is no more than a protest in time of peace against war. In the face of actual war it thrusts the workers like sheep, unarmed and defenseless and without a program, into the slaughter. In our epoch, which is completely dominated by militarism, negative protests against war are of no avail whatever. The proletariat needs a positive program which takes the facts of war and militarism, the characteristic features of decaying capitalism, as the starting point for practical actions.

The first impact of the war in Europe revealed a petty-bourgeois centrist tendency in the Socialist Workers Party which took shape as a faction. Under the leadership of Burnham and Shachtman the minority waged a disruptive struggle in the party and attempted to overthrow the Marxist doctrines in favor of journalistic improvisations. The disruptive struggle of the Burnham-Shachtman faction culminated in their desertion of the party in a typical petty-bourgeois recoil against the discipline of the proletarian majority of the party. The open repudiation of socialism by Burnham within less than two months after he had deserted the party was only the logical sequel to the course he had followed in the party struggle. Burnham's betrayal of socialism confirmed to the hilt the party's characterization of this pretentious mountebank and the petty-bourgeois faction he organized and maneuvered into a split.

Since the party convention the seceding faction has evolved consistently in the direction of traditional left socialist antimilitarism, which at bottom is only a form of pacifism. The resolute struggle of the party majority against the Burnham-Shachtman faction and its decisive victory in the struggle were the necessary conditions for the survival of the party. An unrelenting antagonism to the deserters on every point is no less necessary. The party cannot have the slightest reason for conciliation on any point with the faction of deserters inspired by petty-bourgeois fright before the stern realities and complexities of the developing war.

6. The imperialist war is not our war and the

militarism of the capitalist state is not our militarism. We do not support the war and militarism of the imperialists any more than we support the capitalist exploitation of workers in the factories. We are against the war as a whole just as we are against the rule of the class which conducts it, and never under any circumstances vote to give them any confidence in their conduct of the war or preparation for it—not a man, not a cent, not a gun with our support. Our war is the war of the working class against the capitalist order.

But only with the masses is it possible to conquer power and establish socialism. And in these times the masses in the military organizations are destined to play the most decisive role of all. Consequently, it is impossible to affect the course of events by a policy of abstention. It is necessary to take capitalist militarism as an established reality which we are not yet strong enough to abolish and adapt our practical tactics to it. Our task is to protect the class interests of the workers in the army no less than in the factory. That means to participate in the military machine for socialist ends. The proletarian revolutionists are obliged to take their place beside the workers in the military training camps and on the battlefields in the same way as in the factory. They stand side by side with the masses of worker-soldiers, advance at all times and under all circumstances the independent class point of view, and strive to win over the majority to the idea of transforming the war into a struggle for their socialist emancipation.

Under conditions of mass militarization the revolutionary worker cannot evade military exploitation any more than he can evade exploitation in the factory. He does not seek a personal solution of the problem of war by evading military service. That is nothing but a desertion of class duty. The proletarian revolutionist goes with the masses. He becomes a soldier when they become soldiers, and goes to war when they go to war. The proletarian revolutionist strives to become the most skilled among the worker-soldiers and demonstrates in action that he is most concerned for the general welfare and protection of his comrades-in-arms. Only in this way, as in the factory, can the proletarian revolutionist gain the confidence of his comrades-in-arms and become an influential leader among them.

The total wars waged by the modern imperialists, and likewise the preparations for such wars, require compulsory military training no less than the appropriation of enormous funds and the subordination of industry to the manufacture of armaments. As long as the masses accept the war preparations, as is indubitably the case in the United States, mere negative agitation against the military budget and conscription cannot, by itself, yield serious results. Moreover, after Congress had already appropriated billions for armaments and was sure to pass a conscription bill without serious opposition, such negative agitation against conscription was somewhat belated and easily degenerated into mealy-mouthed pacifism. This proved to be the case with the organizations (Thomasite Socialists, Lovestoneites, etc.) affiliated with the preposterous conglomeration which calls itself the "Keep America Out of War Committee"—a vile and treacherous tool of the "democratic" imperialists. The hypocrisy of their pacifism is indicated by the fact that, simultaneously, they declare themselves in favor of the victory of Britain. Equally treacherous is the purely pacifist agitation of the Stalinists, employed today on behalf of Stalin's foreign policy under the Hitler-Stalin pact; and certain to be abandoned tomorrow when Stalin so orders, if he finds it necessary to switch partners. The pacifism of Browder and the pacifism of Thomas stem from different roots, but are identical in their betrayal of the interests of the working class. Under the rule of a modern imperialism which is already arming to the teeth, an abstract fight against militarism is at best Quixotic.

The revolutionary strategy can only be to take this militarism as a reality and counterpose a class program of the proletariat to the program of the imperialists at every point. We fight against sending the worker-soldiers into battle without proper training and equipment. We oppose the military direction of workers-soldiers by bourgeois officers who have no regard for their treatment, their protection, and their lives. We demand federal funds for the military training of workers and worker-officers under the control of the trade unions. Military appropriations? Yes—but only for the establishment and equipment of worker training camps! Compulsory military training of workers? Yes—but only under the control of the trade unions!

Such are the necessary concrete slogans for the present stage of the preparation of U.S. imperialism for war in the near future. They constitute a military transitional program supplementing the general political transitional program of the party.

7. U.S. imperialism prepares for war, materially and ideologically, without waiting to decide in advance the date when actual hostilities shall begin or the precise point of attack. The workers vanguard must likewise prepare for war without dependence on speculative answers to these secondary questions. The militarization of the country in preparation for war is taking place before our eyes. All our work and plans for the future must be based on this reality.

The first stages of militarization and war present enormous difficulties to our party because we have to swim against the stream. The party will be tested in a preliminary way by its capacity to recognize these difficulties and hold firm when the struggle is hard and the progress slow. Only a party fortified by the great principles and world associations of the Fourth International will be able to do this.

We are not a party like other parties. We alone are equipped with a scientific program of Marxism. We alone retain an unshakeable confidence in the socialist future of humanity. We alone are ready to meet the universal militarism of decaying capitalism on its own terms and lead the proletarian struggle for power accordingly.

The war in its course will utterly destroy all other workers' parties, all half-and-half movements. But it will only harden the bonafide party of the Fourth International and open the way for its growth and eventual victory.

The future belongs to the party of the dictatorship of the proletariat, the party of the Fourth International. It needs only to be true to itself, to hold firm, dig in, and prepare the future.

2. Military Policy of the Proletariat

September 28, 1940

This speech was given as the main political report to the SWP Plenum-Conference held in Chicago September 27–29, 1940. It concluded a two-month discussion on military policy conducted by the ranks of the SWP. The text is from a stenographic report, corrected by Cannon and published in the October 12, 1940, *Socialist Appeal*.

Our first word in formally beginning our deliberations today is devoted to the memory of our greatest teacher and comrade and our most glorious martyr. It is the proposal of the National Committee that we all stand for a moment in silent tribute to the memory of Comrade Trotsky.

We meet for the first time without him. I am sure that as we stood for a silent minute one common thought weighed upon us all. We all realize most poignantly that, whether we are quite grown up to it or not, we now face the appalling responsibility of leading and organizing the world movement of proletarian emancipation without the direct aid of the one who shaped and guided our movement, who instructed us, who raised us up and made men of us and prepared us for this great mission. It is up to us now to show that we have really learned what has been taught to us so patiently and so thoroughly. It is for us to take the tools that have been placed in our hands and use them no more as apprentices but as full-fledged journeymen.

We have confidence that we can do this because we have been left the greatest heritage that any political grouping in the history of the world was ever given. Never before did the workers' vanguard have such complete and thoroughgoing preparation, in a theoretical and programmatic way, as we have received. Especially in the past eleven years since Comrade Trotsky was exiled from the Soviet Union, eleven years so rich in historic events, we have had from day to day and from year to year the aid of his great Marxist brain. With his aid and guidance we have unraveled the mysteries of this epoch and found in every case the strategic and tactical road that leads the proletarian movement to higher ground.

We not only have now the task of leading the movement in this country. We also have on our shoulders a great international responsibility. In the nineteenth century, nearly seventy years ago, Marx and Engels transferred the center of the First International to the United States. Their action was then, so to speak, a symbolic intimation of the future international leading role of America. By a combination of circumstances the prophetic gesture of our great masters has finally been confirmed by concrete reality. The main political center and organizational base of the Fourth International, which is destined to complete the work begun by the First International of Marx and Engels, is in truth lodged here in the United States in the custody of those comrades who are gathered here and those whom they represent in all sections of the country.

A combination of circumstances, rather than any special merit of our own, has imposed upon us this international responsibility. First of all, we were fated to have the greatest amount of freedom for the open and legal development of our movement. While our valiant comrades in one country after another fell under the heavy blows of persecution, were stifled and repressed, we here in America have had now twelve years of uninterrupted preparatory work. We alone of practically all sections of the Fourth International were fortunate in beginning not entirely with new and inexperienced people. We carried over into the new movement of the Fourth International some substantial and experienced cadres who had been tested and who had learned in the Communist movement since 1918, and even before that. Our movement was thus prepared by its past and by these fortunate circumstances to establish an uninterrupted continuity between the movement of the present day and that which preceded it. All these things taken together have equipped and prepared us for the role which we must now play in aiding the further development of the Fourth International in all countries.

This movement is primarily the creation of Comrade Trotsky. He was responsible above all others for formulating its program and assembling its cadres on an international scale. But within the last few years our party has come to the front and played an increasingly important role. More and more Comrade Trotsky came to rely on us as the strongest pillar of the Fourth International. More and more the comrades in all parts of the world came to look at the combination of Comrade Trotsky and the American section as the main guarantee of stability in the leadership of the international party. And now, after the death of Comrade Trotsky, we can be sure that the comrades in all parts of the world—in China, carrying on their work in daily danger of their lives; the comrades imprisoned and in concentration camps in Germany; in illegality in France; in England; in Australia; in South America; in the Soviet Union; everywhere—they are now looking to the American section, to the Socialist Workers Party, to grow up to the level of its historic responsibility and assure the continuous functioning and development of our international movement. That puts a still greater responsibility upon all of us.

We cannot lag any more. Every one of us, I am sure, in the past years felt that if we erred, we had the assurance that we could be corrected by someone wiser than we. All of us, including myself, felt that if we shirked or slumped a little bit now and then, our laxity would be compensated for by the untiring energy of the Old Man. We permitted ourselves more than one luxury. That we cannot indulge ourselves in any more. The burden is on our shoulders. We must carry it. We must give the movement now more than ever in energy, in discipline, in faithfulness, and in efficient work.

We meet at a time of a great change in the world. Before our eyes, almost without our realizing it, there has been brought about a profoundly new world situation. A new period has opened up. The essence of the new situation is that capitalism in its unprecedented decay, in its death agony, has passed over completely from the relative stability and relative peace which characterized it as a growing and healthy social system into a state of permanent crisis, and the permanent crisis is now expressed in permanent war.

At the mass meeting last night I mentioned the new and significant development of the German-Italian-Japanese pact.[1] The announcement of this pact signifies above all other things that the war in Europe is due for an extension into Asia, Africa, and into the Western Hemisphere of the Americas. There is no prospect whatever for any more considerable periods of peace in the capitalist world. Just conjecture for a moment that some kind of peace could be effected in the European war. Nobody could believe that this would be a peace of any stability. It would only be a preparation for a new war of continents, of hemispheres, embracing the whole world. If a sudden, smashing victory of Hitler should enforce a peace with England, as was the case with France, no one would believe this would be the end of the war. If a formal peace should be declared and there should be a lull, during which there should be no war, it would only be an interlude.

We are preparing—our imperialist masters are preparing—night and day to challenge Hitler for world dominion. And Hitler, Mussolini, and the Japanese imperialists are preparing to meet that challenge. The outcome can only be a whole epoch of uninterrupted militarism and war. The proletariat, which is the sole power capable of lifting humanity out of this bloody morass, must face this fact. It cannot indulge in any more daydreams about the peaceful solution of the social problem. The workers' movement was dominated by this illusion for decades, for generations. It was thought

1. Although Japan had been a signer of the anti-Comintern pact with Germany in 1936 and had invaded China in 1937, it did not formally join the Rome-Berlin military Axis until September 27, 1940.

and felt that through the day-by-day work of organizing trade unions, building reformist parties, casting votes, gaining some social legislation, that along these lines, working from year to year and from decade to decade they could gradually improve the conditions of the masses, and glide over peacefully, without violent collisions or shocks, into a new social order called socialism.

The workers can indulge in no such daydreams any longer because the world is on fire with war and militarism. The one big conclusion the proletarian vanguard must draw is this: All great questions will be decided by military means. This was the great conclusion insisted upon by Comrade Trotsky in his last few months of life. In his letters, in his articles, and in conversations he repeated this thesis over and over again. These are new times. The characteristic feature of our epoch is unceasing war and universal militarism. That imposes on us as the first task, the task which dominates and shapes all others, the adoption of a military policy, an attitude of the proletarian party towards the solution of social problems during a time of universal militarism and war.

The prospects of the United States remaining at peace are absolutely zero. You have before you the draft of our resolution on military policy. It has been printed in the internal bulletin and discussed in the branches for the past two months. We have elaborated in this resolution our conception of these new problems and tasks. In the very beginning we take up the question of America's participation in the war. It is completely absurd to imagine that there is some special policy—some legerdemain—that can make it possible for the strongest imperialist power in the world to escape participation in the struggle for the imperialist domination of the world. Nobody believes in this possibility except a few muddleheaded pacifists. And when I say muddleheaded pacifists I do not mean the bourgeois isolationists. I mean the fools, the people who belong completely to yesterday, like the Thomasite socialists, the Lovestoneites, the few religious fanatics.

That wing of the American bourgeoisie going by the name of isolationist are no less aggressive, no less military minded, than the wing which wants intervention right now in the present war.

The *Chicago Tribune* strongly criticizes the Roosevelt policy only because they have a different approach to the war. They think we should begin the struggle, the struggle of American imperialism for world dominion, by conquering first the Western Hemisphere and proceeding next to the East by way of a war against Japan, postponing the clash with Hitler till a later time. The more farsighted, the more conscious and, I am sure, the strongest section of the American bourgeoisie, who are called interventionists, believe that we must begin the struggle for world dominion by intervention in the European war. What divides the two camps at this time is only a matter of strategy. Now that they are confronted by an open military alliance of Germany and Japan their differences can easily be reconciled.

The only question will be how soon and at what point to begin open intervention. As a matter of fact, in all except the formalities of the situation, we are intervening in the European war now as much as we can. We are sending unlimited supplies of military materials to Europe. In my opinion the only reason we are not sending troops is that there isn't any place to land them. The Wall Street heroes and their political lackeys overslept the European situation. They underestimated the rottenness and weakness of the bourgeois democracies of Europe on the one hand, and the military strength of Hitler on the other. They waited too long, until the ports were occupied by the fascists. Nothing remains now but England. England has no room for troops, and there is a growing opinion among American capitalists and military experts that England itself is a lost cause.

When American participation in the war finally begins is only a secondary question. The very fact that we have appropriated approximately fifteen billion dollars in one year for military expenditures before any war was formally started; that we have instituted peacetime conscription for the first time in history—these facts can only indicate that the masters of this country are preparing for an explosion of military aggressiveness on a scale never seen in history before. Imperialist America is out to dominate the world. In its path stands Hitler Germany in the West. In its path stands imperialist Japan in the East. The conflict between these imperialist powers can in no case be resolved by diplomacy or good wishes or half measures, but only as all other things are decided in this epoch—by military force.

Now, confronted with these facts of universal militarism and permanent war, that the biggest industry of all now is going to be war, the army and preparation of things for the army—confronted with these facts, what shall the revolutionary party do? Shall we stand aside and simply say we don't agree with the war, it is not our affair? No, we can't do that. We do not approve of this whole system of exploitation whereby private individuals can take possession of the means of production and enslave the masses. We are against that, but as long as we are not strong enough to put an end to capitalist exploitation in the factories, we adapt ourselves to reality. We don't abstain and go on individual strikes and separate ourselves from the working class. We go into the factories and try by working with the class to influence its development. We go with the workers and share all their experiences and try to influence them in a revolutionary direction.

The same logic applies to war. The great majority of the young generation will be dragged into the war. The great majority of these young workers will think at first that they are doing a good thing. For a revolutionary party to stand by and say, "We can tolerate exploitation in the factories, but not military exploitation"—that is to be completely illogical. To isolate ourselves from the mass of the proletariat which will be in the war is to lose all possibility to influence them.

We have got to be good soldiers. Our people must take upon themselves the task of defending the interests of the proletariat in the army in the same way as we try to protect their interests in the factory. As long as we can't take the factories away from the bosses we fight to improve the conditions there. Similarly, in the army. Adapting ourselves to the fact that the proletariat of this country is going to be the proletariat in arms we say, "Very well, Mr. Capitalist, you have decided it so and we were not strong enough to prevent it. Your war is not our war, but as long as the mass of the proletariat goes with it, we will go too. We will raise our own independent program in the army, in the military forces, in the same way as we raise it in the factories."

We say it is a good thing for the workers now to be trained in the use of arms. We are, in fact, in favor of compulsory military training of the proletariat. We are in favor of every union going on record for this idea. We want the proletariat to be well trained and equipped to play the military game. The only thing we object to is the leadership of a class that we don't trust. We don't want stoolpigeons of the boss as officers in our unions. Just as we don't want them as officers of our unions so we don't want them in the military forces. We are willing to fight Hitler. No worker wants to see that gang of fascist barbarians overrun this country or any country. But we want to fight fascism under a leadership that we can trust. We want our own officers—those who have shown themselves most devoted to their class, who have shown themselves to be the bravest and most loyal men on the picket line, those who are interested in the welfare of their fellow workers. These are precisely the type of people we want as officers. In the period when the whole working class youth is mobilized for war, those are the ones we want at the head of our battalions.

So we simply make our independent demands upon the government. We will join the war as long as the workers do. We will say frankly to the workers in the unions and shops: "We would like to throw over this whole business of capitalist exploitation—military as well as industrial—right now. But as long as you are not ready for that logical solution we will join with you, fight by your side, try to protect the men from useless waste of lives. All that we will do, but we retain one privilege—the right to express our opinion day in and day out: That you must not trust the leadership of your enemy class. Don't forget that the government in Washington is a concentrated representative of the same bosses that you have to fight every day in order to live. It is nothing but the executive committee of all bosses who, together and individually, act as the exploiters and oppressors of the working class. Put no more trust in that bosses' government than you do in the individual bosses at home."

We will fight all the time for the idea that the workers should have officers of their own choosing. That this great sum of money that is being appropriated out of the public treasury should be allocated in part to the trade unions for the setting up of their own military training camps under officers of their own selection; that we go into battle with the consciousness that the officer leading us is a man of our own flesh and blood who is not going to waste our lives, who is going to be true and loyal and who will represent our interests. And in that way, in the course of the development of the war, we will build up in the army a great class-conscious movement of workers with arms in their hands who will be absolutely invincible. Neither the German Hitler nor any other Hitler will be able to conquer them.

We will never let anything happen as it did in France. These commanding officers from top to bottom turned out to be nothing but traitors and cowards crawling on their knees before Hitler, leaving the workers absolutely helpless. They were far more concerned to save a part of their property than to fight the fascist invader. The myth about the war of "democracy against fascism" was exploded most shamefully and disgracefully. We must shout at the top of our voices that this is precisely what that gang in Washington will do because they are made of the same stuff as the French, Belgian, and Norwegian bourgeoisie. The French example is the great warning that officers from the class of bourgeois democrats can lead the workers only to useless slaughter, defeat, and betrayal.

The workers themselves must take charge of this fight against Hitler and anybody else who tries to invade their rights. That is the whole principle of the new policy that has been elaborated for us by Comrade Trotsky. The great difference between this and the socialist military policy in the past is that it is an *extension* of the old policy, an adaptation of *old principles* to *new conditions.* In our conversations with Comrade Trotsky he said he considered the great danger to our movement is pacifism. The taint of pacifism in our movement is in part due to the left-socialist tradition of antimilitarism. In part it is also a hangover from the past of our own movement. We said and those before us said that capitalism had outlived its usefulness. World economy is ready for socialism. But when the world war started in 1914 none of the parties had the idea that on the agenda stood the struggle for power. The stand of the best of them was essentially a protest against the war.

It did not occur even to the best Marxists that the time had come when the power must be seized by the workers in order to save civilization from degeneration. Even Lenin did not visualize the victory of the proletarian revolution as the immediate outcome of the war. Just a short time before the outbreak of the February revolution in Russia, Lenin wrote in Switzerland that his generation would most probably not see the socialist revolution. Even Lenin had postponed the revolution to the future, to a later decade. And a few months later it exploded in all its power in Russia. Acute revolutionary situations developed in one European country after another.

Trotsky pointed out to us that even such valiant and honest antiwar fighters as Debs and others like him conducted a fight against the war as a protest, but never once did it occur to them that the war was directly posing the question of the struggle for power. This protest against the war had a semipacifist character. Our movement was affected by this, especially when it was afflicted with the petty-bourgeois element in the party. You can recall that when we were discussing and arguing with them, the prevailing tendency among them was expressed about as follows: "We want to know, how can we keep out of the war; if the war starts how can we keep out of military service." They were primarily concerned about the various ways of evading the draft. More than one expressed the idea of escape to Mexico.

A group of heroic minorityite students in Chicago bought a small boat and sailed for Tahiti or some such place to hide out there until the war would be over. While millions of young proletarian youth are on the battlefields getting all kinds of experiences, facing all kinds of dangers, becoming hardened and ready for anything, these heroes will be basking in tropical sunshine and waiting for their day of destiny. I suppose when the time comes to make the revolution these people will probably sail back from Tahiti and say: "Here we are, boys, ready to lead you." It is not difficult to imagine the answer they will get from the boys who have already selected their leaders in the test of blood and fire.

Only those who go through hell with the soldiers will ever get close to their hearts and be able to influence them. All those with experience in the labor movement know it takes more than fancy speeches to gain influence with the workers. You must be with the workers. And nine times out of ten, I think every trade unionist will testify, the best asset you can have is to be a good worker in the shop. If the workers say, "He is the best mechanic among us; he does his full share of the work, not because he loves his boss but because he doesn't want to load the work on his fellow workers, etc."—if the workers say that about a man his influence is transferred over into the union, and when he gets up to say a word on the union floor he is listened to.

Absolutely the same psychology will prevail in the army. A man scared, ready to run—he will never be able to lead the worker-soldiers by making a few speeches from his retreat. It is necessary to go with the workers through all their experiences, through all the dangers, through the war. Out of the war will come the revolution, not otherwise. The war manifesto of the Fourth International[2] declares: We didn't want the war—we are not in favor of the war—but we are not afraid of the war. In this very war we will hammer out the cadres of revolutionary soldiers who will lead the struggle.

We must remember all the time that the workers of this epoch are not only workers; they are soldiers. These armies are no longer selected individuals, they are whole masses of the young proletarian youth who have been shifted from exploitation in the factories to exploitation in the military machine. They will be imbued by the psychology of the proletariat from which they came. But they will have guns in their hands and they will learn how to shoot them. They will gain confidence in themselves. They will be fired with the conviction that the only man who counts in this time of history is the man who has a gun in his hand and knows how to use it.

The great advantage of the workers is their mass strength. "Ye are many, they are few," said the poet Shelley. All the oppressed masses need is the will to power. All that is necessary to transform this madhouse of capitalism into a world of socialism is for the mass of the workers and the poor farmers to get the one simple general idea in their heads that they have the power and it is time now to use it. The capitalist class puts arms in the hands of the working class. That will, in the end, prove their undoing.

Now war, as I remarked in my speech last night, destroys a lot of things that are useful and valuable. It is a terrible overhead cost humanity has to pay for the delay in instituting socialism after capitalism has outlived its usefulness. This delay of the revolution has visited a terrible plague upon mankind that is going to destroy not thousands but millions of human lives. It will destroy great accumulations of material culture that took decades of human labor to create. As one small illustration take the city of London today. Here is a great city with centuries of accumulated achievements of mankind being pounded to dust. Nineteen consecutive days of bombing, and it stands to reason that the city is already partially in ruins.

The war destroys a great many things which will take much labor to replace. But war destroys some bad things also. War puts an end to all ambiguity and poses every question point-blank. There might have been room in the past for doubt as to how the workers can best solve the social problem. There were whole generations of workers deluded with the idea that the best way was the gradual peaceful inch-by-inch trade union and parliamentary struggle. By that method they built up great trade unions and political parties with millions of members and tens of millions of votes. These organizations looked very imposing in times of peace. They were very important. But what happened to them, to these organizations, that hadn't learned how to do anything but pay dues one day and vote the next day? The moment they got one violent military blow they were simply finished. They were designed for peace, not for war.

How can anyone respect reformist parliamentarians and vulgar trade unionists after what happened in Belgium, Norway, and France? Millions of people organized, the whole proletariat

2. The formal title of this document is the "Manifesto of the Fourth International on the Imperialist War and the Proletarian Revolution." Written by Trotsky, it was adopted by the Emergency Conference of the Fourth International, held May 1940 in New York. It was published in the *Socialist Appeal* of June 29, 1940, and is reprinted in *Writings of Leon Trotsky 1939–40* (New York: Pathfinder Press, 1973).

virtually organized; paying their dues; contracts signed with the bosses; all equipped with full staffs of well-paid officials and business agents in the unions; many of the officers of long standing, substantial people in the community both physically and socially; everything going fine until the situation changed from peace, which is outlived and outmoded, to war which is the logic of the present day. All these organizations for peace were crushed like eggshells. Nothing of organization remains but the small body of revolutionary people who realized that war was on the agenda and prepared themselves to function accordingly. There is nothing left of the Jouhaux unions in France. Of all his contracts, his business agents, his treasury and his pseudoimportance—nothing is left. One decree of a decrepit General Petain, "We don't want these unions any more," and the game was up.

And that great Socialist Party of Leon Blum, the party that mobilized millions of votes and looked so big in times of peace. The war struck one paralyzing blow, and the French Socialist Party went down and out like a sledged ox in a slaughterhouse. Leon Blum winds up under arrest at Vichy practically like a vagrant picked up on the street and thrown into jail. They are finished people, these reformists, men of the past. Now times call out for new men and a new type of party, a party built for war.

They used to make fun of the Fourth International—this little group talking about war and revolution, which looked insignificant beside their numerically imposing organizations. They boasted of their own importance when their movements were already marked for ignominious death. The Fourth Internationalists, on the other hand, had an idea which contemplated the coming events and they prepared to survive them. I have the great pleasure to report to you that we have received word from our comrades in France—we were all greatly disturbed about the fate of our comrades—we received word that they survived the war up to now, that our comrades had slipped through the nets and were not only safe, but were functioning in little groups and in contact with each other. Even those in jail during the war made their way out at the time when everyone was running, including the jailers. They took advantage of the general exodus and mixed themselves with it and are still there. I am sure the same thing is true in other countries. Those who prepare in their own minds for the war are best qualified to survive and grow stronger. The philistines used to sneer: "The Trotskyites—there are only a few hundred of them." True, but they still exist, more confident than ever. Leon Blum could not today rally together a few hundred Social Democrats in the whole of the occupied and unoccupied territories of France. They were not organized for war. That is why they succumbed to the first blow. Only those parties adapted for war, ready to carry things through to the very end, to a military solution of the problem—only they will be able to survive and conquer.

Now I come to another phase of this problem—the transformation of this society from a peace to a permanent war basis as it affects the trade union movement. One thing is absolutely clear: The days of the old routine reformist trade unions are numbered. They will not be able to survive the war as independent organizations. The trade union movement will be able to survive only insofar as it takes the road of resolute struggle against the capitalist system. The traditional nonfighting trade union in the United States will suffer the same fate as those in France, Belgium, and Norway, unless the revolutionary elements are able to vitalize them from within and inspire them with a spirit of revolutionary struggle.

And similarly the work of our own comrades in these unions has to undergo a change. We ourselves have been affected by the whole general perspective of long years of slow progress. Ninety percent of our trade union activity in the past had to do with little agreements and combinations with progressive and nonprogressive elements in order to gain a few inches in the economic struggle. We have to continue the struggle for immediate demands in the trade unions. It is necessary to continue all the patient day-to-day work, to guard every gain, watch every contract. In this work we collaborate with everybody—whether progressive or reactionary—in the daily interests of the workers.

But at the same time we have to realize, and make the workers realize increasingly, that there is not going to be the possibility in America for a long period of growth and stability of conservative trade unions. Such visions of the trade union bureaucrats represent a mirage. They are thinking in terms of the world of yesterday. America is going into the war with express train speed. The unions will be confronted with this alternative—they will either turn sharply, develop a revolutionary policy, begin a struggle for power hand in hand with the revolutionary wing of the army, or they will cease to exist. At best they will be relegated to mere appendages of the government, having no independent power. It is in this tone that we must speak louder in the unions and in the factories.

We have to look over our own party. All those comrades of the party who are in the conservative trade unions, who have in one way or another begun to succumb to that stifling atmosphere, who have begun to develop tendencies to avoid struggle and let well enough alone—all those party comrades who are sinking into that quagmire must be pulled up short. They must be reminded that the one most important thing in this epoch is to build a revolutionary party. Only a revolutionary party can inspire the unions to meet the test of the new times. We have to insist more than ever upon the party responsibility of every comrade.

Your strength in the unions is the strength of your party. Don't forget it. All these collaborators of the day; all these trade union militants who look so good in normal, peaceful times, who are good enough for a local strike but have no general concepts—how quickly these people can be transformed under the pressure of the social crisis. Only those will be able to stand up in the coming period who are fortified by great general ideas—not otherwise. You will have some bad disappointments if you believe for one moment that a man who has not yet broken his allegiance to capitalism in general will be able to stand up under the pressure of war. Not at all. Some of our comrades have already had some very painful experiences along this line. Those people can stand up under pressure who have anticipated pressure and can see beyond it to the goal of the new society.

Above all, we have to develop our party as a party of a new type. All the old party organizations were built for peace. They can't survive in this new epoch of universal militarism. The only party that can survive is the one that adapts itself to universal militarism and aims at the struggle for power. It can't be a sprawling, slow-moving, undisciplined organization. It must be highly centralized, with iron discipline in its ranks. It must be able to function, if necessary, under all kinds of persecution. It needs a strong leadership. We have to select out of the ranks tested and trusted people for leading positions and give them full authority. Only so will we be able to move fast and strike hard as a united, disciplined organization.

During the past year we made gains of historic significance. While Comrade Trotsky was still alive to help us we had the possibility of fighting out in our ranks a fundamental struggle which prepared us to build the party of a new type. We had people who set up a great howl about "bureaucratism." They wanted a party where one could do as he pleased; have the honor and badge of the Fourth International without any personal responsibility. And if the party at any time demanded anything of them, they raised a hue and cry about the injustices they were suffering. When these milksops cried about "bureaucratism" they really meant to protest against centralism and discipline. I thought many times, and I said many times to comrades, that the grievance the real proletarian revolutionists in the party held against us was that the accusations of the petty-bourgeois minority were not even half true.

The workers in the party want discipline. They want centralization. They want a party that doesn't permit anybody to make a fool of it. They want a party that demands of every leader that he put his whole life, his whole time, including his personal life, at the disposal of the party. Our movement is not playing for fun. It aims to take power in this country. For that we need a hard party, a firm party. It is a great advantage for us that we got rid of this petty-bourgeois opposition. We improved the composition of our party; we got rid of a lot of windbagism. We got rid of a lot of deadwood and are now in a position to take some real steps forward.

It is time now to bring the struggle with the petty-bourgeois faction to a definitive conclusion. You know the minority refused to accept the decisions of the convention. In order to be perfectly fair and give them time to think it over we allowed them a period of nearly six months of suspension, not expulsion, to accept the decisions of the convention majority and restore their party standing. They haven't availed themselves of this exceptional concession. In the meantime they have developed politically far away from us as a typical left-socialist, pacifist clique. Their ideological leader, Burnham, has renounced socialism. We haven't anything in common with them politically. They have more than used up the credit balance of probation we allowed them. We don't want any ambiguity and confusion in the public mind regarding them and us as two wings of the same movement. It is the unanimous recommendation of the National Committee that the suspension of the convention minority be changed to unconditional expulsion at this conference.

Our second recommendation is that we begin a closer checking up of party responsibility, discipline, and loyalty without permitting any panic in the ranks. We have two things to fear now, and we must steer a course between them. One is carelessness and irresponsibility, and the other is supercaution, a spy hunt, and general jitteriness in the organization. The second is by far the greater danger. We are proposing a measure that will tend to eliminate both of them. I have talked about a party that says it will stop at nothing short of the struggle for power and will fight to the end to overthrow capitalism. Such a party cannot exist with a leadership that is scared for itself or afflicted with nervousness of any kind.

We are under great pressure and will be under still greater pressure. We know that we are dealing with a murderous machine in Stalin's GPU. We know that Comrade Trotsky was not the first, and probably will not be the last, victim of this murder machine. Our party must also expect persecutions from the Wall Street government. Realizing all this, some comrades have wondered if we couldn't do something to preserve our leaders from danger—perhaps put them on ice, I suppose. From the very first hour since the assassination of Trotsky we have conducted a resolute struggle against this psychology. Scared people are not going to be able to lead anybody. One who takes part in the revolutionary movement by that fact has to encounter certain risks. Millions of young American workers are going to be thrown into the war. Many of them will lose their lives. These are dangerous times. But they are dangerous for everybody, not only for us. Revolutionists must face the hazards of our time, and not fear them. A good one-half or three-fourths of the objective of persecutions and assassinations is to terrorize others. Nobody can terrorize us. We will try to be careful, but not afraid.

I had an interesting talk with Comrade Dobbs about these two dangers of nervousness and carelessness. He agreed with me that jitteriness is worse than carelessness. "A careless man," he said, "is good as long as he lasts, but a jittery man is no good at any time." That is profoundly true. We must use the necessary caution and save ourselves as much as possible. But if you create an impression in front of the workers that you fear the hazards of the struggle you can never lead them. You can do without a lot of things in a revolutionary party but you can't get along without courage.

Now then, on the other hand, we have to check up on carelessness. We want to know who is who in the party. We don't want to have any universal spy hunts because that is worse than the disease it tries to cure. Comrade Trotsky said many times that mutual suspicion among comrades can greatly demoralize a movement. On the other hand, there is a certain carelessness in the movement as a hangover from the past. We haven't probed deeply enough into the past of people even in leading positions—where they came from, how they live, whom they are married to, etc. Whenever in the past such questions—elementary for a revolutionary organization—were raised, the petty-bourgeois opposition would cry, "My God, you are invading the private lives of comrades!" Yes, that is precisely what we were doing, or more correctly, threatening to do—nothing ever came of it in the past. If we had checked up on such matters a little more carefully we might have prevented some bad things in the days gone by.

We are proposing that we set up a control commission in the party. We are fully ready for that now. This will be a body of responsible and authoritative comrades who will take things in hand and carry every investigation to a conclusion one way or the other. This will do away with indiscriminate suspicions on the one side and undue laxity on the other. The net result can only be to reassure the party and strengthen its vigilance. We think the whole party now, with the petty-bourgeois riffraff out of our way, is ready for the appointment of such a body.

We have to strengthen our professional staff. We don't pretend to be a party of glorified rank and filers. The only reason we haven't got ten, twenty, thirty, or forty more people devoting their whole time, their whole energy, to the party is that we lack the resources for it. We need more money to engage more functionaries full time. This conference has to decide how big a forward step in this direction it feels able to take. We are not coming here with a proposal for specific quotas. We want each delegation to confer and decide what they can raise in, say, two months' time. Our general plan is that, as several branches have suggested, we raise a "Trotsky Memorial Fund" to build the party. We think it is a good plan. If it meets with the approval of the conference we can adopt a resolution to that effect.

We want to build the party henceforth in a more balanced way than in the past. In the past we gave an inordinate amount of our resources to the press. We had to do that. Propaganda had to go ahead of organization and prepare the way for it. In the next period we want to bend the stick a little for organization on the general principle of dollar for dollar—one for press and one for organization.

Since the last convention we have taken certain steps in this direction. You comrades in the auto field know we maintained qualified comrades in the field continuously. The same is true in other fields. The important step taken in St. Paul will have a national meaning for all of us. It shows the growing tendency of serious comrades to regard the party as the most important thing of all. I refer to the action of Comrade [Grace] Carlson in resigning her civil service job and accepting a post as party organizer. This is a good example. We should raise as much money as possible to put to work for the party on a full-time basis a great number of qualified party workers. It is appalling how many capable people we have who have to devote only a small portion of their time to the party because the necessary job of making a living takes so much of their time and energy. That is all right for the old party, but not for us.

3. Summary Speech On Military Policy

September 28, 1940

These excerpts from Cannon's summary of the discussion of his report on proletarian military policy at the SWP Plenum-Conference in September 1940 were published in the *Socialist Appeal* of October 26, 1940. The stenographic transcript was corrected by Cannon and this is the only version now extant.

In summary, I will take up the questions in reverse order of their importance. The Stalinist question is a question of tactics and is by far secondary to the main problem of our military policy. Nevertheless, it has considerable importance. The discussion has shown one thing clearly, that there is in our ranks today very little misunderstanding of the fundamental aspects of the question of Stalinism. That is far different from the situation a year ago.

It is important to remember in this connection that our fight with the petty-bourgeois ideologist Burnham began over the question of the characterization of the Stalinists. It will be recalled that almost two years ago, at the time of the auto crisis, the first real clash with Burnham and his satellites was precipitated by their attitude toward the split in the auto union. Despite the fact that the great mass of the auto workers were going with the CIO—and thereby at that time with the Stalinists—Burnham wanted to divert our support to Martin, even in the direction of the AFL, on the theory that the Stalinists were not really a part of the labor movement.[1]

The thing came to a head again over the invasion of Poland when Burnham wanted the party to take an outright stand against the Red Army on the theory that the Soviet Union is "imperialist." The issue grew sharper with the Finnish invasion.[2] Then, when Browder was indicted by the government on an obviously trumped-up passport charge, Burnham opposed any defense of Browder on the ground that he did not represent any legitimate labor tendency. He overlooked the fact that as an agent of the Soviet bureaucracy, Browder indirectly represented the biggest labor organization in the world, that of the Soviet state.

Burnham in this case was fundamentally motivated by the pressure of democratic imperialism in the United States. The Stalinists were for the moment at loggerheads with the Roosevelt administration, and the "intransigence" of the Burnham faction against the Stalinists simply represented a cheap and easy form of adaptation to the clamor of the bourgeois democrats. Their opinions were shaped against any kind of recognition of the CP as a tendency in the labor movement. We haven't heard such an expression here today from anybody.

---

1. In January 1939 the United Auto Workers split into two factions, one led by Homer Martin, which called a convention in Detroit, and one led by Walter Reuther and the Stalinists, which called a convention in Cleveland. Burnham, who was acting national secretary of the SWP while Cannon was working in France for the Fourth International, proposed to support the Martin forces even though they were headed for a break from the CIO and reintegration into the AFL. His policy was rejected by the party's auto fraction which advocated support to the CIO gathering in Cleveland.

2. Two weeks after the German invasion of Poland, after German troops had encircled Warsaw, Russian troops invaded the country from the east on September 17, 1939. This led to the partition of Poland between Nazi Germany and the Soviet Union. Moscow then demanded territorial concessions from Finland. When these were refused, the Soviet Union bombed Helsinki on November 30, 1939, and sent an invasion force against the Finnish Mannerheim Line. After a series of initial defeats at the hands of the Finnish army, the Russians staged a massive assault that broke through the defenses. An armistice on Russian terms was signed on March 13, 1940.

Comrade Morton gave us a speech here today which was very informative about his experiences in the CIO union of Electrical and Radio Workers. He said something that we must heed—that the Stalinist rank and file in this union do not distinguish between us and the red-baiters, that they tend to regard us as a part of the general reaction. If that is true, we must take heed and correct such an impression.

First of all in the press. Our press must have a more precise line, a line that cannot be misunderstood. On each and every important occasion it must be made clear to the readers of our press that, while we are irreconcilably hostile to Stalinism—more now than ever before—we recognize that it does represent a current in the international labor movement, and as such we defend it against the attacks of the red-baiters. Our press is our most important medium of clarification. But the press campaign must be reinforced by united-front proposals to the Stalinists on suitable occasions which provide us the possibility of approaching the Stalinist workers and advancing the revolutionary cause.

Of course we must not forget that the present line of the Stalinists is only a year old. I will be very much surprised if it has another year to last. It was the opinion of Comrade Trotsky that Moscow is already turning in the direction of the Allies, and particularly in the direction of the U.S. The Soviet Union is caught in a vise between Japan on the one hand and Nazi Germany on the other. If the Axis powers suffer military reverses, if American imperialism moves more aggressively against them, Stalin is very apt to shift over into the orbit of democratic imperialism led by the U.S. You can be sure, in this event, that the line of the Stalinists in this country will very soon change accordingly.

Such a prospect does not speak against approaching the Stalinists with united-front proposals on the basis of their present line. The more deeply we penetrate their ranks on a united-front basis in connection with their pseudoradical policy, the better possibility we will have to influence the workers against the swing back to bourgeois democracy and the Popular Front ballyhoo when the bureaucrats make the switch.[3] Such an overnight reversal of policy will inevitably provoke a crisis in the CP. We should strive to be in a good position to influence the revolting elements—and this time they will be the best, not the worst—in a revolutionary direction. Everything speaks in favor of a serious, carefully worked out, realistic, and practical united-front policy. It is obligatory that we devote a properly proportioned amount of our time and energy to the Stalinists.

But let us not go crazy over this issue. One could notice a slight tendency in the discussion to overemphasize this secondary tactical question at the expense of our main business, that of orienting the party for a military policy which has nothing in common with the policy of the CP. We must not begin to dance around this question like jitterbugs. We must not paint up the CP and make it appear to be something different than it is. We should correct our one-sided policy of the past, but not overcorrect it. There is a danger of our making a sort of panacea of united fronts with the CP.

I got a little bit scared today when I heard some of the speeches. I had a horrific vision of the party pacing back and forth and around in circles and so preoccupied with CP united fronts that we would not have anything else to do. Whiskey looks like tea but cannot be consumed so freely without bad effects. This business of united fronting with the CP is also a strong medicine. We must condition ourselves to the self-control of the man who can take it or leave it alone. Don't forget that Stalinism is an agency of imperialism no less than the bureaucracy of Green and Lewis. It is only another variety. Like the traitors of traditional reformism, the Stalinist bureaucracy also tries to defend its own interests against the imperialists. It is this contradiction in each case which opens the way for the united-front tactic. But never forget that the main blows of Stalinism are directed against the international working class.

Some comrades raised the question a little falsely, I think, today. They asked: "Who represents the main danger right now? What is the main danger?

3. The Comintern and the American CP abandoned their radical stance the day after the German invasion of the USSR in June 1941. Thereafter they sought alliances with liberal bourgeois politicians in the imperialist democracies and subordinated all class-struggle issues to the campaign to produce for the war effort. In the United States the CP openly supported Roosevelt and advocated a no-strike pledge in industry for the duration of the war.

Is it represented by the out-and-out patriots of the Green and Hillman type? Or is it the CP?" And they came to the conclusion that it is the jingoes, not the CP. That only shows that the CP is an even greater danger than we realize; its duplicity creates a little confusion even in our ranks. Stalinism is the greatest danger to the international revolutionary movement precisely because the Stalinists discredit the great Russian Revolution and sow confusion and demoralization in the ranks of the proletarian vanguard which had rejected traditional reformism. A momentary diplomatic maneuver of Stalin—itself inspired by treachery—must not create the impression in our ranks that perhaps the CP is not as great a danger today as it was yesterday. Stalinism is treacherous to the core. It is the main obstacle in the path of the proletarian revolution. Our attitude towards Stalinism is that of irreconcilable war. We can conceive of the united front only in the sense of a flank attack against our most perfidious enemy.

The crux of the Stalinism question can be summarized under these five points:

First, where is the main reservoir of future recruiting for the revolutionary party in this country? Is it in the ranks of the CP? Or is it in the ranks of the half-awakened working class in this country that has not been defeated and that has not been corrupted? We consider it self-evident that the main reservoir for recruiting is in the ranks of these non-Stalinist workers. It is only incidental recruiting that can be expected out of the Stalinist party. This is also an important source, but it is not the most important. Every move we make in regard to Stalinism has to be weighed by the criterion whether it will help or harm our possibility of recruiting in the ranks of the young, uneducated but militant proletariat.

Second, we have to be more careful, more precise, and more militant in distinguishing our criticism of Stalinism from the attacks of the red-baiting jingoes. We must begin in earnest to emphasize this difference in our press. We have to clarify the whole problem for our membership, for our readers, for the Stalinist workers who sometimes read our press. We must make it clear on every occasion, sharply and categorically, that we have nothing in common with red-baiting attacks on the Stalinists by the capitalist newspapers, the old-style labor skates, and the Social Democrats.

The third point: Our chief problem in the political field is neither blocs with the Stalinists against the progressive jingoists nor blocs with the progressive jingoists against the Stalinists on incidental day-to-day problems in the unions. Our main problem is to bring forward and develop more clearly and precisely the independent line of the revolutionary party.

The fourth point: In the course of development, we will look for and take advantage of suitable and practical opportunities for united-front actions directed toward the CP workers. But this must not become the dominant side of our activity with regard to them. We will write ninety-nine attacks against the perfidies of the CP to one move that we will make in the direction of the united front with them. And even at the moment of approaching them for a united front, we will never relax for a moment, nor allow any worker to get an idea for a moment that this tactic signifies any kind of reconciliation, or any softening of our attitude towards the treacherous murder machine of Stalinism.

The fifth point: I am not as optimistic as some comrades about the number and quality of the recruits we will get from the CP. There are some members in our organization—quite a few—who came to us from the Stalinists in recent times and who have developed into good revolutionists. We've also had the experience of recruiting Stalinists more than once, more than ten times, who tried to become revolutionists, but who had become so demoralized, and to some extent so corrupted, by the CP that they were not assimilable. One of the greatest curses of Stalinism is the enormous demoralization, disorientation, and corruption of the minds of the advanced militant workers it has brought about.

Now I come to the decisive and basic question with which our party occupies itself, the question of military policy. During the discussion some comrades have asked: Was our old line wrong? Does the resolution represent a completely new departure and a reversal of the policy of the past? It is not quite correct to say that the old line was wrong. It was a program devised for the fight against war in time of peace. Our fight against war under conditions of peace was correct as far as it went. But it was not adequate. It must be extended. The old principles, which remain unchanged, must be applied concretely to the new conditions of permanent war and universal militarism. We didn't visualize, nobody visualized, a world situation in which whole countries would be conquered by fascist armies. The workers don't want to be conquered by foreign invaders, above all by fascists. They require a program of military struggle against foreign invaders which assures their class independence. That is the gist of the problem.

Many times in the past we were put at a certain disadvantage; the demagogy of the Social Democrats against us was effective to a certain extent. They said, "You have no answer to the question of how to fight against Hitler, how to prevent Hitler from conquering France, Belgium, etc." (Of course their program was very simple—the suspension of the class struggle and complete subordination of the workers to the bourgeoisie. We have seen the results of this treacherous policy.) Well, we answered in a general way, the workers will first overthrow the bourgeoisie at home and then they will take care of invaders. That was a good program, but the workers did not make the revolution in time. Now the two tasks must be telescoped and carried out simultaneously.

The main thing is that we must operate not under the old conditions of peace, but under the new conditions of universal militarism and war. We cannot avoid the new circumstances; we must adapt our tactics to them. In times of strike, we urge the workers to stay out of a plant. But when the majority decides to go back, we have to go back with them and accept with them, for the time being, the exploitation of the bosses. Sometimes the defeat of a strike goes so far as not only to smash a legitimate union but to drive the workers into the bosses' company union. We are against company unions; but if the workers are driven into them we go along and try to work there in the interests of the proletariat. Analogous tactics must be applied also in questions of war and militarism.

We had a great Marxist for a teacher, and a part of his genius was his never-failing application of Marxist tactics. He always took the existing situation, in its totality, as the point of departure. The Bolsheviks set out in 1917 to overthrow the whole capitalist world. They did overthrow the Russian bourgeoisie, but the other countries remained under the domination of the international capitalist class. So, at a certain point, the Bolsheviks drew the balance and said: "Here is the situation as it exists in reality. We cannot overthrow the other imperialist bandits at present. The workers are not yet ready. Therefore, let us open trade relations with the imperialist countries, gain a little breathing space, and overthrow them tomorrow." Comrade Trotsky was prompted to elaborate and extend our tactics by the new situation in the world. A party which fails to adapt itself to this situation, to existing war, can play no role whatsoever.

One comrade here tried to justify a policy of antimilitarism. His remarks were, to my opinion, a reminiscence of departed days. Antimilitarism was all right when we were fighting against war in times of peace. But here you have a new situation of universal militarism. It is obvious that all over the world everything is going to be settled not by mass meetings, not by petitions, not by strikes, not even by mass demonstrations in the streets. Everything is going to be settled by military means, with arms in hand. So, can we now be antimilitarists? By no means! Just the contrary. We must say: "All right, the situation, not of our making, is that military force decides. There is only one thing left for the workers to do. That is to learn how to be good fighters with modern weapons." So we antimilitarists of yesterday become positive militarists today. The comrade who tries to represent our position today as still antimilitarist is, in my opinion, decidedly wrong.

I raised this question in our conversations with Comrade Trotsky. After he had elaborated his ideas, I put the question to him and asked him to make his answer as sharp and categoric as possible. I asked: "Can we call ourselves militarists?" And he said, "Yes. It might not be tactically advisable to begin with such a proclamation, but if the pacifists accuse you of it, if you are accused of being a militarist, you take the platform and say, 'Yes, I am a proletarian revolutionary militarist.'"[4] This

4. Cannon is quoting here from memory. Trotsky's exact words were: "Yes—in a certain sense—we are proletarian so-

doesn't contradict the somewhat different attitude we took in somewhat different times—when the possibility of preventing war by revolution could not be excluded.

Was the fight of the social-pacifist elements against conscription right in this last period? No, it was not right. It overlooked realities and sowed illusions. The workers were for conscription. The conscription bill was carried without any serious opposition whatsoever. The fight as we conducted it, for workers' control, was 100 percent correct. We are positively for conscription, but we do not want conscription of the workers by the bosses. We want conscription of the workers by a workers' organization. If some horrified muddlehead of a pacifist asks: "Do you really mean it? Do you want to compel every worker to take up arms and learn how to use arms?" We answer, "Yes, that is exactly what we mean." How do we justify such compulsion? By the necessities of the class struggle which justify everything. There is nothing new in such an attitude. A certain amount of compulsion has always been invoked by the labor movement against the backward, the slackers.

For example, trade unions always strive to make membership compulsory. The intelligent, loyal, and serious workers join the union voluntarily. Then they say to the backward, to the ignorant, and to the scab-hearted: Join if you will, peacefully, but join this union or else stay out of that factory. That's compulsion for you, my boy. We cannot allow your ignorance or mistaken conception of individual interest to interfere with the class interests as a whole. What is a picket line? Well, some that I have seen at least, had aspects of extraordinary persuasion. I have seen picket lines of such a nature that if anyone wanted to argue about it, he didn't even get a chance to argue. He either stayed out or got knocked out. Compulsion in the class war is a class necessity. We didn't invent it. It must be applied also to military training.

An interesting question, asked by some workers, was reported here: "How can you tell the workers to put themselves under the control of the unions for military training when the unions are controlled by people like Lewis and Green and Hillman?" Well, if we wait until the unions are led by the Fourth International, we lose all sense of the dynamics of their development. Green and Lewis and their similars—the whole upper bureaucracy of the labor movement at present—are agents of the capitalists in the labor movement, but they are not the same thing as the bosses. Their sole base of existence is the labor movement; and in spite of all the bureaucratism of the unions, they are subject to certain pressures, certain controls from below. When the worsening of conditions, supplemented by our agitation, raises a wave of radicalization in the masses, the workers will solve the problem of leadership in the workers' regiments as well as in the unions.

We always take the workers' organizations as they are. We join them as they are, support them as they are, try to remodel them from within. Of course, the very idea of a Lewis or a Green heading the military instruction of workers is farfetched. Correctly understood, our fight for military training under trade union control is a mortal struggle against the reformist, nonfighting bureaucracy. The adoption of our policy, or even a strong movement in favor of it, would spell the doom of the present leaders. Nobody would believe these scoundrels are fit for such a serious enterprise as the instruction of workers for military action.

In 1917, following February, the soviets of Petrograd and Moscow were controlled by the Social Democrats and the Social Revolutionaries, that is, men of the stripe of Lewis and Green, Hillman and Dubinsky; no better and no worse. In spite of that, because the soviets embraced the workers, Lenin raised the slogan: "All power to the soviets." In the course of that fight for all power to the soviets, the Bolsheviks won to their side the majority of the workers. And almost coincidentally with the uprising, the workers threw out the Mensheviks and Social Revolutionaries and placed the Bolsheviks at their head. That's the way things have to be conceived in this question also.

The question of the referendum on war in connection with compulsory military training was raised by one of the comrades. This question was propounded to the Old Man in a letter from Gold-

cialist revolutionary militarists. Possibly we should not use it at first. Wait until we are called militarists by Thomas or someone like that, and then make a polemical reply. Thomas has called us militarists. Yes, we can be called militarists in a certain sense. Then we can use it with this explanation" (*Writings 1939–40*, p. 343 [2012 printing]).

man, and answered by him. The Old Man said: "I don't see why we should drop the demand for a referendum on war. Before they actually enter the war, an agitation for a people's referendum is an excellent means of showing up their fake democracy."[5] It is a means of agitation against them. It is not so simple and automatic; one does not exclude the other.

Comrade Trotsky also answered the question whether our slogan of workers' defense guards is superseded by our military policy. He said he did not see why. He thought they were interrelated. Of course at the present time, the emphasis is entirely on the question of penetrating the military organizations. But, as the crisis develops, all kinds of reactionary attacks will be made on the unions. Gangs will be organized to break them up. The union members will be under the constant necessity to protect themselves. The workers must be on guard to protect their unions. The slogan of workers' defense guards can be raised at an appropriate time, not in contradiction to our military policy, but in correlation with it.

On the question of the role of women in the party after conscription. We must not get the idea that all our people will be in the army. Roughly speaking, the same percentage of our party will be in the army as the percentage of their class of the same generation. We have a young party. You will learn from Comrade Dobbs's comprehensive organization report that the average age of our party is twenty-nine years. This means that perhaps a majority of our men comrades are going to be in the army sooner or later. Some of our leading people will be taken out and in their places women comrades will come forward. We already have indications that we are not without resources in this field. And don't forget we have a few old codgers who are beyond the draft age. Maybe the party can make use of them. Lenin once said, and I always sympathized with him, that when a revolutionist reaches the age of fifty he should be shot. When men get older they usually get tired and conservative. But there are exceptions to all laws, and we come in under the exceptions. If we have the correct policy, and if we have the conception that every member of our party is potentially a leader, potentially a general in the army of the revolution, we will not lack leadership.

Comrade Birchman mentioned the question of the Negro workers in the militarization. Our attitude toward the Negroes in war, like our attitude toward all other questions, is the same as in times of peace. Our line is the class line. We stand for absolutely unconditional equality for every race and nationality. That's a cardinal principle of communism. We have to fight for and defend this principle under all conditions, including the conditions of militarism.

How do we work in a conscript army, someone asked. We work the same way as in a shop. Indeed, the main purpose of industry now is supplying the army. Where would you draw the line? There is hardly an industry that won't be mobilized either for the manufacture or transportation of materials for the army. The masses are in the army, or working to supply the army. The workers are subjected to military exploitation. We go in and defend the interests of the slaves of military exploitation, just as we go into the factory and fight against capitalist exploitation there. Our basic line everywhere is the class line.

The second point is to be careful, cautious. Make no putsches, make no premature moves that expose us and separate us from the masses. Go with the masses. Be with the masses, just as the Bolsheviks were in Kerensky's army.

Why can't we do that here? And how otherwise can we do it? How otherwise, in a world dominated by militarism, can we see our way to world salvation except through military means? And how can we get these military means except by penetrating the army as it exists?

We have one great assurance. I repeat what I said at the mass meeting. We have our opportunity before us in this country. Even if war is declared and a military dictatorship is instituted, even if all kinds of repressive measures are decreed—we must always remember that

5. The letter Cannon is referring to, dated July 9, 1940, is reprinted in *Writings 1939–40* under the title "On Conscription." The precise wording of the paragraph Cannon quotes from memory is: "I don't see any reason why we should renounce the slogan of a people's referendum on the war. It is a very good slogan to unmask the futility of *their* democracy in such a vital question as the war."

a dictatorship of the police and military forces, instituted by fiat, cannot be the same thing as a fascist dictatorship based on a mass movement mobilized over years of time after the workers have muffed their chance to take power. Before fascism can come in this country on a mass basis, according to the historical law elucidated by Comrade Trotsky, the great mass radicalization of the workers will take place. The workers here, as everywhere, will have the first chance to take power. That is all we need. We will have our chance, and we will not miss it.

4. Militarism and Workers' Rights

Published November 30, 1940

This was the second of three articles in the *Socialist Appeal.*

Our resolution on military policy proclaims no new principle, but attempts to apply the old principles of Bolshevism to the new conditions. In line with all the programmatic documents of the Fourth International, the resolution says: "The imperialist war is not our war and the militarism of the capitalist state is not our militarism. . . . We are against the war as a whole just as we are against the rule of the class that conducts it, and never under any circumstances vote to give them any confidence in their conduct of the war or preparations for it—not a man, not a cent, not a gun with our support. Our war is the war of the working class against the capitalist order." (*Socialist Appeal,* October 5.)

So much for the principled position of Trotskyism, which alone among all the tendencies in the international labor movement remains consistently revolutionary in times of war as well as in times of peace. But, despite our opposition, we have the militarism and tomorrow we will have the war in full scope. That does not change our principle, but it imposes upon us a certain line of tactics since we do not want to remain aloof as mere oppositionists. We do not rest content with general opposition to capitalism and general advocacy of the socialist revolution and simply repeat our ultimate aims as a set of soul-saving formulas. We seek in each and every situation to devise the tactical slogans around which we may carry on continuous and effective agitation leading toward the goal. The problem of the hour is to find a realistic basis for our irreconcilable class agitation in the arena of war and militarism which now, and for a whole epoch, will dominate the world. This is the aim of our resolution on military policy.

Our military program is intended as a program of agitation. In order to be effective such a program must take into account not only the objective circumstance (the epoch of militarism), but also the present consciousness and mood of the workers. The American workers are against war, they are fearful of war, yet they are convinced in their bones that it is unavoidable and that the millions of young men who are being drafted and sent up for military training are destined to be cannon fodder. A comrade writes from Buffalo: "A large section of the working class, and perhaps all of it subconsciously, regards the draft for what it is—going to war. Even the National Guardsmen who left town last month were accompanied by weeping mothers and sweethearts."

The workers like to hear the promises of Roosevelt and Willkie that American boys will not be sent into foreign wars, but the great mass of them do not believe a word of it. Neither do they believe the isolationist and pacifist liars who say it is possible under capitalism to "keep America out of war."

The workers are profoundly impressed by the fate of the European countries which have been overrun by Hitler's army. They hate and fear fascism. So far they see it incarnated only in the foreign foe, and they are ready if necessary to go to war against it, especially if the war is presented to them, as it surely will be, in the guise of "defense" against a "foreign" attack. Facing the prospect of war it is obvious to the serious-minded workers that military training is needed. That is why they submitted universally to conscription; without enthusiasm, it is true, but also without any serious opposition. This attitude of the rank and file of the American working class is a thousand times more practical and realistic than that of the pacifist muddleheads who proclaim the necessity of socialism and yet oppose compulsory military training—in a world gone mad with militarism.

Our military resolution takes the foregoing circumstances, objective and subjective, as its point of departure and attempts to show the workers how to carry on their daily struggle against the bosses over into the new field of militarism.

The American workers have made great advances in the last six years. Millions of new recruits have been drawn into the trade union movement for the first time. They have had to fight every inch of the way to gain the smallest concessions, and then to fight all over again, and continuously, to keep them. In the course of these fights the workers have developed a fervent devotion to their unions. They have learned to hate and distrust the bosses who directly exploit them and the police and local authorities who help the bosses.

In strike after strike the militant American workers have demonstrated that they have no fear of direct clashes with these local authorities and police. But in their overwhelming majority, the workers still think of the national government as something different. They respect it and at the same time they fear it as a remote power, which cannot be combatted. The average militant trade unionist, who considers a battle with local cops as a part of the day's business in a strike, is inclined to flinch away from any conflict with "the man with the whiskers," the popular name for the federal government and its police agents.

"You can't strike against the government"—this is not only the dictum of Roosevelt, but also the feeling of the great majority of workers at the present time. Some of them think they have a right to do it, as was shown by the strikes against the WPA,* but the great majority approach any prospect of a conflict with the federal government with the feeling that "you can't get away with it." These illusions of the workers are the ace card up the sleeve of the American imperialists.

A letter from a Toledo comrade highlights this attitude: "I and other comrades have noticed in agitating at employment offices on our military program the following response. While workers agreed that military training is needed and express distrust of the methods of the present conscription bill, they are extremely skeptical of the *possibility* of getting the unions to control training or of winning union conditions in the army. 'You can't strike against the government.' 'If you agitate in the army you will be shot.' 'You need trained military men to have good training.' These are the three most common answers. . . . Even some of the politically developed sympathizers of the party say that our program has value only in an *agitational* sense but that it cannot be accomplished." (My emphasis.)

By such expressions—which are quite typical—the workers express the mistaken opinion that the class struggle ends when they leave the arena of the union and the factory and enter the new arena of war and militarism. They do not anticipate in advance the tremendous new experiences which are destined to make such a powerful impression on their minds, and that in a comparatively short time. Even the reported remarks of some of our sympathizers to the effect that our program "cannot be accomplished," reveal an unconscious tendency to accept as permanent a situation which is radically changing before our eyes and which will continue to change with increasing speed and sweep. Respect for the status quo is out of tune with the times. War and militarism will uproot the workers from the old environment in which their present convictions were formed, impose new and terrible experiences upon them, and compel them to think in new terms.

The workers have yet to learn that the government, which now appears as a sacrosanct institu-

* In the summer of 1939 Roosevelt ordered massive layoffs in the Works Progress Administration, the New Deal public works program established to provide jobs for the unemployed. At the same time, hours were lengthened and pay was cut. Some 500,000 of the 2.5 million workers affected went out in a spontaneous nationwide strike in July. The largest and most effective strike of the WPA workers took place in Minneapolis under the leadership of the Federal Workers Section of Teamsters Local 544. A police attack on massed pickets on July 14 left one worker dead and seventeen wounded. This was followed by grand jury indictments against more than 150 strikers for "conspiracy" to deprive people of employment under the WPA. Three trials held in Minneapolis in October and November resulted in thirty-two convictions. The three longest sentences were handed down against Max Geldman, Ed Palmquist, and Leslie Wachter, who each served one year in the federal penitentiary.

tion standing above the classes, is in reality the executive committee of all the bosses. Experience under the conditions of militarism and war, aided by our agitation, will teach this necessary lesson in the coming period. In the course of these developments our program, if we present it with simplicity and clarity, will not only have success in an "agitational sense"; the awakening workers will pass over its extremely modest and elementary demands as advancing troops pass over a bridge to a new point of vantage.

The army of conscription will be different from the comparatively small standing army we have known, and the change will be all for the better. The "volunteer" army has been recruited for the most part from the ranks of the half-starved unemployed. They have been isolated from the people, helpless and unable to get a hearing. It was customary to think of these soldiers as having no human rights whatever, no means of redress. "If you agitate in the army you will be shot." Contemptible are those opponents of compulsory military service who, at the same time, directly or indirectly support this monstrous militarism of the "volunteer" variety.

In the army of conscription the situation will be radically changed. It will consist of millions of young workers—the proletariat in arms! They are accustomed to certain rights. Their mighty numbers will confer a sense of power upon them. It will not be possible to treat them like cattle for any length of time without creating a profound discontent in their ranks.

Our military transitional program is not for a day, but for tomorrow, for a long time. If only a part of the militant workers take interest in it and regard it as a good thing if it could be accomplished—that is already a gratifying initial success. It is up to us then to convince these workers that our demands are reasonable and practical in the present situation, and fully within their rights, as indeed they are.

Our aim, it must always be remembered, is not to convince quibbling factional opponents who wage a fictitious political struggle in the form of literary exercises, but workers who take the question, as they take all questions, seriously. That is why we hinge our agitation around illustrations from the life they know, that of the factory and the union. Their class attitude in the factory is the product of their experience, aided by the agitation of the more conscious elements. The right of the workers to organization, to have union officers of their own choosing, to be represented by shop committees of their own trusted people—these precious and necessary rights were not conferred upon our workers by benevolent bosses or an impartial government. In fact, they also were once "illegal," and more than one worker has been "shot" for advocating them. The workers' conviction that they need these things in the factory, in order to set limits to oppression and exploitation, is the result of their experience.

Their skepticism regarding the possibility of realizing analogous conditions in the field of militarism arises from the fact that for them it is as yet unexplored territory. But they will soon discover that the oppression, exploitation, and class discrimination, which are the substance of their daily lives as workers, reappear also in the Prussianized militarism of the capitalist state in a form that is more intensive, more brutal, and more contemptuous of human life. The military experience of the workers will come powerfully to the aid of our program, giving it a burning actuality, and make it the banner of their first struggles for a minimum of class independence and self protection. Our program anticipates this experience and attempts to prepare the minds of the workers for a speedier and more conscious reaction to it.

Our slogans carry the class line into the new conditions of militarism. In the factory a militant trade unionist wouldn't trust an employer or an agent of the employers as far as he can kick an anvil in his bare feet. But in the military machine, in the present setup, the officer corps from top to bottom is dominated by people of this boss type—class enemies who regard the workers in the ranks as cannon fodder, and have no regard for their welfare and safety. Why shouldn't the workers, in such a situation, put forth the demand for officers from the ranks of the workers and the unions?

Haven't the workers, who are risking their lives for "democracy," the right to a little democracy for themselves? Out of the billions of dollars of federal funds appropriated for military purposes, why shouldn't a certain sum be earmarked for the establishment of special camps to train workers to become officers? What's wrong about such a demand? And, for that matter, what is "illegal" about it? Indeed, if a serious militant worker who hates and distrusts the bosses and their agents for good reason will stop to think about it, he must be impressed by the extreme modesty of the demands of our transitional program. They represent not the last word, but rather the first. Most workers today have the illusion that the class lineup, which confronts him in the factory and on the picket line, is by some miracle eliminated in the domain of war and militarism. Our program of transitional demands, proceeding from the Marxist principle which never recognizes a suspension of the class struggle in the class society, is designed to break this illusion, this fetish. That is the purpose of our agitation around the program.

In my speech to our Chicago conference, I devoted a big section to our agitational approach to the workers who think it necessary to defend the country against fascism by military means, but imagine it has to be left in full charge of the bourgeois rulers. I argued against this prejudice in terms and by means of illustrations which I thought might be effectively employed by our party agitators. I summed up a whole section devoted to such arguments with the following statement: "The workers themselves must take charge of this fight against Hitler and anybody else who tries to invade their rights. That is the whole principle of the new policy that has been elaborated for us by Comrade Trotsky. The great difference between this and the socialist military policy in the past is that it is an *extension* of the old policy, an adaptation of *old principles* to *new conditions*."

From a reading of the text of my speech it is clear beyond possibility of misunderstanding that I was arguing against the prejudices of the workers and not against any principles hitherto maintained by our movement. On the contrary, I took pains to assert that our new concrete practical slogans are simply "an extension of the old policy, an adaptation of old principles to new conditions." My speech as a whole as well as the resolution adopted at the Chicago conference and the published letters and comments of Comrade Trotsky on the subject are all permeated with this idea. We stand, now as before, on the principles of Bolshevism and we aim to advance these principles by a transitional program in the military epoch.

Anyone who wants to conduct an honest dispute with us must begin by stating our actual position fairly and honestly and then criticize us from one of two standpoints: (1) the principles of Bolshevism are wrong and, likewise, the practical slogans designed to apply them; or, (2) the transitional program violates the principles of Bolshevism on war.

Shachtman, writing in *Labor Action* (November 4) employed a different method of attack, a method designed not to clarify, but to confuse. At the beginning of his article, as the first "point" which sets the tone and shapes the character of this article as a whole, he "lifts" my above-quoted statement out of its context and tries to make it appear that I am arguing not against the prejudices of the workers but against the *principles* of the modern Trotskyist movement! Then, with mock seriousness, he asks: "Of *which* old policy is our military program an extension?"—and solemnly pretends that I may have been speaking of the policy of the "Liberals, social-democrats and Stalinists." Then, after explaining to us that "Trotsky above all taught the movement that the workers themselves must take charge of this fight against Hitler," he ends the first "point" and premise of his article with the devastating question: "If that was the 'whole principle of the *new* policy' what was the principle of the 'old' policy?"

But I had explained in the sentences he quoted, and can only repeat here again, that we are not enunciating any different principle but simply attempting to apply "old principles to new conditions." But Shachtman obviously calculates that by the time he gets to the end of his juggled and misapplied quotation the casual and unsuspecting reader will be too muddled and confused to know the difference. To answer him it is only necessary to go back and show what we really said and what we really meant. The interested reader, who takes the trouble to read the quotations in their context—and that is an absolutely necessary precaution whenever Shachtman is "quoting"—can get the matter straight. He will also get an insight into the polemical methods of Shachtman which became so notorious in the factional struggle which he conducted jointly with Burnham against Trotsky and the majority of our party. He became known to the adult members of our movement as an unscrupulous "twister" of quotations and a perverter of historical incidents to serve factional contentions.

In his lengthy attack on the military policy adopted by our party, Shachtman runs true to form from beginning to end. The dubious methods which he employed in his premise are maintained throughout the article. Misrepresentation is followed by falsification and reinforced with a spice of outright literary forgery. In debating with Shachtman one needs not a pen but a pair of hip boots and a shovel in order to dig down and clear away the filth which he piles over the essence of every dispute. It is not a very agreeable task but in the line of duty, I shall return to it again, insofar as the exposure of these methods of the political underworld helps to facilitate the explanation and clarification of our military transitional program to workers who are seriously and honestly interested in the question—the most important and burning question affecting their lives.

III. 1945: WHEN U.S. TROOPS SAID 'NO!'

A Hidden Chapter in the Fight Against War

by Mary-Alice Waters

This article first appeared in the November-December 1965 issue of the *Young Socialist*, published by the Young Socialist Alliance. It was later published as a Young Socialist pamphlet and widely distributed throughout the years of the anti-Vietnam War movement. It has been reprinted from *New International* no. 7 (1991).

The war in Vietnam has had profound effects on the entire American population. As the war continues to escalate step by step toward a massive land war in Asia, the opposition among the U.S. population also rises steadily.

This opposition is reflected among the troops themselves, who are more and more voicing their hesitations about fighting in Vietnam. It is in this context that the post–World War II troop demonstrations in the U.S. Army take on special historical significance.

It is accurate to call this a "hidden chapter in the fight against war," because the vast majority of our generation is unaware that the greatest troop revolt that has ever occurred in a victorious army took place at the end of 1945 and the beginning of 1946. The central issue was whether U.S. troops would be demobilized, or whether they would be kept in the Pacific to protect Western interests from the growing colonial revolution.

The typical American college textbook makes at best a passing reference to the "Bring us home" movement. A good example is found in *The American Republic* by Hofstadter, Miller, and Aaron (p. 641): "At the end of the war, strong pressure arose within the army and among civilians for the return of American soldiers from overseas. The government responded so quickly that for a time it seemed that we might be incapable of even occupying the countries we had defeated." The text then goes on to state that this "impaired the United States position in international affairs."

This is the officially endorsed interpretation of the troop revolts and their consequences. American military officials said the same thing in order to defend themselves against the angry demands of the troops and their supporters in the United States. But the GIs had another point of view on demobilization. A pamphlet issued by the Soldiers' Committee in Manila during the height of the demonstrations declared:

> According to a War Department spokesman, demobilization is proceeding at alarming rapidity. Alarming from whose point of view? Alarming to generals and colonels who want to go on playing war and who do not want to go back to being captains and majors? Alarming to businessmen who stand to make money having their investments rebuilt at army expense? Alarming to the State Department, which wants an army to back its imperialism in the Far East?

The conflicting interests expressed in these two quotations generated a mass movement that changed the entire course of postwar history.

Resentment among troops explodes

When V-J Day brought an end to the war in the Pacific,[1] the American troops expected to be speedily returned to the United States. Quite naturally, they felt there was no longer any need for fifteen million men in arms and that they should be released.

---

1. September 2, 1945, the day the Japanese government formally surrendered to the Allied powers, became known as V-J Day (for Victory in Japan). V-E Day (for Victory in Europe) was May 7, 1945.

Contrary to their expectations, however, the army command started transferring combat troops from Europe to the Pacific. The official explanation was that troops were needed for occupation duty. Congress was immediately flooded with petitions and letters from the GIs protesting this action. Even the White House announced on August 21, 1945, that it had received a protest telegram from 580 members of the Ninety-fifth Division stationed at Camp Shelby, Mississippi.

The Ninety-seventh Infantry Division, which had already spent five and a half months in Europe, was ordered to the Pacific. En route across the United States the soldiers displayed signs from the train windows saying, "Shanghaied for the Pacific," "We're being sold down the river while Congress vacations," and "Why do we go from here?" Two reporters who tried to interview soldiers on the train were arrested by military police under the pretext that troop movements were still classified information. The reporters were released several hours later, after the Twin Cities military security officer reprimanded the troops' commanding officers for exceeding their authority.

Throughout the fall of 1945 the campaign to bring the men home increased as families and friends held mass meetings across the country, and as resentment among the troops grew stronger. Columnist Drew Pearson reported on September 15, "Gen. Harry Lewis Twaddle, commander of the Ninety-fifth Division, Camp Shelby, Mississippi [the same group that had earlier protested to the White House] assembled his troops to explain occupation duty in Japan. The boos from the soldiers were so prolonged and frequent, it took him forty minutes to deliver a fifteen-minute speech."

By December, the resentment among the troops had reached explosive proportions. On Christmas day in Manila 4,000 troops marched on the Twenty-first Replacement Depot headquarters carrying banners demanding, "We want ships." The demonstration, touched off by the cancellation of a troop transport scheduled to return men to the United States, lasted only ten minutes. But the high point of the day occurred when the enraged depot commander, Col. J.C. Campbell, thundered, "You men forget you're not working for General Motors. You're still in the army." At that time there were 225,000 workers on strike against General Motors at plants across the United States. Since the GI demonstrations coincided with the greatest labor upsurge in U.S. history, the obvious similarities between the actions of the soldiers and the actions of the striking workers back home drew comments from many quarters.

The New York newspaper *PM* carried a January 13, 1946, dispatch from Nuremberg, Germany, saying:

> The fact is the GIs have strike fever. Almost every soldier you talk to is full of resentment, humiliation, and anger. . . . The GIs now feel they have a legitimate gripe against their employers. If the gripe does not include a wage scale, that is purely a minor consideration. They don't like their conditions of work, they don't like the length of their contract, they don't like their bosses.

On December 26, the day after the large demonstration in Manila, Colonel Krieger, an army personnel officer in the Philippines, assured 15,000 men in the replacement depots that they would be swiftly returned to the United States. On January 4 Lt. Gen. Lawton Collins, director of Army Information, admitted that shipping was available to bring back all eligible men overseas in three months.

Within days, however, *Stars and Stripes,* the widely read army newspaper, carried an announcement by the War Department that Pacific demobilizations would be *cut* from 800,000 to 300,000 per month due to the difficulties in obtaining replacements.

The GIs were infuriated. Their mood was well expressed by a soldier whose letter was read into the *Congressional Record* on January 23, 1946. He wrote, "First it is no ships, now no replacements; are we going to sit by and let them blackmail our families and hold us hostages to push through their compulsory military training program?"[2]

On January 6, 1946, thousands of these "hostages" demonstrated at different points in Manila.

---

2. Legislation authorizing compulsory military training (conscription) was enacted in September 1940 and expired in March 1947. After a lapse of a year, peacetime conscription was instituted with the passage of the Selective Service Act in June 1948.

One group was dispersed at Quezon Bridge and another broken up by military police as it approached Lt. Gen. William D. Styer's headquarters.

The demonstrations continued on January 7. More than 2,500 men marched four abreast to the general's headquarters carrying banners reading, "What does eligible mean?" "Service yes, but serfdom never," and "We're tired of false promises, double-talk, and double-crossing." They distributed mimeographed leaflets saying, "Redeployment has been deliberately slowed down to force compulsory military training. . . . The State Department wants the army to back up its imperialism."

That night, according to various reports, between 12,000 and 20,000 soldiers jammed into the bombed-out shell of the Philippine Hall of Congress to continue the demonstration and listen to speakers angrily denounce U.S. aggression in north China and the Netherlands Indies (Indonesia), and demand that the Philippines be allowed to settle its own internal problems.[3] A UPI dispatch from Manila on January 7 described the capital as "tense."

The demonstrations spread

As news of these mass protests spread, the wave of GI protests began to sweep around the world. On January 7, the second day of demonstrating in Manila, 2,000 GIs staged a mass meeting at Camp Boston, France, demanding a speedup in European demobilization. That same day, 6,000 soldiers on the Pacific island of Saipan wired protests against the slowdown in demobilization, and on Guam 3,500 enlisted men of the 315th Bombing Wing of the Twentieth Air Force staged a hunger strike. The following day on Guam, 18,000 men took part in two giant protest meetings. From Hawaii, Alaska, and Japan, thousands of cablegrams flooded into the United States. Directed at friends, families, Congress, churches, veterans' groups, and unions, the message demanded that pressure be put on the War Department to bring the troops home.

In Yokohama, Japan, 500 GIs met to plan for larger demonstrations. In Reims, France, 1,500 gathered to protest "illogical explanations" of the demobilization slowdown. In Paris, posters reading, "Don't let our Manila buddies down. Meeting, Arc de Triomphe, 8:30," drew over a thousand GIs who paraded down the Champs-Élysées to the American embassy. In Germany a telegram signed by one hundred GIs demanded:

> Are Brass Hats to be permitted to build empires? Why? . . . The evident lack of faith of our friends and neighbors is causing bitter resentment and deterioration of morale of men in this theater. It is to be hoped that our faith in democratic procedure is not finally lost.

From London, 1,800 enlisted men and officers of the Eighth Air Force demanded in a telegram:

> We want an explanation of delayed return. . . . *New York Times* says all U.S. troops who have not been redeployed have venereal disease or have volunteered. Ambiguous replies from congressmen and three canceled shipping dates do not help. We are tired, homesick, disgusted men . . . eligible for discharge December 1, 1945. In the European theater over thirty months.

At Andrews Field, Maryland, 1,000 soldiers and WACs[4] booed down their commanding officer when he tried to explain the delay in discharging them.

On January 9 the protests continued to spread. In Frankfurt, Germany, a demonstration of 5,000 was met at bayonet point by a small group of guards and some twenty were arrested. Five thousand soldiers demonstrated in Calcutta, India, and 15,000 at Hickam Field in Honolulu. In Seoul, Korea, several

3. Japanese forces occupying the Philippines were defeated by the U.S. armed forces in 1944–45. The Philippines, however, remained a U.S. colony, as it had been since 1898. The U.S. government immediately launched a military campaign to crush the Hukbalahap (People's Army against Japan) guerrilla forces, which had organized resistance to Japanese occupation throughout the war. The guerrilla movement was advocating a sweeping land reform in the countryside. The Philippines was granted independence on July 4, 1946. The U.S. Army, however, continued to conduct military actions against the rebel forces, who were dispersed and defeated by 1954.

4. The Women's Army Corps, known as WACs, was a U.S. Army organization created in 1942 to enlist women for duty in the military. It was formally dissolved in 1978.

thousand soldiers issued a resolution stating, "We cannot understand the War Department's insistence on keeping an oversized peacetime army overseas under present conditions."

At Batangas, Philippines, 4,000 soldiers voted funds for full-page ads in U.S. papers demanding the removal of Secretary of War Robert Patterson. Simultaneously, a service newspaper issued in Hawaii bore the headline: "Patterson Public Enemy No. 1."

As the GI demonstrations developed greater organization and militancy, the protest within the United States deepened too. For months the troops had been rubber-stamping the mail sent to the United States with slogans such as: "Write your congressman—get us home" and "No boats, no votes." They had been carrying on a vigorous letter-writing campaign themselves, writing Congress, families, friends, and newspapers demanding they be released and asking others to write letters too. In the midst of the GI revolt, Sen. Elbert D. Thomas, head of the Military Affairs Committee, complained to the press: "Constituents are on [the congressmen's] necks day and night. The pressure is unbelievable. Mail from wives, mothers, and sweethearts demanding that their men be brought home is running to almost 100,000 letters daily." And that figure did not include direct appeals from the servicemen!

As the wave of mass demonstrations began to subside, the issues became broader and the soldiers protested against other abuses. On January 13, 1946, 500 GIs in Paris adopted a set of demands that a UPI dispatch characterized as "a revolutionary program of army reform."

The Enlisted Man's Magna Charta, as this program was called, demanded:

1. Abolition of officers' messes, with all rations to be served in a common mess on a first-come, first-served basis.

2. Opening of all officers' clubs at all posts, camps, and stations to officers and men alike.

3. Abolition of reserved sections for officers at recreational events.

4. Abolition of all special officers' quarters; requirement that all officers serve one year as enlisted men, except in time of war.

5. Reform of army court-martial boards to include enlisted men.

In addition, these soldiers demanded the removal of Secretary of War Patterson and elected a committee to present the Magna Charta to a Senate investigating committee scheduled to come to Paris two weeks later. Their final action was to establish the "GI Liberation Committee" and urge everyone to return to their units and organize for further actions.

Officers unable to curb revolt

The administration of Democratic Party President Harry Truman was well aware that this massive GI revolt represented a serious challenge to the American military system. The army of World War II was not designed to permit criticism from the ranks. GIs who protested to their congressmen or participated in similar actions left themselves open to severe reprisals. But the massive character of the GI protests after World War II did not give the authorities much leeway. They could not victimize the leaders without stirring up even larger protests; at the same time, it was difficult to crack down on hundreds of thousands of men at once. Yet from the military's point of view, the situation was critical and the rapidly dissolving discipline had to be halted somehow. When privates and sergeants started requisitioning planes and jeeps to carry elected GI representatives to meetings with congressional investigating committees to talk about arranging transportation home, the officers knew they were in trouble.

The military used a soft hand at first. It merely "requested" that all complaints go through normal channels and imposed greater censorship on service newspapers. On January 11 the staff of the *Daily Pacifican,* an army newspaper in Manila, printed a statement that "new restrictions on freedom of expression imposed from above no longer enable us to bring full news and full truth to our GI readers."

Demonstrations spread geographically and broadened in scope, however, as indicated by the Paris meeting where the Magna Charta was proclaimed. Furthermore, the military had no intention of immediately living up to the promises it had made to pacify the soldiers. A UPI dispatch on January 16 announced, "The U.S.S. *Cecil,* carrying veterans to the United States, left Manila one-third empty, the Navy disclosed today." The Manila Soldiers' Committee on that same day, January 16, announced plans for another mass demonstration.

At this point the army decided things had gone too far. On January 17, Chief of Staff Gen. Dwight Eisenhower issued an order banning further soldier demonstrations. A similar order was issued by Gen. Joseph McNarney, commander of U.S. forces in the European theater, who stated that "further meetings may prejudice the prestige of the occupation forces."

Lt. Gen. Robert Richardson, Jr., ordered a court-martial for any soldier or officer in the mid-Pacific who continued to agitate for speedy demobilization, and confined to quarters three leaders of the Honolulu protests while the army "investigated" their remarks about the demobilization policy. Other minor reprisals followed, primarily in the form of transfers and threats of disciplinary action. Two men were removed from the staff of *Stars and Stripes* and sent to the island of Okinawa—considered the "Siberia of the American army"—for signing a joint protest against official muzzling of the paper.

Leaders of the Manila Soldiers' Committee were also transferred to Okinawa. One of these leaders was Sgt. Emil Mazey, former president of the militant Briggs Local 212 of the CIO United Auto Workers. Mazey had led the fight at the 1943 UAW convention to revoke the no-strike pledge and introduced a resolution to form a labor party. Although his recent history hasn't been so inspiring—Mazey is now secretary-treasurer of the UAW and UAW president Walter Reuther's right-hand man—the leading role he played in the "Bring us home" movement was indicative of the close interrelationship between the militant labor movement and the GI revolt at the end of the war.

Workers in army and unions unite in struggle

A conscript army of millions depends on workers and farmers for its human raw material. Many of the men who served in the U.S. forces during World War II had been part of the great labor battles of the late 1930s and had been deeply affected by them. Thousands upon thousands of them had taken part in the CIO organizing drives that had transformed the labor movement, and they had learned the methods and tactics of mass struggle from their experiences. They had gained organizational ability and knew the power of united action. These lessons and the abilities of men like Emil Mazey were used with great effectiveness by the rebelling troops.

At almost every base where soldiers demonstrated, they also began to organize themselves. One news item after another reported that "the soldiers elected representatives to present their demands" or "the GIs chose a committee to plan further action." The highest point of organization was reached by the Manila Soldiers' Committee. On January 10, 1946, 156 delegates—each elected by different outfits in the Manila area, and representing 139,000 soldiers—held their first meeting. The delegates unanimously elected a chairman and adopted a program. The chairman appointed a central committee of eight, which according to the *New York Times* (January 11) included "two officers and is widely representative of creeds and backgrounds." In addition to Emil Mazey, the group was composed of a Black soldier from North Carolina, a white soldier from Alabama, a Jewish soldier, another of Italian background, and regional representatives from different sections of the United States.

The protesting soldiers were as conscious of their allies in the unions as Colonel Campbell had been when he reminded the soldiers that they were not working for General Motors. The outfit stationed at Batangas, Philippines, headed by Mazey, sent an appeal to the United Auto Workers asking for support. The cablegram was immediately made public by the union, and R.J. Thomas, then president of the UAW, issued a statement saying:

> I have the utmost sympathy for the outraged feelings of these GIs. The War Department having made a public commitment on the rate of discharge, that commitment should be carried out in full at least in nonhostile countries. What soldiers and sailors do we need to occupy the Philippines? To ask the question is to expose how ridiculous it is.

The CIO council of Los Angeles called a demonstration in front of City Hall and then marched to picket the Chinese consulate on January 5 in order to show their support for the GIs' demands.[5] Many

5. The bourgeois Kuomintang government at the time, led by Chiang Kai-shek and backed by U.S. military forces, was conducting a war against the revolutionary upsurge sweeping China.

unions passed resolutions similar to the one passed by the Akron CIO council, which stated, in part:

> WHEREAS committees of soldiers on Manila and other fields of occupation have requested the aid of the labor movement in speeding their return to their homes and families;
>
> THEREFORE BE IT RESOLVED that the Akron Industrial Union Council joins in the soldiers' protests against the slowdown in demobilization and gives support to the millions of workers in uniform who long for peace, for home, and for a return to normal life; and
>
> BE IT FURTHER RESOLVED that the Akron Industrial Union Council is in full accord with the demonstrating soldiers who protest against being used to protect the wealth and foreign properties of such antilabor corporations as Standard Oil and General Motors.

These would be surprising words to hear from the U.S. labor movement today. But in 1946, while the troops were demonstrating abroad, the unions on the home front were engaged in a struggle for their very existence. These two fights were really twin battles in the same war.

From 1941 to 1945 the labor movement in the United States operated under severe restrictions imposed by the Roosevelt government with the assistance of the labor bureaucracy. A War Labor Board was established that settled all disputes by compulsory arbitration. Hours were lengthened and wages were frozen at the prewar level. A War Manpower Commission was established with control over some 2.3 million federal employees, in addition to workers in many of the industries classified as "essential." Civil liberties were severely curtailed and outspoken opponents of the war, such as leaders of General Drivers Local 544 in Minneapolis and members of the Socialist Workers Party, were jailed under the Smith Act.

All sizable political forces in the country—including both capitalist parties and the Stalinist and social democratic tendencies in the workers' movement—united in support of the war drive and in denouncing any attempts by workers and Blacks to protect their rights. The leadership of both the AFL and the CIO enthusiastically pledged to enforce a no-strike policy for the duration of the war. The field was wide open for the employers to launch an all-out attack on the gains made by the unions during the thirties. They were not long in taking advantage of this opportunity. As Adm. Ben Moreell, chief of the U.S. Bureau of Yards and Docks, told an October 1942 meeting of the AFL Building and Construction Trades Department in Toronto:

> I will admit that no one can live without labor, but they certainly can live without labor unions. They are living without them in Germany, and in Italy and in Japan, and they seem to be doing right well—at least for the moment—and, in my opinion, they will damn well live without them here if all of us don't get in there and pitch.

As the war drew to a close, the bitterness of the workers over wartime restrictions on their rights and the attempts to prevent them from using their organizations to fight effectively to defend themselves against speedup and safety violations reached explosive proportions. Within six months after V-J Day, there were more than 1.7 million men and women on the picket lines in the United States demanding shorter hours and wage increases to compensate for the soaring cost of living.

The employers, remembering the post–World War I era, hoped that the millions thrown out of jobs by the cutback in war production plus the millions of returning veterans could be used to break the unions. But the labor situation in 1945 was far different from that of 1919. The industrial union organizing battles of the 1930s had transformed the U.S. labor movement and begun to break down divisions from Jim Crow segregation within the unions, especially the CIO. Consciousness of the need for labor solidarity was qualitatively greater than following World War I.

Also during the war the unions had fought for and won job guarantees, full seniority rights, and other benefits for their members in the armed forces. Union consciousness among the leaders of the troop demonstrations helped to assure that veterans would be sympathetic to organized labor. As a result, returning veterans could not be mobilized as a strikebreaking force. They joined the picket lines instead, and fought with the unions for pay raises and a decent standard of living. It was a common sight to see men marching under banners that read: "This entire group—veterans of World War II," and "Veterans demand 18½ cents an hour."

American troops refuse to crush colonial revolts

One of the most important results of the "Bring us home" movement was that it served notice that the U.S. troops would not allow themselves to be used against their brothers, either at home or abroad. The resolutions, letters, and telegrams written by the GIs give a clear indication of their mood. They protested being used to back what they themselves labeled American imperialism in the Far East and resented the role of protecting business interests abroad. What was behind these accusations? What were the American troops being used for that created such bitter resentment?

The events in Indochina are an excellent example. At the Potsdam conference it was decided that northern Indochina—what is today North Vietnam—would be awarded to Chiang Kai-shek's government as a sphere of influence, and that southern Indochina would be given to the British.[6]

Immediately following V-J Day, throughout all of Vietnam the anti-Japanese guerrilla forces led by the Viet Minh rode to power on the wave of a popular revolution and established the Democratic Republic of Vietnam.[7]

When the British occupation forces arrived in the south in September 1945, the Ho Chi Minh government welcomed them with open arms, only to find that the British had no intention of allowing Vietnam to become an independent nation. As the British were having their own troubles in India, Burma, and elsewhere, they returned control of the former French colony to Paris. French troops, collaborating with the Japanese officer corps that had only weeks before been "the enemy," launched a military campaign to wipe out the Vietnamese liberation army.

U.S. troops stationed in the Far East were well aware that Washington was aiding the effort to subjugate the Vietnamese people and reimpose French colonial rule. In addition to other material aid, many U.S. troopships, instead of bringing American soldiers home, were used to transport French reinforcements to Indochina. The New York newspaper *PM* carried the following story on November 12, 1945:

> Victory ships *Taos* and *Pauchag* [left Marseilles] October 31, each carrying more than 1,000 troops to Indo-China. The crewmen of the *Taos* signed on in New York with the understanding that they were to proceed to India to bring American troops home. Upon their arrival [in Marseilles] they learned they were also to be used to carry French troops to the Orient.
>
> Prior to the sailing of the *Taos* and the *Pauchag,* three other [U.S.] Victory ships left France bound for French Indo-China carrying French troops.

The Indochinese story was repeated in the Netherlands Indies (Indonesia). With the conclusion of the war against Japan, the Indonesian nationalist forces set up a government and proclaimed their independence. The Dutch launched a campaign of extermination against them that can easily be compared to the atrocities committed by the United States in Vietnam today. An AP dispatch on December 30, 1945, pointed out that American aid to the Dutch was considerable:

> Two thousand American-trained and -equipped Dutch marines arrived off Batavia [Indonesia] today. Trained at Quantico, Va., Camp Lejeune, N.C., and Camp Pendleton, Calif., and fully supplied with American equipment, the marines are considered among the finest troops in the Netherlands armed forces.

6. A meeting of the leaders of the main victorious Allied powers (Washington, London, and Moscow) was held in Potsdam, Germany, in July–August 1945 to carve up conquered territory and assign economic and political domination to one of the victors.

7. The Viet Minh, the League for the Independence of Vietnam, had waged a struggle against Japan to free the country from colonial rule. In September 1945, an independent Vietnam was proclaimed, with Ho Chi Minh as president. When French troops began to return that same month, the Viet Minh resumed the struggle, driving out the French in 1954.

An extremely bitter U.S. marine stationed in China described how the soldiers felt about American aid to the Dutch in a letter to his father read into the *Congressional Record* by Rep. Charles W. Vursell of Illinois on December 3, 1945. The GI asked:

> Is our navy to be used for ferrying supplies to the Dutch in Java or for getting our troops home? . . . We have a great fleet, but when a group of ships carrying United States troops are stopped at Hollandia,[8] the troops ordered off, and supplies for Java put aboard, then it is time to call a halt. That little story we got from our First Marine Division news sheet.

Why was the U.S. government so concerned with the situation in the Netherlands Indies? The December 28, 1945, *United States News* explained it by saying:

> If the Javanese people are successful in their challenge to Dutch rule, the effect may be felt through a large part of Asia. Already, in Sumatra, Malaya, Siam [Thailand], and French Indo-China, there are evidences of unrest. . . . [The outcome of the events in Java] may determine what happens to the white man's position in neighboring areas inhabited by hundreds of millions of people.

The U.S. government was vitally concerned that these hundreds of millions of people and their countries, rich in natural resources, should not be lost to American economic domination. Several months before the war was over, Senator Tunnel, in a speech to Congress on February 15, 1945, spelled it out very clearly: "It would be an anomalous position for the United States to occupy, after putting up the men, the money, and enduring all the sacrifices which these mean, to have our country precluded from the markets we have liberated."

Events similar to those in Indochina and Indonesia occurred all over the Pacific, causing no small amount of bewilderment among American troops. A *New York Times* editorial on November 25, 1945, summed up the situation by saying:

> After the war the fires of nationalism broke forth and the resulting violence produced the paradox of 500,000 or more Japanese troops in Southeast Asia being deliberately kept under arms. . . . A British spokesman described them as "good troops" who fought well.

Gen. John Reed Hodge, the commander of American forces in Korea, told newsmen, "We had to leave the Japanese some small arms as protection against the Koreans since it is our duty to maintain order." He went on to add, "As a matter of fact the Japanese are my most reliable source of information." The brutality of the thirty-five-year Japanese colonial enslavement of the Korean people was notorious. The collaboration of U.S. military commanders with the hated Japanese officer corps to "maintain order" subjected U.S. GIs, who thought of themselves as liberators, to growing hostility.

Is it any wonder the American soldiers began to ask what they were being used for in the Pacific? Their allies suddenly became their enemies, and the officer corps of their former enemy became an ally.

American GIs in China

The most blatant use of American troops to suppress the colonial revolution occurred in China. At the end of the war national liberation forces under the leadership of the Chinese Communist Party were supported by the vast majority of the population, but Chiang Kai-shek's troops still controlled part of south China. The United States immediately moved in American soldiers to support Chiang and try to defeat the Red Army and suppress the vast revolutionary tide that was sweeping China. China was *the* great prize market of the Pacific, and men like Senator Tunnel did not want the United States to be excluded. According to the U.S. *Foreign Policy Bulletin* of November 30, 1945, the strength of Nationalist [Chiang Kai-shek] troops "is reinforced by the presence in north China of over 50,000 United States marines, who have made possible the entrance of Chungking divisions by holding certain cities for them until their arrival,[9] jointly patrolling these centers

8. Hollandia, today Djajapura, is the capital of the Indonesian province of West Irian.

9. Chungking (Chongqing), a city in south central China, served as the capital of the Chiang Kai-shek government during World War II.

with the central [government's] troops thereafter, and guarding stretches of railway in the Peiping-Tientsin [Beijing-Tianjin] area."

How did the American soldiers feel about being used this way? A pilot in the Army Air Force at Kunming, China, wrote a bitter letter printed in the New York newspaper *PM* on December 2, 1945:

> We hear news reports daily over the radio about the Chinese war and the United States intention of staying out. We know now that our own country lies even as German Nazism lied to the German people.

He then went on to explain how American pilots were ordered to paint over the insignias on their planes before they flew missions.

The marine who wrote the letter that was entered in the *Congressional Record* on December 3, by Representative Vursell (quoted earlier), complained:

> Today General Wedemeyer stated that the marines would remain in north China until the "unsettled affairs are settled." . . . That means we are protecting the Chinese Nationalists from the Communists. That is the truth. We are preventing the Communists from controlling this area until the Nationalists get here. In short, we're deciding what government China should have. We are doing exactly what we told Russia not to do. No wonder they don't trust us in Russia.

After asking why Wedemeyer and Truman were using repatriation of the Japanese forces as a pretext for intervening in the Chinese revolution, the marine went on to say, "Dad, if I could only impress you with the bitter hatred that exists among the marines over this, perhaps you could understand how we feel."

Why did U.S. troops revolt?

Today, U.S. troops are again fighting in Asia. They are being used in a colonial war even more brutal and destructive than those that followed World War II. Their morale is low, and most do not like what they are doing. But their resentment has not yet reached the heights it did following the Second World War. Why did soldiers refuse to fight then?

First of all, they were just plain tired of fighting. They had had enough and wanted out. But this does not adequately explain their rebellion. Had they been convinced of the need to fight, and had they felt it was their duty to crush the growing colonial revolution, they might have done so. However, five years of wartime antifascist propaganda could not be wiped out in a matter of months. World War II had been described as a war to liberate subjugated people from the yoke of fascism, as a war to destroy a system that practiced genocide, as a war against Nazi totalitarian oppression of the working class and its organizations.

At the end of the war, when the Allied powers tried to reconquer their former colonies, the American soldiers simply said, "No, this is not what we fought and died for." In an open letter to President Truman, an army psychiatrist warned of a "psychological breakdown" among the troops as a result of "being used to stifle the very democratic elements they hoped to liberate." Another reason the soldiers refused to go on fighting was that "the great fear" of communism had not been ingrained in them yet. The Soviet Union had been an ally in the fight against fascism, and the American troops were not convinced of the need to fight their former friends.

Another significant aspect of the troop revolt was the racist character of U.S. foreign policy, as well as the completely racist organization of the army. The World War II army was still totally segregated, assuring that Black troops would get the hardest and dirtiest menial assignments. One result of this was that many of the construction battalions assigned to the Pacific after the war were all-Black units. This meant that delayed demobilization hit them hardest.

Throughout the war, strikes and demonstrations against the Jim Crow practices of the military had mounted, as Black troops refused to accept that the "fight for democracy" meant postponing the struggle against racist abuses.[10] In March 1945, the Thirty-fourth Seabee Construction Battalion went on a hunger strike. In another instance, a Black unit of the Women's Army Corps went on strike

10. For a week-by-week account of this struggle, taken from the pages of the *Militant*, see C.L.R. James et al., *Fighting Racism in World War II* (New York: Pathfinder Press, 1980).

at Fort Devons against menial labor assignments. The women were all court-martialed and sentenced to one year at hard labor and dishonorable discharges.

The Port Chicago disaster has gone down in history as one of the most grisly consequences of Jim Crow practices in the armed forces. Port Chicago, California, was a major supply depot on the West Coast, and the navy crews that loaded ships were almost entirely Black. On July 17, 1944, one of the ammunition ships being loaded in the harbor exploded, and 327 men died, the majority of them Black sailors. When those who survived were ordered back to work, most of them refused because of the obviously unsafe working conditions. In retaliation, the navy shipped hundreds of them off to the Pacific. In the largest mass trial in naval history, fifty were court-martialed on charges of conspiracy to mutiny. Every single sailor court-martialed received a sentence of at least eight years at hard labor, and several received as many as fifteen years.

Such examples give an idea of the racism that was institutionalized in the U.S. armed forces and contributed to the fact that Black troops were less than enthusiastic about being used to subjugate Asia. They knew from long, bitter history the racist attitudes that made wholesale slaughter of nonwhite people "acceptable" to the military command.

Historical consequences of troop revolt

The mass demonstrations by soldiers to "Bring us home," brief as they were, had far-reaching consequences in the post–World War II era.

First, *they did force the U.S. government to demobilize the troops.* More than 12 million men and women were serving in the armed forces at the end of the war, and by midsummer 1946 this had been reduced to 3 million. By June 1947 it was down to 1.5 million troops. The strength of the revolt, its size and depth, and the massive support it received within the United States brought about a near disintegration of the American military machine. The government had no choice but to disband the large draftee army.

Second, the revolt gave notice to the military that the entire concept of a permanent, disciplined, peacetime conscript army could not be easily foisted on the American population. It is hard for our generation to comprehend this fact, but a conscript army never existed, except during large-scale wars, prior to our lifetimes! The charges made by the soldiers that they were being used as hostages in the military's campaign to force universal military training made it evident that the people of the United States wanted no part of such a program; it was two years before Congress could safely pass a law instituting universal military training. Madison Avenue advertising techniques had to swing into high gear before Americans "bought" the idea.

Third, the "Bring us home" demonstrations made it clear to the U.S. ruling class that a new political propaganda campaign was needed and had to begin immediately if working people in the United States were to be convinced of the worldwide "communist menace" and a military force rebuilt adequate to play a counterrevolutionary role wherever needed. When American troops rebelled at fighting the Chinese Red Army and "Communist" guerrillas, it was time for antifascist slogans to be replaced by anticommunist propaganda; the struggles of the colonial people for independence had to be transformed into "Communist conspiracies." In 1947 the new militarization drive began.

Fourth, the troop revolt postponed the entire postwar time schedule as proposed by British prime minister Winston Churchill and U.S. president Harry Truman for the war against the Soviet Union. The U.S. troops served notice that they would no longer fight, and it took time to generate the Cold War witch-hunt campaign, that reactionary assault on democratic rights whose target was the U.S. labor movement. As a result the Soviet Union gained a breathing space to recover from the war, to begin to rebuild its industrial capacity, and to develop into a nuclear power. The colonial revolution was able to advance and the United States was prevented from trying to militarily crush the Chinese revolution in the last half of the 1940s. The victory of the Chinese revolution in 1949 and the fact that the United States no longer had a nuclear monopoly contributed to the stalemate in Korea in the opening years of the 1950s. The U.S. government was prevented from gaining a military victory in Korea; the workers' state in the northern part of the country was not rolled back.

The stalemate in Korea and the unpopularity of that war in turn made U.S. working people loath to enter the Indochinese war on the side of the French in 1954. This, and the French government's decision to turn down the offer, were the main factors that prevented U.S. president Dwight Eisenhower from asking Congress for permission to use nuclear weapons already en route to Vietnam at the time of Dien Bien Phu in 1954.[11]

Fifth, the close ties that existed between the "Bring us home" movement and organized labor made it evident that millions of returning soldiers would not be antiunion and could not be counted on to serve as strikebreakers. This gave a tremendous boost to the labor struggles occurring in the aftermath of the war. It meant that the CIO made significant gains in the immediate postwar period. Although, the Cold War red-baiting campaign served to split and seriously weaken the unions, and the class-collaborationist leadership left them hog-tied, the unions were not physically destroyed as were the working-class organizations of Germany, Italy, Spain, and Japan under fascism. Had such a defeat occurred in the postwar era, the working class would probably not yet have recovered. A case in point is Spain, where thirty years after the defeat of the Spanish workers, the unions are only now beginning to rise again.[12]

Sixth, the struggle for Black rights was given impetus by the "Bring us home" movement. The inclusion of Blacks on the soldiers' committees and the interracial solidarity against the most blatantly racist aspects of American foreign policy served to encourage the freedom struggle within the United States as well as abroad.

And seventh, the "Bring us home" movement is graphic proof that the working class in the United States is capable of mass action on political questions, that working people are not concerned only about their stomachs.

Finally, the postwar troop revolt has tremendous significance for those of us involved in the antiwar movement today. One of the most important questions being discussed by Americans who are opposed to the war in Vietnam is the challenge of how to reach the troops, of how to explain to them why we are opposed to the war and why they should not have to fight and die in a war that is not in their interests. The "Bring us home" movement provides some answers to that question.

"Bring the troops home" is the demand the GIs themselves will raise. It is the slogan that will mobilize the hundreds of thousands of men and women we must mobilize in order to stop the war. Demands to negotiate a settlement, or to call a cease-fire, or to send in the United Nations—which for the soldiers simply means exchanging a brown helmet for one that is UN blue—will be recognized by the troops as a subterfuge for continuing the war.

When the GIs have had enough, they will want out and nothing less. They will then organize and mobilize themselves. But this will not happen in isolation. It can occur only as an integral component of deepening class struggle at home—when the GIs know that their determination is matched by the action of millions at home to achieve the same end. Then, history has already shown us, GIs can unite in the kind of actions that will shake the very foundations of U.S. foreign policy and the U.S. military machine.

As the number of conscript troops in Vietnam grows, their response to the demand "Bring the troops home" will increase. We should raise this demand continuously and settle for nothing less. Our uncompromising fight at home will let them know they are not alone in their dissatisfaction with the war in Vietnam. To every man, woman, and child, every soldier and civilian, the antiwar movement must say, "Bring the GIs home now!"

---

11. In April 1954 U.S. rulers discussed ordering massive bombing to help lift the siege of Dien Bien Phu, a village in northwest Vietnam where freedom fighters were nearing a decisive victory over the occupying French forces. U.S. aircraft carriers armed with nuclear weapons were deployed off the Vietnamese coast, and the Republican administration of Dwight Eisenhower considered their use as a possible part of the operation.

12. Following a three-year civil war, fascist forces led by Francisco Franco had ousted Spain's republican government by March 1939. The Franco dictatorship remained in power for more than thirty years.

EXPAND YOUR REVOLUTIONARY LIBRARY

Labor, Nature, and the Evolution of Humanity

The Long View of History

FREDERICK ENGELS, KARL MARX, GEORGE NOVACK, MARY-ALICE WATERS

Why is it important to know that social labor, transforming nature, has been the motor force of humanity's evolution for millions of years? Because without that knowledge, working people are unable to see beyond the capitalist epoch, beyond the class exploitation that warps all human relations, ideas, and values. The dictatorship of capital had a beginning . . . and it will have an end. But only the revolutionary conquest of state power by the working class can open the door to a world free of capitalism's dog-eat-dog social reality. A world built on human solidarity. A socialist world. $12. Also in Spanish and French.

Women's Liberation and the African Freedom Struggle

THOMAS SANKARA

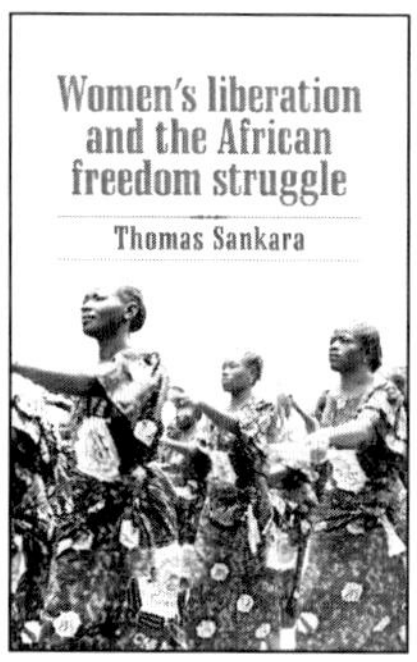

"There is no true social revolution without the liberation of women," explains the leader of the 1983–87 revolution in the West African country of Burkina Faso. $5. Also in Spanish, French, and Farsi.

Women in Cuba: The Making of a Revolution Within the Revolution

VILMA ESPÍN, ASELA DE LOS SANTOS, YOLANDA FERRER

The integration of women in the ranks and leadership of the Cuban Revolution was intertwined with the proletarian course of the leadership of the revolution from the start. This is the story of that revolution and how it transformed the women and men who made it. $17. Also in Spanish, Farsi, and Greek.

W.E.B. Du Bois Speaks, 1920–1963

Speeches and Addresses

A comprehensive collection of speeches by the Black rights advocate and scholar. 2nd of 2 vols. $20

By Any Means Necessary

MALCOLM X

"The imperialists know the only way you will voluntarily turn to the fox is to show you a wolf." In eleven speeches and interviews, Malcolm X presents a revolutionary alternative to this reformist trap, taking up political alliances, women's rights, US intervention in the Congo and Vietnam, capitalism and socialism, and more. $15

Fighting Racism in World War II

FROM THE PAGES OF THE *MILITANT*

An account of struggles against racist discrimination in US war industries, the armed forces, and society as a whole from 1939 to 1945, taken from the pages of the socialist newsweekly, the *Militant*. These struggles helped lay the basis for the proletarian-based civil rights movement that followed. $20

Malcolm X Talks to Young People

"The young generation of whites, Blacks, browns, whatever else—you're living at a time of revolution," said Malcolm in 1964. "And I for one will join with anyone, I don't care what color you are, as long as you want to change this miserable condition that exists on this earth." Four talks and an interview in the last months of Malcolm's life. $12. Also in Spanish, French, Farsi, and Greek.

Marianas in Combat

Teté Puebla and the Mariana Grajales Women's Platoon in Cuba's Revolutionary War, 1956–58

TETÉ PUEBLA

Brigadier General Teté Puebla, the highest ranking woman in Cuba's Revolutionary Armed Forces, joined the struggle to overthrow the US-backed dictatorship of Fulgencio Batista in 1956, when she was fifteen years old. This is her story—from clandestine action in the cities, to serving as an officer in the victorious Rebel Army's first all-women's unit. The fight to transform the social and economic status of women in Cuba remains inseparable from its socialist revolution. $10. Also in Spanish and Farsi.

Capitalism and the Transformation of Africa

Reports from Equatorial Guinea

MARY-ALICE WATERS, MARTÍN KOPPEL

Describes how, as Equatorial Guinea is pulled into the world market, both a capitalist class and a working class are being born. Also documents the work of volunteer Cuban health-care workers there—an expression of the living example of Cuba's socialist revolution. $10. Also in Spanish and Farsi.

The History of the Russian Revolution

LEON TROTSKY

How, under Lenin's leadership, the Bolshevik Party led millions of workers and farmers to overthrow the state power of the landlords and capitalists in 1917 and bring to power a government that advanced their class interests at home and worldwide. Unabridged, 3 vols. in one. Written by one of the central leaders of that socialist revolution. $30. Also in French and Russian.

Maurice Bishop Speaks

The Grenada Revolution and Its Overthrow, 1979–83

The triumph of the 1979 revolution in the Caribbean island of Grenada under the leadership of Maurice Bishop gave hope to millions throughout the Americas. Invaluable lessons from the workers and farmers government destroyed by a Stalinist-led counterrevolution in 1983. $20

Democracy and Revolution

GEORGE NOVACK

The limitations and advances of various forms of democracy in class society, from its roots in ancient Greece through its rise and decline under capitalism. Discusses the emergence of Bonapartism, military dictatorship, and fascism, and how democracy will be advanced under a workers and farmers regime. $17

To See the Dawn

Baku, 1920—First Congress of the Peoples of the East

How can peasants and workers in the colonial world achieve freedom from imperialist exploitation? By what means can working people overcome divisions incited by their national ruling classes and act together for their common class interests? These questions were addressed by 2,000 delegates to the 1920 Congress of the Peoples of the East. $17

Cosmetics, Fashions, and the Exploitation of Women

JOSEPH HANSEN, EVELYN REED, MARY-ALICE WATERS

How big business reinforces women's second-class status and uses it to rake in profits. Where does women's oppression come from? How has the entry of millions of women into the workforce strengthened the battle for emancipation, still to be won? $12. Also in Spanish, Farsi, and Greek.

Lenin's Struggle for a Revolutionary International

Documents, 1907–1916; The Preparatory Years

The debate among revolutionary working-class leaders, including V.I. Lenin and Leon Trotsky, on a socialist response to World War I. $30

America's Revolutionary Heritage

Marxist Essays

GEORGE NOVACK

A materialist explanation of the American Revolution, Civil War and Radical Reconstruction, genocide against the Indians, rise of American imperialism, first wave of the fight for women's rights, and more. $23

Labor's Giant Step
The First Twenty Years of the CIO: 1936–55
ART PREIS

The story of the explosive labor struggles and political battles in the 1930s that built the industrial unions. And how those unions became the vanguard of a mass social movement that began transforming US society. $27

Teamster Rebellion
FARRELL DOBBS

The 1934 strikes that won union recognition for truckers and warehouse workers in Minneapolis and helped pave the way for the working-class social movement that built the industrial unions. The first of four volumes by a central leader of these battles. $16. Also in Spanish, French, Farsi, and Greek.

The Jewish Question
A Marxist Interpretation
ABRAM LEON

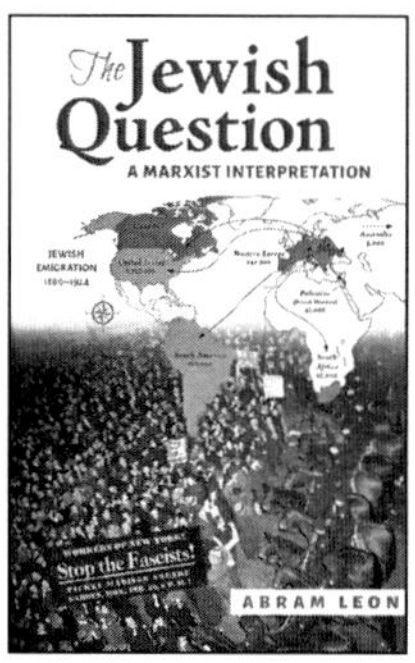

Why is Jew-hatred still raising its ugly head? What are its class roots—from antiquity through feudalism, to capitalism's rise and current crises? Why is there no solution under capitalism? The author, Abram Leon, was killed in the Nazi gas chambers. Revised translation, new introduction, and 40 pages of illustrations and maps. $17. Also in Spanish and French.

Are They Rich Because They're Smart?
Class, Privilege, and Learning under Capitalism
JACK BARNES

In battles forced on us by the capitalists, workers will begin to transform our attitudes toward life, work, and each other. We'll discover our worth, denied by the rulers and upper middle classes who insist they're rich because they're smart. We'll learn in struggle what we're capable of becoming. $10. Also in Spanish, French, Farsi, and Arabic.

U.S. Imperialism Has Lost the Cold War
JACK BARNES

The collapse of regimes across Eastern Europe and the USSR claiming to be communist did not mean workers and farmers there had been crushed. In today's sharpening capitalist conflicts and wars, these toilers are joining working people the world over in the class struggle against exploitation. In *New International* no. 11. $14. Also in Spanish, French, Farsi, and Greek.

The Revolution Betrayed
What Is the Soviet Union and Where Is It Going?
LEON TROTSKY

In 1917 workers and peasants of Russia were the motor force for one of the deepest revolutions in history. Yet within ten years a political counterrevolution by a privileged social layer, whose chief spokesperson was Joseph Stalin, was being consolidated. The classic study of the Soviet workers state and its degeneration. $17. Also in Spanish, Farsi, and Greek.

The Fight against Fascism in the USA
Forty Years of Struggle Described by Participants
JAMES P. CANNON AND OTHERS

In 1939 some 50,000 people in New York City responded to a call by the Socialist Workers Party to answer a pro-Nazi rally of 20,000. "The question of how to fight fascism was answered in thunderous tones by the magnificent demonstration which raised the cry: Workers Defense Guards to crush the fascist danger!" $5

We Are Heirs of the World's Revolutions
Speeches from the Burkina Faso Revolution, 1983–87
THOMAS SANKARA

How peasants and workers in this West African country established a popular revolutionary government and began to fight hunger, illiteracy, and economic backwardness imposed by imperialist domination. They set an example not only for workers and small farmers in Africa, but their class brothers and sisters the world over. $10. Also in Spanish, French, and Farsi.

BUILDING A PROLETARIAN PARTY

In Defense of Marxism

Against the Petty-Bourgeois Opposition in the Socialist Workers Party

LEON TROTSKY

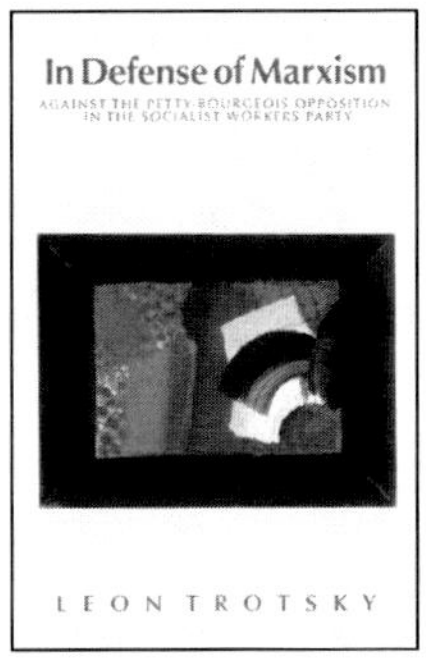

A reply to those in the revolutionary workers movement in the late 1930s bending to bourgeois patriotism during Washington's buildup to enter World War II. Trotsky explains why only a party fighting to bring workers into its ranks and leadership can steer a communist course. In the process, he defends the materialist and dialectical foundations of Marxism. $17. Also in Spanish.

The Struggle for a Proletarian Party

JAMES P. CANNON

"The workers of America have power enough to topple the structure of capitalism at home and to lift the whole world with them when they rise," Cannon asserts. On the eve of World War II, a founder of the communist movement in the US and leader of the Communist International in Lenin's time defends the program and party-building norms of Bolshevism. $20. Also in Spanish and Farsi.

Revolutionary Continuity

Marxist Leadership in the United States

The Early Years, 1848–1917

Birth of the Communist Movement, 1918–1922

FARRELL DOBBS

"Successive generations of proletarian revolutionists have participated in the movements of the working class and its allies . . . Marxists today owe them not only homage for their deeds. We also have a duty to learn what they did wrong as well as right so their errors are not repeated." —*Farrell Dobbs*. Two volumes, $17 each.

The History of American Trotskyism, 1928–38

Report of a Participant

JAMES P. CANNON

$17. Also in Spanish and French.

The Transitional Program for Socialist Revolution

LEON TROTSKY

The Socialist Workers Party program, drafted by Trotsky in 1938, still guides the SWP and communists the world over. The party "uncompromisingly gives battle to all political groupings tied to the apron strings of the bourgeoisie. Its task—the abolition of capitalism's domination. Its aim—socialism. Its method—the proletarian revolution." $17. Also in Farsi.

Socialism on Trial

Testimony at Minneapolis Sedition Trial

JAMES P. CANNON

The revolutionary program of the working class, presented in response to frame-up charges of "seditious conspiracy" in 1941, on the eve of US entry into World War II. The defendants were leaders of the Minneapolis labor movement and the Socialist Workers Party. $15. Also in Spanish, French, and Farsi.

Their Trotsky and Ours

JACK BARNES

To lead the working class in a successful revolution, a mass proletarian party is needed whose cadres, well beforehand, have absorbed a world communist program, are proletarian in life and work, derive deep satisfaction from doing politics, and have forged a leadership with an acute sense of what to do next. This book is about building such a party. $12. Also in Spanish, French, and Farsi.

What Is to Be Done?

V.I. LENIN

The stakes in creating a disciplined organization of working-class revolutionaries capable of acting as a "tribune of the people, able to react to every manifestation of tyranny and oppression, no matter where it appears, to clarify for all and everyone the world-historic significance of the struggle for the emancipation of the proletariat." Written in 1902. $8

THE CUBAN REVOLUTION AND WORLD POLITICS

From the Escambray to the Congo

In the Whirlwind of the Cuban Revolution

VÍCTOR DREKE

Dreke was second in command of the internationalist column in the Congo led in 1965 by Che Guevara. He recounts the creative joy with which working people have defended their revolutionary course—from Cuba's Escambray mountains to Africa and beyond. $15. Also in Spanish.

Red Zone

Cuba and the Battle against Ebola in West Africa

ENRIQUE UBIETA GÓMEZ

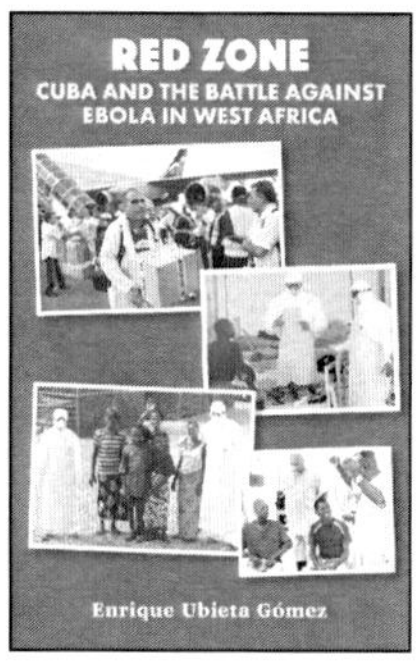

When three African countries were hit in 2014–15 by the Ebola epidemic, Cuba's revolutionary government sent what no other country even pretended to provide: more than 250 volunteer doctors, nurses, and other medical workers. This firsthand account of their actions shows the kind of men and women only a socialist revolution can produce. $17. Also in Spanish and French.

The First and Second Declarations of Havana

Nowhere are the questions of revolutionary strategy that today confront men and women on the front lines of struggles in the Americas addressed with greater truthfulness and clarity than in these uncompromising indictments of imperialist plunder and "the exploitation of man by man." Adopted by million-strong assemblies of the Cuban people in 1960 and 1962. $10. Also in Spanish, French, Farsi, Arabic, and Greek.

Bolivian Diary of Ernesto Che Guevara

Guevara's day-by-day chronicle of the 1966–67 guerrilla campaign in Bolivia, an effort to forge a continent-wide revolutionary movement of workers and peasants and open the road to socialist revolution in South America. $23. Also in Spanish.

Our History Is Still Being Written

The Story of Three Chinese Cuban Generals in the Cuban Revolution

ARMANDO CHOY, GUSTAVO CHUI, MOISÉS SÍO WONG, MARY-ALICE WATERS

"What was the key measure to uproot discrimination against Chinese and blacks in Cuba? It was the socialist revolution itself." New edition sheds light on Chinese Cubans' involvement in Cuba's internationalist course, including in Africa and Latin America. $15. Also in Spanish, French, Farsi, Greek, and Chinese.

Cuba and the Coming American Revolution

JACK BARNES

This is a book about the struggles of working people in the imperialist heartland, the youth attracted to them, and the example set by the Cuban people that revolution is not only necessary—it can be made. It is about the class struggle in the US, where the revolutionary capacities of workers and farmers are today as utterly discounted by the ruling powers as were those of the Cuban toilers. And just as wrongly. $10. Also in Spanish, French, and Farsi.

Cuba and Angola: The War for Freedom

HARRY VILLEGAS ("POMBO")

The story of Cuba's unparalleled contribution to the fight to free Africa from the scourge of apartheid. And how, in the doing, Cuba's socialist revolution was strengthened. $10. Also in Spanish, Farsi, and Greek.

Che Guevara Talks to Young People

Guevara challenges the youth of Cuba and the world to work. To become disciplined. To join the vanguard on the front lines of struggles, small and large. To become a different kind of human being as they fight together with working people of all lands to transform the world. $12. Also in Spanish and Greek.